KEPT IN CZECH

Margaret Austin

ISIS
LARGE PRINT
Oxford

First published in Great Britain 2009
by
History into Print
An imprint of Brewin Books Ltd.

Published in Large Print 2010 by ISIS Publishing Ltd.,
7 Centremead, Osney Mead, Oxford OX2 0ES
by arrangement with
Brewin Books Ltd.

British Library Cataloguing in Publication Data
Austin, Margaret.
    Kept in Czech. - - (Reminiscence)
    1. Austin, Margaret.
    2. Austin, Margaret - - Marriage.
    3. Austin, Fred.
    4. Foreign spouses - - England - - Dudley - -
    Biography.
    5. Czechs - - England - - Dudley - - Biography.
    6. Dudley (England) - - Biography.
    7. Large type books.
    I. Title II. Series
    942.4'93082'092–dc22

ISBN 978–0–7531–9564–2 (hb)
ISBN 978–0–7531–9565–9 (pb)

This book is dedicated to the memory of my parents, who gave me life and so much more.

Contents

Prologue 1

1. My Early Days 5

2. War and a Move to The North-East 36

3. Grammar School at Last 59

4. Return to Cleethorpes 74

5. October, 1947 86

6. Christmas in Paris 124

7. My Finals Year 132

8. Cooks for a Month 139

9. Training to Teach 150

10. Wedding Preparations 158

11. Adventures on Honeymoon 166

12. Newly Weds in Leicester 173

13. Peritonitis is No Joke 190

14. Our House in Lardenne 197

15. Easter in Spain 204

16. Farewell France! 212

17. Life and Death in Birmingham 219

18. A Lake Side View for Our Babies 239

19. Children Are Not All Alike 250

20. Caravan Adventure 279
21. The Children Grow and Flourish 287
22. Affairs of Fred's Heart 310
23. Margaret Looks Back 329
     The Colam Family Tree 338

Prologue

Once it was established that I would be able to accept the place I had been offered at University College, Leicester without being a burden to my parents and after being interviewed by an important official at the Education Offices in Lincoln, where it was confirmed that I would be financially independent, my mother and I were engrossed in the purchasing of new clothes. In my mother's eyes, this was principally a matter of underwear and nightwear, bought lavishly but leaving precious few of the clothing coupons available to us. The luxuries proved to be the several jumpers I knitted myself and the "housecoat" made by our ex-baby sitter, who had served an apprenticeship in dressmaking. She also made up a cut-out dress, bought from the *Woman* magazine, which was pale blue, though its full-length zip was black, for, at that period of post-war austerity, only black and white zips were available. It was to give me a phase of notoriety later, I fear. All my needs were furnished with generosity by my mother and her last contribution was a great luxury — a packet of chicken sandwiches from Woolworths for a meal on my journey to Leicester by train. Dad gave me an alarm-clock, and sandwiches and clock were packed in the new Marks & Spencer hold-all which I carried with me. The bulk of my clothes and books had been despatched in a newly-purchased trunk on a Pickfords van — all of this because there was no car.

My mother could sense that I was feeling apprehensive and she offered to accompany me to Leicester. The suggestion was promptly refused — surely, would-be University students would not be so chicken-hearted as to need Mummy's hand. I was, nevertheless, full of trepidation and this was overtaken by blushing embarrassment when my alarm-clock bell sounded in the crowded compartment. Half-way through my journey, I was ravenous, but could not face the "shame" of eating sandwiches in public. Furtively, I fished the packet out of the hold-all and took myself to the smelly toilet, where I swiftly ate my meal and then ashamedly crept back to my seat. What a fool I was!

The train pulled into the LNER station in Leicester and, as I stepped out into what seemed to be a crowded metropolis, I was, once again, faint-hearted and hailed a taxi — thus making substantial inroads into my limited spending money. It was, however, a great relief to enter College Hall — a house previously occupied by the Attenborough family, where I was informed that several of the single rooms were not completed and mine was one of them. Thus, I spent a substantial part of the first term with several other freshers who, like me, were to share a large bedroom, once the refuge of one of the Attenborough sons.

After the evening meal, it suddenly dawned on me that I had forgotten to send a telegram to my mother to reassure her that I had survived the journey. I asked the Warden if I could send it from a Hall phone, but she refused permission, instructing me to walk to the LMS station on London Road, almost to the centre of town. I stumbled outside and turned right instead of left, as she had instructed me, thus falling into some prickly shrubs. I was virtually at screaming pitch by the time I had telegraphed home and realised how broke I was rapidly becoming. Would I ever get to enjoy my existence in Leicester? We shall see!

In conversation with some of the other newcomers, I learned that all of the Arts Freshers were to see Dr. Bryan, Dean of the Faculty, the following morning for a brief interview. With the other girls I had become acquainted with on the previous evening, I joined the queue and waited to fulfil this duty. As we moved slowly towards his office, my attention was drawn to a group of noisy young men further along the line and to one in particular, whom the others found very entertaining. The sound of their laughter resounded along the corridor every time he turned to gaze upon our group and to pass some comment or other. I felt that he was looking directly at me and I have never forgotten my reaction to his behaviour. My head drummed with one thought only: "You look as though you are used to getting what you want, but you won't get me!" Well, one cannot always be right.

CHAPTER ONE

My Early Days

I was born on June 12th, 1929, my mother having abandoned the bread dough she had placed in front of the kitchen fire to rise, in order to deliver her fourth child, with the help of Grannie Carlton, a totally unqualified but very competent midwife, trusted by all the women in the neighbourhood to deal with the birth of their babies. The latter also completed the bread-baking after delivering me and promptly became my attentive godmother. On the self-same day, as I later discovered, the superbly gifted, but so tragic Anne Frank was also born, sadly not destined to survive into adulthood. Her premature death in Bergen-Belsen did not prevent her from producing her literary legacy which, I have always found, offers such an honest and illuminating picture of the thoughts and emotions experienced, I imagine, by most teenage girls. What an amazing talent was so cruelly extinguished by typhoid and the evil deprivations of life in Auschwitz and Belsen.

It was in No. 10, Daubney Street, Cleethorpes that I first saw the light of day. My mother always commented on the intense heat of that June day and her unwillingness to have even a sheet to cover her because of the temperature. My parents had had the good fortune to rent the house some years before my birth, when it was a newly-built property, in which they could enjoy what must have seemed to them palatial accommodation, after their prolonged stay in a bedsit in the home of a Grimsby skipper whose wife had a heart of gold, a lively personality and a stentorian voice — a consequence I believe, of her deafness. On my mother's 21st birthday, this lady, of towering height and weatherbeaten complexion, known to all as Pearce, heard my mother weeping in her room. She went in without ceremony and bellowed: "What's the matter, Giddywilk" (According to Pearce, every member of the human race went by the name of Giddywilk). My mother admitted that my father was out job-hunting, since he had, as was his wont, very recently walked out from his place of work because some minor matter had displeased him. Mum was there with two small babies, but without a bite of food on her shelf, nor any money to replenish her stores. She was immediately instructed by Mrs. Pearce to follow her downstairs and was quickly presented with a sumptuous breakfast of bacon, egg, fried bread and whatever else could be mustered. Mum always claimed that she could not have had a better birthday meal anywhere else. By the time that they were ready to move to more spacious accommodation, my parents were expecting another baby.

Although she could never have found a more caring landlady and companion, when she left her bedsit, Mother must have felt she was embarking on a life of luxury in that terraced house, with its amenities of three bedrooms, a bathroom which contained a bath with cold, running water only and three rooms downstairs, with a scullery and its built-in "copper" for boiling the weekly wash or for heating a large quantity of water. From this source, my father drew buckets of extremely hot water and toiled through two downstairs rooms and then up the stairs, so that we could all have a deep, hot bath. When he was away from home, as he often was during the thirties, leaving no one to heave those hazardous buckets upstairs, we were bathed in a zinc bath on the large table in the room that we always called the kitchen — a far cry from today's kitchens. It had a wide, built-in range, with an oven on one side and a ring which could be pushed over the fire and on which there was usually a large, black kettle emitting steam — at least, during the colder months, when there was a fire in the grate. During the summer months, the same kettle resided on the sole gas-ring in the scullery — the only room downstairs where there was running water, cold again, but very useful, nevertheless. I must not forget to include, as our final luxury, an outside water-closet, which was of great daytime value, but which had to be superseded at night by chamber-pots, which Mum always referred to as "Jeremiahs" or "Jerries". As the fear of war increased in the late thirties, I had a recurring vision of hordes of German soldiers descending upon us, each brandishing a chamber-pot, because, in those days, the Germans were always alluded to as "Jerry" but my ability to

7

distinguish between the two uses of the word did not yet extend that far.

We felt our own outside "lavvy" was very advanced each time that we visited my mother's parents in Boston. Their house had no bathroom, a minute kitchen with two gas-rings and an outside "convenience", which consisted of a large open bin with a wooden seat over it. As the days passed, the bin became fuller and fuller, occasionally giving the impression that it would overflow, but I do not think it ever did. Regularly, a large cart visited the road and some really tough men came to heave out the disgusting bin and pour its contents into some alternative receptacle on the cart. I always thought those strong-stomached bravehearts had the most unpleasant job in the world.

To return to life in Cleethorpes — my parents had two tiny children before they moved into their first home. The eldest was Clarice Gertrude, born in 1915, quickly followed by Evelyn Ivy in 1917; two years later, Stanley Frederick was born in 1919. My mother never made a secret of the fact that, at that stage, she had hoped that Stan's arrival would complete her family. I mentioned earlier that my father's short fuse led to his frequently relinquishing his job. My mother detested the insecurity to which this characteristic gave rise in her life, though she readily admitted that he was always willing to find another position and was promptly employed by another firm, since he had a good reputation as a competent fitter. However, his unreliability gave her a great deal of anxiety, terrified as she was of ever getting into debt. She pinched and scraped, avoided every risk and gradually and proudly invested in new sticks of furniture. It was, however, a very slow process and even when I was six or seven, some years after moving to the house, the front room was still unfurnished, except for the sideboard my father was painstakingly making. He had advanced ideas and fitted into that work of art a turntable for their small collection of seventy-eights. He included a loudspeaker, for the front of which he cut out a complicated fretwork. I was very often with him as he toiled, accompanying his exertions with my outspoken repetition of "Stop grunting, Dad!"

They were not very prosperous in those days but, generally speaking, I believe no-one ever went hungry in the family. However, my parents had to face a terrible tragedy just when life must have seemed to be developing more smoothly for them. Evelyn, their adored second child, fell ill one November day when she was aged eight and was dead within twenty-four hours: her death certificate stated that she had lost her life from a severe attack of tonsillitis, which caused heart failure. It was strange for me to learn, years later, from an outside source, that, within the same week, there were three other child deaths in the same vicinity, all of which were said to have been caused by diphtheria. My mother steadfastly refused to listen to that story.

My mother's attitude to another pregnancy must have changed after this dreadful experience and eventually when Clarice was thirteen and Stan was ten, I came on the scene: I was always assured that I received a rapturous welcome, being lifted up and cuddled incessantly, according to my parents, and to this they attributed the development of a dangerous infection in my eyes. Apparently, I had to have daily drops in both eyes — administered by our doctor — for a long period of time. In pre-National Health days, all of this brought heavy expenses on the parents' shoulders, but our dear, kind Dr.Tabois employed a "doctor's man" who called at the house every Friday to collect a weekly payment towards their debts. They finally paid off the last of their debt when I was ten years old. However, I was led to believe that, because I was being outrageously indulged as a tiny baby, it was a good thing for all the family when my younger sister, Mavis, joined us in 1932 to share the limelight.

Travel, as we know it now, is a regular part of our lives but, as children, Boston, Lincs, the birthplace of both my parents, would be as far as we went, on visits to our grandparents. I have memories, too, of my mother telling me that she took me on an outing to Sandringham when I was only a few months old and, some time later, on a trip to Lincoln with her old friend, Pearce, where they tasted horse-radish sauce for the first time, much to Pearce's horror.

The earliest memory I have of a friendship must precede the birth of my younger sister. My constant companion was a pet duck which occasionally succeeded in following me into the house, an intrusion which instantly evoked the disapproval of my houseproud and scrupulously clean mother, who

10

unceremoniously removed the creature and incarcerated it with the other poultry in the lean-to which was supported by a low garden wall. I was two years and ten months old when Mavis was born, but I still have a crystal clear memory of the day of her christening. Perhaps it has remained so vividly with me because of the intense indignation I experienced on that occasion: I am still unforgiving about the petty ploy my mother concocted to deny me any involvement in that visit to the church. Two houses away from ours, lived an invalid lady, Mrs. Middleton. I never saw her out of the bed she occupied in the "middle room" downstairs. I loved that lady, for she always had time to talk to me and would readily accept my calling on her, when I would always inquire about her health. As the christening party was ready to leave for church, I was urged to go and inquire after Mrs. Middleton's well-being. The latter must have been told of the plan, because I remember that she chatted to me at length, so that, when I returned home, I discovered that I had missed the special occasion which I had anticipated with an inflated conception of its magnitude.

My childhood misdemeanours stand out in my memory with great clarity. One of my favourite habits was to climb to the top of the brick pillar which formed one of the back garden gate-posts. I recall being perched there one scorching day and being assailed by a tremendous thirst. Hastily, I descended from the pillar and ran to the pantry. I knew that, on the wide shelf, there would be the customary bowl of milk and that I could just about reach it. As I dragged it to the edge of the shelf, I tipped the bowl to drink from it, or so I thought. My height and strength did not prove equal to such a task and, suddenly, the inevitable disaster occurred — my unexpected inundation was not as enjoyable as Cleopatra's baths must have been for her, especially as I was quickly rewarded by an uncomplimentary flood of recriminations and a whack on the backside from an irate mother who bemoaned the total loss of her day's purchase of milk. Our milk was delivered each morning by a milkman who dragged a large churn around the houses. When the lid was removed, a pint measure with a long, hooked handle was exposed. It was fascinating to watch the pints of milk being ladled out into the housewives' waiting receptacles. Another interesting diversion provided by a tradesman from time to time was when the chimney-sweep was called to the house: his face was masked with soot, so that his eyes always seemed to sparkle more than anyone else's. We crowded around as he pushed his brush into the chimney and skilfully inserted rod after rod into the stem until, eventually, he would ask the children to run outside to await the emergence of the brush at the top of the chimney, whereupon we were to run back to him to say that it was visible. During our absence, he had secured covers round the fireplace: "To save cleaning up, Missus," he would always say. When the job was done and he had left, the housewife could see that his precautions had not exactly been effective. The black face of the chimney sweep was more than matched by that of the coalman who, once a week, bent double, slouched into the corner of the scullery, where the open coalhouse was located, so that he could empty the sack of coal that was resting on his back Breathing in all that coaldust and bearing such a heavy load must have taken a great toll on the health of those who tackled that work. In those days, the coal arrived in carts drawn by horses, rather than on lorries: even the lemonade was delivered by similar vehicles. The carts had lights burning on their sides as twilight was descending and this all created a wonderful and mysterious picture. At such a time, a man could be seen turning on the gas for our street-lights every evening. When the horses and carts arrived in daylight, keen eyes watched attentively and, as soon as a horse deposited its droppings on the road, the men would rush out with their spade and bucket, hopeful of being the first to arrive at the coveted means of fertilising their garden.

I realise I was twice a thief from my Mum in those early days. After the milk adventure, I furtively attempted the production of a home-made "goodie" as we called sweets, by helping myself to a couple of teaspoonsful of cocoa and two of sugar, mixing the two and secreting my treasure in an empty sweet-bag, which I hid in the outside lavatory. Because nothing was ever hidden for very long from the piercing and vigilant eyes of my mother, my crime was swiftly uncovered and my secret hidden treat gave rise to another whack on my backside, when she discovered the reason why there had been scattered cocoa on her usually spotless pantry shelf. In my next childhood crime, my sin was shared with another little girl whose name now eludes me. We were playing in a favourite location — Sidney Park, Cleethorpes — when we wandered into the formal flower-bedded area, resplendent with glorious annual blooms in all their summer colours. We were carrying our tiny "shopping" baskets and were both unable to resist the temptation to fill them with the flowers. When I returned home, I placed mine in a jam-jar of water, which I then put on an outside window-sill. Mum must have recognised the source of my acquisitions but, for once, she restrained her anticipated reprimands. A similar misdemeanour took place when I was on a Sunday School trip to the village of Holton-le-Clay. The "treat" began with a ride for all the children on the open back of a smelly fish lorry — it was, after all, during the impoverished years of the thirties and we were all from simple but caring homes. Looking back on it, I wonder how such a perilous mode of transport was considered appropriate for a crowd of young children. Soon after our arrival, I wandered away from the field where we had been deposited to enjoy simple little races and other diversions, to walk into the lane which ran alongside our playground. On the far side of the lane was a pretty little garden fronting a tiny cottage. There were roses growing and some of the blooms were on the lane side. Once again, I was unable to resist stealing some flowers and was just trying to sever the first of my choice when a sweet little elderly face appeared behind the rosebush and its owner said very kindly, "Just wait a moment, dear and I will get my scissors to cut you some." My heart somersaulted, but I waited to accept her generosity. I really do think that her wisdom in handling me on that occasion gave rise to a stronger conscience and finally put an end to my nefarious activities.

I was able to enjoy other activities, too. I do not know how it was acquired, but I was given a "boneshaker" of a second-hand bicycle, with instructions to ride it only in the very wide passageways that ran behind our house in Daubney Street and the backs of the parallel properties in Phelps Street. I spent hours trying to master that wretched bicycle, frequently falling off and grazing a knee or an elbow. I would rush home, yelling and my mother would produce a large tin box from the cupboard under the stairs, to find, I suppose, the universal cure, Germolene. On the last, daring attempt to master my boneshaker, I fell and both knees started to pour with blood. I rushed into the house, but my unanswered yells did not produce my mother. Taking the law into my own hands, I found the treasure-box, but could locate no pink tin. However, there was a cream tin of similar size and shape. Having finally succeeded in opening it, I wiped away the red flood with a not overclean handkerchief and daubed both knees liberally with the pleasant-smelling, white cream. Shortly afterwards, my mother returned from a quick visit to a tiny shop in the vicinity and was astonished to see the results of my independence. She asked what I had covered my injuries with, so I picked up the tin once more. She exploded into laughter and told me I had used the coconut ointment with which she tried to make her very thin hair thicken up. She teased me that I would now grow a beard on each knee.

15

My favourite hobby at this time was sewing. I had a bag of "patches" which was made up from "fents" that my mother bought me for a penny at the Lancashire Fent shop on Cleethorpes Road, Grimsby. From these prized materials, I made tiny clothes for my two-inch celluloid dolls, bought regularly from Woolworths. They were constantly having to be replaced because they dented so easily. For a while, the dent could be removed by inserting a pin in its middle and gently easing the celluloid back up. There was, however, a limit to the number of pin-holes the tiny doll could sustain.

Having a wonderfully patient and partially deaf teacher at school — Miss Edwards — whom we all, boys and girls alike, adored, we girls were carefully taught simple embroidery. I loved it and was often bought a traycloth or chairback with a simple design on to embroider. My mother would proudly give the finished product to a relative — very frequently to her mother, our lovely grandmother. Miss Edwards was always especially kind to me, partly because I was the "top" girl in her class, but also because my sister Evelyn had died when she was a member of that class. Our teacher also tried her hand at drama and I was thrilled to be cast as the princess in *The Sleeping Beauty*: one of her efforts in dramatic production. I recall her demonstration of the elegant posture to be adopted by Prince Charming when he was to revive me from my hundred years' sleep with a royal kiss. My prince, a boy called Dennis, used to practise our kiss after school, as we loitered about the Junior School entrance, awaiting the emergence of our older friends through these gates.

In that little school there was a tradition, I imagine, of doing little productions of plays with us. In the Infants class before I went to Miss Edwards, I recall participating in a play and wearing the black "dressing-gown" kimono, heavily embroidered with a gold dragon on the back. I still have this treasure which my father brought back from his prolonged stay in the Mediterranean, working as a Chief Petty Officer in the Navy and spending time in both Palestine and Egypt. The dressing-gown must, however, have been produced in and exported from China. The water-pitcher, on the other hand, which Dad also brought, is Egyptian and was not costly — he exchanged it for a pair of socks with some trader or other. This relic of our family past I also still possess. Although I no longer know the duration of his absence from home which seemed to my younger sister and me interminable, the recollection of my mother reading extracts of his letters to us is still very dear to me, as indeed is that of his return: the display of all the treasures he had brought back with him from the Middle East was enchanting for us.

I still treasure the Palestinian pen and ink-stand of which my mother was so proud. There was a velvet cover for the back of the settee my mother had recently purchased: we thought this a splendid thing — it had a lion design on it. He also brought a lovely little coffee service in its own silk-lined case and a full dozen tea-service which was regarded with great awe by the

17

family. My sister Mavis and I received little chain bracelets with discs bearing pictures of Malta, where Dad had bought them on the ship's homeward journey: I still have the wreck of mine.

Soon after my father's return, my brother Stan, who had been paternal towards me and had taught me how to tell the time when I was quite young, bought himself the smallest accordion on the market: I seem to recall it was a twenty-four bass. Stan had a vision that he would play wonderful music on this instrument, but his repeated failures with a book called a tutor became too disheartening and he passed the problem on to me. He booked lessons with a local young lady who knew at least the rudiments of reading music and playing simple tunes with both hands on the piano accordion. I must have produced reasonable noises, because Dad decided I should be promoted to a more capable teacher, Miss Ivy Robinson, who, as well as giving lessons, ran a quite successful accordion band. As the members of this band included all age groups, I was very soon made a member. My uniform, consisting of black satin trousers and a red velvet jacket with black lapels, was duly made for me in a shop specialising in such things. Needless to say, my first accordion was unsuitable for this new situation, so it was replaced by a Galanti one hundred and twenty bass. On one occasion we were performing in what, I suppose, was a Working Men's Club: we were on a stage, on very high stools, onto which I had to be lifted. Whilst the curtains were still closed, the slippery surface of my trousers conspired with that of the stool to bring about my downfall. My father, seated in the front row of the auditorium, was horrified to see my feet suddenly appearing under the stage-curtain and rushed to my aid. He found me very confused, having received a severe bump under the chin from my prized and disproportionately large new instrument.

The new accordion was Dad's Christmas present to me and I was thrilled when we went to collect it, because the shopkeeper gave me a book of Christmas Carols with music and words. This memory of Christmas Eve reminds me of the treats in those years. Dad took Mavis and me after tea into the dark night on Freeman Street, Grimsby. We had a stroll around Woolworths — a great adventure for us — and then to the still open and busy market almost opposite. To children, this was an astonishing and exciting spectacle because each stall had two or three carbide lights guttering and hissing and emitting flames and a smell which I associated with my father's much-prized bicycle, known to all by its pet name, Black Bess, which also relied on a similar noisy and pungent lamp. The reason we were allowed this annual treat was to liberate my mother, who was busy preparing the turkey and its accompaniments for the following day, as well as a mountain of queen cakes and other great luxuries of the same ilk.

My mother was a typical product of her class, being adept at feeding us well on what was usually a tight budget. There was always a hot, cooked meal every lunchtime, sometimes made of simple, inexpensive ingredients, such as "pig's fry", costing sixpence from Dewhurst's, a once-weekly regular. On one occasion, she asked me to go for it and was furious when she discovered that they had taken advantage of the child shopper to wrap up some rubbish. She immediately rewrapped my purchase and returned to the shop, bursting with indignation. Needless to say, with my mother on the rampage, the "rubbish" was quickly replaced by an exceedingly generous sixpenny "fry". She also managed to give us teas that we found delicious: she scorned mothers in the vicinity who fed their children bread and jam and, because we heard her frequently voicing this scorn, I suppose we also became prejudiced against such humble fare. We often had an old plate or saucer she had placed in the range oven, piping hot and containing an egg, half a tomato and a small chunk of cheese, all deliciously cooked, this being a great favourite with all the family. Our teas were always complemented with a large plate of bread and butter; I was often in trouble for hiding the crusts under the rim of my plate. Needless to say, I was always forced to eat them. Our favourite tea was composed of half a tiny tin of Nestle's thick cream and an equal amount of jam on our plates. We could eat the ingredients separately or beat them together — I found that cream so blissful that I firmly resolved that, when I was a married lady, I would have a whole tin to myself every day. Crusts were not the only thing which I regularly hid: at lunchtime, cabbage was quite often our second vegetable. Since I did not find it agreeable, I would bury it among my mashed potato and ate it that way, because, with a mother like mine, you ate it without argument.

Just as she budgeted so well with our food, she displayed the same ability to provide us with Christmas and birthday presents, with which we were always delighted. She would spot what we were admiring in shop windows and return, in our absence, to pay weekly instalments on the toys, which were never taken from the shop until the final payment was made. Her policy and fear of debt were instilled into me not by what she said, but by the example that she steadfastly set. She had had, as a young mother, an experience by which she was scarred all her life. She bought something quite expensive, she felt, from a nearby shop and did not retain the receipt. She was unscrupulously pursued by the proprietor, who threatened her with a court case because he claimed her purchases were still owing, so she paid him for the same thing a second time. From that time on, she never disposed of a receipt. I remember a large spike, packed tight with old receipts mantled with dust and retained for many a long year.

The nastiest event in my childhood occurred when I was aged about eight or nine. A largish group of girls, of which I was one, had been playing on our beaches on a long summer afternoon. As we were dawdling back home along the sands, a similar sized group of boys followed us, hurling at us what they and we considered insults, innocent though they must have been. As we approached a footbridge over the railway (known to us as the Sands Bridge), eager for the last word, as ever, I paused to respond with similar insults. I then turned to the footbridge to discover that my wiser friends had already disappeared over it and were probably on the road on the other side of the railway. I set off over the bridge and, in the far corner, before the steps leading down to the road, a man was lounging. As I approached, he attracted my attention and I saw that he was exposing himself: I was terrified, screamed and backed away, falling down several steps, to the sound of his diabolical laughter. When I reached the road, my friends had all disappeared once more. I started to walk home, when I was promptly greeted by Eileen, "a big girl", who saw my distress immediately. As her home was only a few houses away from mine, she walked there with me and told me to tell my mother straightaway what had occurred. As soon as Mum spotted me, she realised that something was amiss, so I reluctantly told her about the incident, for I really felt that I had done something dreadful. My father and brother-in-law were both home from work and were immediately informed. They asked me for a description of the man, which I proferred in a child's vocabulary, after which they took to their heels to find him. My mother and I followed and, when we arrived at the bridge, we met another lady and her child, who had had a more sinister experience. As they were confiding in us, a police car appeared, whereupon the second mother offered them a room in her house which was nearby, as a private space to occupy whilst they were questioning the two children. I was terrified, I remember clearly, to go into the room where two policemen were waiting, even though I was accompanied by my mother. I recall very clearly how, at that age, my vocabulary did not measure up to the demands of the situation: when asked about the criminal's appearance, I told them that he had a purple chin. I thought about this description for months afterwards and eventually indicated to my father a man with a similar complexion. He told me the words I had needed were "dark-shaven". When they asked me to describe this man's actions, my childish version of the episode found this expression: "He was showing me his tail". I believe the man was later caught, but I am not really clear about that.

Not long after this experience, I was involved in an entertainment with the band and, as ever, was chaperoned by my attentive father. Dad was approached by a man from the audience and told, "You have a very wary little girl" and the man went on to describe how he had noticed me as the youngest of the entertainers and had asked me if he could buy me a bottle of lemonade. Apparently, I had taken to my heels and had run off to find my father straightaway: I continued, for several years, to be filled with trepidation when approached by strange men. My final remaining memory of a problem with my association with the band emerged after a practice in the rooms Miss Robinson rented. My mother was always knitting us new outfits and, that evening, I was clad in a newly-knitted skirt and its matching jumper. I took off the accordion and, to my horror, saw that something on the instrument had pulled several stitches into loops on the front of the jumper. It was treated as a minor tragedy when it was revealed to my mother. A similar accident occurred with a red check summer dress she had toiled over when making it on her treadle sewing-machine and with which I was very impressed. However, a group of the local children were involved in a game which consisted of running across the street — we took advantage of the lack of traffic in those days — and leaping onto the low walls with metal railings set into them in front of the houses opposite. The object of the game was to hang on and be the last to be above ground level. Just how I managed my downfall I do not understand but, somehow, I had, in the process of jumping up, caught the bottom of the dress on one of the spikes of these railings. When I leapt off a sickening noise of new material tearing was heard. Eileen, the girl who had helped me home after my distressing encounter on the Sands Bridge, once more came to my rescue and quickly stitched the tear together. Of course, it did not escape the eagle eyes of that matriarchal figure and, as usual, I was soundly reviled for playing such stupid games and practising so iniquitous a deceit, with Eileen's complicity. Mum was not a tyrant really, even though such was our perception of her on sensitive occasions.

In those days, one of the favourite distractions of the neighbours — especially the women — was chatting over the garden walls. I remember eavesdropping on one such conversation when my mother and her neighbour were discussing Miss Doodson, a teacher at Reynolds Street Secondary School. In the eyes of the pupils and their parents, she really did rule with a rod of iron. My mother was insisting that, when her children reached the age to transfer to that school, she would take up the cudgels with the offender, if she was as intimidating towards her children as her reputation suggested. I broke into the conversation rudely forgetting what we were frequently told — "Children should be seen but not heard" — with my own vision of my future, announcing with absolute conviction, "But I am not going to Reynolds Street. I shall go to the Grammar School". My prophecy proved more accurate than my mother's.

Meanwhile, my primary education was still continuing at Barcroft Street where I had loved every minute of the school day with three outstanding infants' teachers. Of the many memories remaining with me, I particularly treasure the one of Miss Selby, our reception class teacher, who taught the whole class, boys and girls alike, to knit, by providing us with thick wooden needles and balls of cream "wool", which closely resembled soft string, and training us into the correct procedures with both, as we chorused in unison: "In, over, through and off". She succeeded very well with this instruction in knitting and also in encouraging us to make little calendars decorated with Father Christmases: these were intended to provide us with Christmas presents for our mothers on Christmas Day. How this simple offering was prized, at least in my home! Our gentle teacher was very kind to all her pupils and her compassion extended to a large group of children who had chronic, rather disgusting, dirty, dripping noses. She had a huge bag hanging on our classroom door, in which she stored oddments of rag torn up from old garments. She frequently rescued children from the shame and embarrassment of the unpleasant "green candles", as we referred to them with childish insensitivity, by providing them with rags to wipe away the offending mucus (our ubiquitous present-day tissues did not become available until several decades later).

Another lovely lady took over responsibility for our group, though I think she was only permitted to be with us briefly because of the regulations which prevented female teachers from continuing after marriage. I imagine that our dear Mrs. Swan was what we now call a supply-teacher. We all found her utterly charming and she won my heart by giving me the highly coveted task of glueing up pictures and cut-outs onto the large rolls of paper unfurled and pinned around the walls. I was even awarded a title: "Little Miss Sticker-on". Whilst I was still in Mrs. Swan's class, I overheard many conversations in which my fellow-pupils were discussing the activities of their elder siblings, who were involved in the "scholarship" and who had either succeeded or failed in that pursuit. I had noticed, in the classroom of the eldest pupils in the Infants' School, a very large model yacht on the top of a tall cupboard. In my innocence, I decided that must be the scholarship and, as our house was very close to the beach, I assumed that, at some stage, I would have to sit on the vessel and sail it on the estuary. The idea petrified me and I was convinced I was destined to fail this test. I had a few extremely distressing nightmares about attempting this ordeal. Fortunately, when a neighbouring child succeeded in passing the scholarship, the true meaning of the word was explained to me. I have already described the adorable Miss Edwards and it was from her "top" class that we were promoted to the ranks of the Junior School. Needless to say, there emerged another teacher to be worshipped. Miss Allen interested us in wide-ranging topics, the contents of which have long remained with me. We set about enthusiastically making a model of a mediaeval monastery which, I fear, was never completed. We were daily drilled in mental arithmetic and Miss Allen expanded our knowledge of world geography. We shared her interest in the Royal Family, especially the visit to Canada of George VI and Queen Elizabeth: we learned the words and music of "Oh, Canada" and "The Maple Leaf", which we sang with gusto. Prior to that, in 1935, when we were still "infants", we had celebrated the Silver Jubilee of King George V, when we proudly wore something red, white and blue during the festivities. I sported a blue beret with lace running through, displaying those special colours. To mark the occasion, all the schoolchildren in Cleethorpes were presented with small tins of biscuits, which had pictures of the King and Queen decorating the top. Mine remains intact, or almost, since my mother decreed that such precious biscuits should not be consumed. I did try eating one several years later and found it to be rather stale. At some later date, Cleethorpes was given the status of "Borough"; once again the children were given a trophy — this time a booklet about the new borough — and this, too, remains in my possession, as does the book about the royal family, given to us to commemorate the coronation of King George VI. There was a mug too, but that was broken, much to my regret.

Our next teacher was Miss Ball, a tiny woman, with a hunchback that was never remarked upon by her loving pupils. She entranced us with her tales of the holiday she had had in France and I was so thrilled when she rewarded me with a red thimble because I had done some pleasing sewing under her supervision. I prized that thimble for many years because Miss Ball had purchased it in France. It was that same teacher who drilled us in the ten commandments and I was terrified as we repeated the seventh until we had it by heart. My interpretation of "adultery" was that one had to avoid becoming an adult and I was perplexed as well as fearful, for I could not fathom how to avoid this sin.

In those days, many local children had displayed a tendency to be absent on Friday afternoons and it was realised, after the investigations by the "Board Man", that their mothers were sending them to Grimsby Docks to collect their father's pay, the fathers being on trawlers far out at sea. It was eventually decided that this absenteeism had to be dealt with, so the Friday morning session was extended to compensate for lost afternoon hours; playtime was extended by, I suppose, ten minutes, to allow pupils to consume a packed lunch they had been instructed to bring to school. Miss Ball directed us in this affair and told us to bring a serviette to put on our desks as a miniature table-cloth. By the time I reached home and was relating these instructions to my mother, the word "serviette" totally eluded me — we children, for the most part, had no experience of such luxuries in our working-class homes of the 1930's. As a result, I assured my mother that I had to take a "theatre" to school with my lunch. After a grilling about the purpose of this object, she was able to solve what I had been told and a serviette was duly begged or borrowed from a neighbour: I used that acquisition reverently, as it was made of white damask linen and had a blue border!

Our lunches were placed by my mother in the usual miniature shopping-baskets, of which my sister and I were very proud. We had different requests as to what we would like to eat: I loved hard-boiled eggs, in particular. One Friday, we must have picked up each other's basket in error and, when I came to open the one I had, I discovered I had Mavis's. Miss Ball told me to rush to the Infants School and exchange the basket for my own. The Infants classes always started their lunch-hour before us, nevertheless, I asked my sister to get my basket and handed her hers, still complete with food. She was a little while gone and eventually returned with my basket — quite empty! I asked her where my food was and she replied, "Oh, I ate it before you came". "Give me yours back, then", I responded. "I can't. I have eaten that as well". Tearfully, I returned to my beloved Miss Ball. Although teachers at that time, I believe, received pitiful salaries — especially the women, who did not receive equal pay — she quickly provided me with part of her lunch, so that I had my introduction to Macvita biscuits, which seemed to me

29

to be the most delicious treat that I had ever tasted. It is not surprising, when we recall such compassion, that our teachers were so highly respected and affectionately regarded.

Our great treat of the week came on Saturday mornings, when we queued at the cinema for the children's entertainment: I think we paid threepence to gain admission. As we queued outside, the older children regaled us with stories of what would happen if Mussolini invaded our country, as he had already overrun Abyssinia. We were dejected to learn from these "knowledgeable elders" that, during World War One, German soldiers had performed dreadful cruelties on the Belgians, making the adults stand in bowls of scalding hot porridge, whilst their babies were thrown into the air and impaled on the soldiers' bayonets. Our informants went on to say that we could expect similar treatment here if Mussolini came, predicting solemnly that the Germans might join them as well. We were accustomed, of course, at that time, to hearing Adolf Hitler bellowing terrifyingly on the radio and these stories preyed upon my mind, as did the searchlights that I could see every night through my window, sweeping the sky. My mother recognised that I was becoming more and more withdrawn and nervous and she questioned me about my fears. Once more, I was taken to Dr. Tabois who, after listening patiently to my mother's account of my symptoms, lifted me onto his desk and took both my hands in his. He talked to me at length, offering me all kinds of reassurance with the utmost patience. Whatever he prescribed as medication,

I do not know but, years later, my mother told me that he was treating me for a "nervous breakdown" as it was then called. My memory of him is that he was one of the kindest, gentlest people I have ever known.

My health problems seem trivial when I think of the sufferings of a boy living almost opposite, across the passage behind our back garden. He seemed to me, when I first became aware of him, to be very fortunate: many "uncles" visited their home and one was a permanent resident there. The latter always gave all the children a penny whenever they walked past, so I thought that family must enjoy great wealth. However, one bright sunny day, I saw a relaxing chair made up as a bed in their back garden and, lying on it, was the son, Sidney, always referred to as Siggy. He was a shadow of his former self but could still feebly raise his hand in a wave and offer the sweetest of smiles as we passed by. One day, the day-bed and Siggy were no longer there and soon we saw a hearse outside the front door of the house where this victim of tuberculosis had lived to about the age of fifteen. There was a sombre sadness in the neighbourhood for many days, strongly resembling the oppressive cloak of sorrow in which the town was enveloped whenever trawlermen were lost at sea. In those days, townspeople shared both sadness and joy. When the war actually came, my brother, who was in the Royal Naval Reserve, was called up straightaway and directed into the minesweeping service, which is where converted trawlers were used. The boy who had died had an elder brother, Roddy, a good friend of my brother. One day, when they were on minesweeping patrol in the North Sea, Stan and his fellow sailors saw a trawler drifting. Pulling alongside, they saw no human movement. Some of the younger men clambered on board, where they witnessed a terrible scene — all the seamen riddled with bullets. It was especially horrible for Stan because he found Roddy propped against a door, dead, as were all his shipmates. They had been "strafed" by a German fighter-plane. How that family suffered adversity! I still remember the letter my brother wrote, giving his moving description of this heartrending experience and yearning to share his sorrow with us.

The Walker family, living next door to the Newmans and opposite to us, were a colourful group. By the time that 1939 arrived, I think they had six or seven children, the first of whom was the only daughter. She won great respect when she, together with a boy called Thomas Parker from the other end of the passage, passed the "scholarship" — one to attend the Girls' Grammar School, the other to Clee Grammar for boys. When I saw the adulation they received and their school uniforms, I was even more resolved to follow in their footsteps, having begun to grasp what was required of us in the "scholarship" and realising, with great relief, that no water was involved. Joyce Walker was, as far as I remember, the only one in the family, before the war, to achieve this success and she later qualified as a nurse. Chatting with my mother one day, when I had just learned that Maurice, the fourth child, was suffering from "quinzies" I was adding up the number of children in the Walker household and, when

I had named six, I added, "So that makes eleven". My mother asked me why I had added five and I pointed out sagaciously, "Well, we must now include Maurice's quins". That story was repeated to all and sundry whilst I blushed, as I had, by then, had my error explained to me.

There were two weddings in our family when Mavis and I were still children and enchanted to act as bridesmaids. Clarice's was the first. We had the glory of becoming aunts when I was seven and Mavis was four. My sister had given birth in 1936 to Byron, a most beautiful baby, and then, in March, 1938, his brother Kenneth was born. My brother was very young when he married Norah and their first-born, Brian, came on the scene very close to the time when Kenneth arrived. We were so thrilled with all of these beautiful babies. It was the presence of babies that gave rise to two nicknames for me: "Daw-Daw" was how Mavis had addressed me when she first began to talk, whilst to Byron I was "Elly". When Kenneth came home from the maternity home, I rushed in from school, bursting with excitement to inspect my new nephew and was in deep disgrace when I commented that he was like Donald Duck. He looked rather strange to my childish eyes because he was born with two front teeth.

I very much enjoyed visits to a nearby non-conformist Sunday School and the occasional treats we had there. From time to time, we were regaled with a "magic lantern" show, a primitive form of film presentation, and the most memorable event was the Christmas Party at the associated Seamen's Mission in

33

Grimsby, where we enjoyed games of "Blind Man's Buff", "Musical Chairs", "Oranges and Lemons" and "Here we go round the Mulberry bush", to mention but a few. We each had a prize of an orange and an apple to take home after the festivities, as we did also on the Saturday morning before Christmas Day, when the cinema show for children was concluded. The manager of the cinema distributed the fruit at the door.

We were a fortunate generation, in that the street could be used so safely as a playground, especially on long summer evenings. The big boys or fathers would often turn a clothes-line into a skipping-rope for the girls — several of us, therefore, being able to skip in unison. Frequently, a group would form for a game of "Hide and Seek" and, at other times, we would draw a "Hopscotch" on the pavement and organise a competition. We also tried to put on little entertainments for each other and I possessed my "treasure box" of discarded adult finery, including very high-heeled shoes which were much too big for us. One day, my mother proudly returned from her Freeman Street shopping expedition, bearing a large, flat box which she gave to me. I was enraptured to find inside a new "bridal" veil and headdress which were destined for my dressing-up box. What a prize! I am sure she had discovered a great bargain.

My father gave me another very much appreciated present — a brand new Hercules bicycle. I imagine that my parents were concerned about the frequent falls from the old boneshaker to which I had continued to succumb. At that time, I was entrusted with a house-key when I left for the afternoon session at school, on those days when my mother thought she might not be back from her shopping expedition in time to unlock for us. I was firmly instructed to do my accordion practice before going out on my new bicycle, but temptation began to overwhelm me: I would take out the accordion, drape the duster over it as usual, to make it appear that the duty had been performed and rush off to enjoy my new acquisition. On one occasion when I did this, however, I was furtively tiptoeing out of the room towards my forbidden goal, when a thunderous voice bellowed "And where do you think you are going, young lady?" My mother had caught me out again and I was much reviled for my untrustworthiness. Over the following years, that bicycle proved far more useful to me than did my musical instrument, although the latter was also well used for quite some time.

CHAPTER
TWO

War and a Move to
The North-East

As war loomed nearer, my father acquired the best job of his life when he was appointed civil inspector of armaments. At first, he worked at Woolwich Arsenal but, by August 1939, he had been transferred to Vickers Armstrong, located in Scotswood, a sprawling suburb of Newcastle which edged the northern bank of the river Tyne. Apparently, he was anxious about our future safety if we continued to live on the east coast, so close to Grimsby docks, but he had the good fortune to find a thirties vintage semi-detached house to let, located not too far from Blaydon-on-Tyne and occupying a site on the fringes of the parkland, originally on the Clavering estate, where their ancestral home still stood. Our chattels were quickly packed so that, on her forty-fourth birthday, my mother, her two young daughters and a large cage full of her beloved budgies, all settled into a compartment of an LNER train which took us to Darlington, where we changed into a train for Newcastle. Dad collected us at the station, bought us a meal and then guided us to the bus which took us to Axwell Park — we had landed in paradise and were destined to remain there until June, 1945. As well as shepherding her two younger children to seats on the train, mother found a guard, to whom she handed over the huge, home-made cage full of outraged budgerigars, accustomed to inhabiting her much-loved aviary. The latter, dismantled, was taken to accompany the house contents in a freight container, collected from our Daubney Street home by lorry and transferred onto a flat railway wagon to be transported to "The Croft", Shibdon Road, Blaydon-on-Tyne.

On what remained of the walls surrounding the Clavering estate where we lived in Axwell Park, we could find a crumbling stone gatepost, on which was proudly embossed the Clavering family emblem — a severed hand! We were assured by many local people that this symbol testified to the supposed origin of how the Claverings acquired the land. Their ancestors — believed to be Vikings — benefited from the traditional ruling that whoever placed a hand first on some newly discovered territory had an indisputable right to claim it for his own. One of the Claverings was so enraptured with what lay before him and was so filled with longing to possess this beautiful tract of land that he cut off his hand and threw it across the waters of the river Derwent along which they were sailing: he thus ensured, as the hand landed on the nearby bank, that the much-desired prize became his. I know little of any other fame attributed to this family except that, on a building as one entered Blaydon — probably the Town Hall — there was a plaque which honoured the memory of Napier Clavering, a successful Victorian general, I believe.

By the time we came to live there, the Clavering house had obviously been sold and converted into a school where boys were detained because of their criminal records. We all, rather cruelly, knew it by the name of "Naughty Boys' School", the term "Borstal" not being in current use at that time. Uniformed, the boys were regularly paraded on Sundays, marching to attend a church service in Blaydon, but otherwise, except for rare mishaps, they were kept very much confined on the premises or its immediate environs. They were, I think, encouraged to assist with the upkeep of their gardens.

The parkland closer to our house had lovely facilities to offer children — a boating lake, not much used for that purpose in those wartime days, clogged as it was by weeds, but a good source for sticklebacks and other tiny fish like minnows, as well as the occasional eel. When frozen over in the winter, it was a hazardous but inviting place to attempt to become proficient with the ice-skates that the local children seemed to have found among their Christmas presents: however, skating was nigh on impossible because the surface of the lake was never smooth. Behind the houses near ours, there was some unused land with a small hillock that was perfect for our toboggans when the winter snows covered it over. As ever, our father concocted a clumsy sledge for us, whereas the other children had more prestigious, less bulky sledges and scorned ours. Beyond, was a piece of woodland which we thought was perfection.

There, bluebells bloomed profusely in the spring, as did occasional wild daffodils and purple primroses which were known to us as "dusty millers", the derivation of which remained a closed book to me. I found wild arums there and, on the hill just outside the woodland, vetches and shepherd's purse flourished. Stretches of bracken took over as it came to its gradual end. The boating lake was bordered by pink flowers which we called "milkmaids" and there were ample supplies of "bread and cheese leaves" — I think from hawthorn trees, of which there was an abundance. A ubiquitous tough grass invaded every available spot and this, if split carefully down its middle and then stretched tightly between two thumbs, allowed you to blow through and produce a strong, squeaky noise. There were so many stimuli to encourage my early addiction to flowers and the gifts of a bountiful nature: even pink rhododendrons had taken to the wild at the top of the sand quarry — another hazardous hunting-ground. The trees in the field adjacent to the lake were good for climbing and the "shaky" bridge, further along the lake from our fishing place, was a constant temptation to the more daring children — of late, my younger sister has furtively admitted to being one of the foolhardy. Often the children would gather in the field behind our house and play a primitive form of cricket. My most vivid recollection of these games is one of my own inattention as wicket-keeper, thus falling victim to the boy next door's careless batting: I really do believe that I saw stars that evening as his bat hit my face instead of the ball.

Before all of these pleasures could be enjoyed, we had to familiarise ourselves with a wider area than the park. Our mother, always a great walker, marched us into Blaydon so that we could investigate its facilities. Her chief interest, to discover a grocery, was soon satisfied and remained a source of delight to her for the following five years. She particularly appreciated the friendly welcome she received in Walter Wilson's from the jovial manager and his friendly staff. She displayed both astonishment and pride when several Tynesiders complimented her on her children's speech. We also explored the town for a school and were duly enrolled in the primary school. Several of our local playmates did not attend the same school because of their Catholic faith, but they came with us on the bus into Blaydon to attend the nearby Catholic primary. As soon as war was declared, the school day was restricted to mornings only, as there was a fear, I believe, that many children could be killed when massed together, should there be an air-raid. I am not sure, but I think that the final year-group were permitted to attend only three mornings a week at first.

As soon as my father knew that war was inevitable, he provided my mother and the two of us with some sort of digging implement and, wielding his own spade, instructed us in the art of excavating a "dugout" which, he claimed, could save our lives once hostilities began. We succeeded in producing a rectangular pit which remained a useless monument to my father's ingenuity until it was overgrown with weeds and was really quite valueless. At that time, he owned a shotgun which he planned to use for shooting rabbits, but never did. Of the other function which he foresaw for the weapon, we received due warning. If the Germans entered our locality, he would shoot us all so that the invaders would not practise their evil habits on his beloved family. In due course, many of the heaps of dug soil were replaced and Dad indulged his next enthusiasm — "Digging for Victory". His efforts did produce lovely vegetables, far more useful to us than the empty hole we had all worked on so diligently.

When we were finally able to go to school, the buses into Blaydon were always tightly packed with people, no matter what time of day one boarded them. I remember with great pleasure and admiration the curriculum which Miss Reid, our teacher, offered to her charges. We were admirably taught in English and Arithmetic, as well as in Geography, History, Music, Art and Crafts. She stimulated great enthusiasm for all these pursuits. New horizons were opened to me, but I confess to her complete failure with me in Art — I remained as hopeless as I had always been. We had one lesson each week with another teacher, whose name sounded like Miss Pears. She guided us in the skill of copperplate handwriting, in which she achieved with me as dismal a result as those of my artistic efforts. It was, however, a great joy to return to the more tender care of Miss Reid after half an hour of torture with her severe colleague, who never employed our Christian names: we were to her "Little girl" and our surname. The rapture of once again opening our copies of Pitman's Common Sense in English was a great relief.

We tackled vocabulary exercises and grammar tests, all of which I found absorbing but, above all, we were allowed to take home these precious manuals in order to learn quite lengthy passages from Shakespeare — *When icicles hang by the wall* and "How now, spirit, whither wander you?" — as well as poems, such as *The Fiddler of Dooney*. It was with this little book that I also learned to prize the Fables of Aesop and many other treasures. Miss Reid was very advanced in her methods and had a lovely little collection of books which she called her library. We were permitted to borrow one of these to take home to read and it was thus that I read a book about Dartmoor and a child's frightening encounter with a ferocious-looking man, clad in a strange yellow suit, daubed with large white arrows. I failed completely to understand this story, but was much happier with my next borrowing — *Lamb's Tales from Shakespeare*.

Miss Reid taught us the art of making bowls from papier-mache and puppets, the heads of which were formed by placing an old tennis-ball inside the foot of a discarded stocking. The rest of the body was gradually added by stuffing newspaper into the stocking. There were, however, much more serious tasks on the horizon. Miss Reid's class was the "top" class and it must have included about forty children of all abilities. Nevertheless, we were all informed that we were to learn about the scholarship examination and would probably be entered for it, if our parents wished it. Because of the limitations of our hours in school, it was decreed that the examination would be limited to two tests, as opposed to the wider-ranging tests hitherto. For preparation, we were given exercises of the type that we could expect when the portentous day arrived. Many years later, I came to understand that we had taken an intelligence test and, I think, exercises examining achievements in Arithmetic and English. I have no recollection of taking the test itself, except for one morning of combined apprehension and excitement. But I do remember an interview with the Headmistress, Miss McKinnon, a stern, tall lady, known to all and sundry as the "Yacht", because she was said to sail grandly around Blaydon. To my astonishment, I found her amazingly gentle and reassuring. She also revealed this characteristic to me on another occasion, when I had fallen and sprained my ankle on the stone staircase, commiserating warmly as she bandaged my injury.

I was later summoned to this august presence and quaked with fear when she complained bitterly of my sister's lack of academic achievement, asking me — a mere ten year-old — how I accounted for her lack of ability in reading. Totally perplexed, yet anxious to protect my younger sister, I assured her that, in Cleethorpes, she wouldn't have been taught to read at her age. I had no idea what had hampered Mavis's progress really, but it was a matter of family solidarity to defend her, if possible. The "Yacht" must have decided that I was a complete fool, but she did not say so and was later jubilant when she heard that I and three or four other girls from my class had passed the examination for the Grammar School. One of the successful few was a lovely but rather tragic girl who was ill-clad and never looked particularly clean, but was extremely gifted and whose artistic talents far outstripped all of those other would-be artists in the class. Despite her achievement in the examination, her parents decided that they were unable to allow her to go to the Grammar School because of the need to purchase uniform and all the accoutrements required: PE dress, hockey stick, tennis racquet and several other items. I think it was the same child who walked to Axwell Park each week, bearing bundles of firewood produced from chopped-up crates, begged from shops. My mother, tenderheartedly, bought a good proportion of her wares and gave her little gifts in addition. The whole population had been issued with gas-masks by this time and our family had become proud possessors of leather or Rexine cases to replace the government issue of flimsy cardboard boxes in which the masks had arrived. For some reason, I had acquired two such new cases, so our little "Woodgirl" as Mum called her, was given my spare case. Apparently, she was enchanted with this gift. At a later stage, my mother saw the child looking longingly at the budgies in the aviary: the following week, she presented the child with a cage, no longer in use, a young bird and a bag of birdseed. We hoped that the little thing would survive, but Mum said it was worthwhile whatever happened, because of the rapture and incredulity which the girl displayed on receiving the treasure.

This inability to ignore the needs of others must have quickly been noted by the tramps who frequently passed through our area. Mum faced a steady stream of these men, for they had heard they would be given a hunk of bread (and cheese, if the ration stretched to it) and a delicious mug of hot cocoa at our kitchen door. She would also add a penny or two, until a neighbour informed her that she had seen at least two of Mum's recent protegees lying helpless in the shrubs beside the road leading up to the wood, with an empty bottle of methylated spirits alongside. Thus, my mother was compelled to restrain her generosity, because she nursed a lifelong hatred of drunkenness. Her compassion, however, remained. On one occasion, there was a knock on our back door and, when my mother opened it, she saw an emaciated man, shivering pitifully and clutching a large, rolled-up rug. He demonstrated his poverty by opening his jacket and revealing a totally unclad and bony chest. He told her he needed to sell the rug in order to buy food for his children. Needless to say, his appeal did not fall on deaf ears and soon he was pocketing the paltry sum for which he had asked: the rug now adorned our sitting room floor. It was obviously quite new and my mum came in for a thorough berating when Dad came home that evening. He pointed out to her that she had probably committed a felony by buying stolen goods. Both parents were unwilling to risk incriminating themselves or a possibly innocent man so, as far as I recall, the rug remained on our floor and lasted quite a few years, the police never having been informed of the incident.

A Mr. Hughes, who lived nearby — a gentle, kindly man, afflicted with palsy (that was my mother's name for his condition) — used to take a group of children once a week along the blacked-out roads to a tiny Methodist chapel in Blaydon, where we attended a class called "Christian Endeavour". It was quite eery finding our way along obscured pavements when there was no moon or brilliant starlight. On one occasion, one of the older boys — a rather refined young man — crashed into a barely discernible lamp-post in the murky darkness and, with his usual courtesy, exclaimed, "Oh, dear! I do beg your pardon". Guessing what had caused his mishap, the rest of the children predictably exploded into loud, cruel laughter. The blackout often presented such problems. Once, in the safety of the little school-room behind the chapel, we were told that we would shortly be entered for a Scripture examination to test our studies. We were advised to study carefully several chapters of the gospels and, eventually, the examination evening arrived. I remember what pleasure I took in scribbling away and my joy when, a few weeks later, I discovered that I had passed the examination with honours. I still possess my certificate recording that achievement. I also have the letter my parents received, confirming that I had been successful in the entrance examination for my lovely new school.

The religious life of the Catholic children seemed very mysterious to us: once a week they went to confession. We were inquisitive enough to probe into this and were told that they had to tell the priest about all their sins. They then explained that, if they prayed with their rosaries, which they proudly displayed to us, all the prayers decreed by the priest, they would be absolved. This absolution seemed very unjust to me — we Protestants would be amassing a huge burden of sin, whereas the Catholics could jettison theirs every Thursday! However, my greatest quandary was what sins I could confess to, if the opportunity ever arose. My mother had dealt with my misdemeanours rigorously and had transformed me into a good little girl, or so I believed.

Another very remunerative Catholic custom soon also came to our attention. If one passed the Catholic church as a wedding party was emerging — a frequent event on a Saturday morning — a man in the company would hurl handfuls of threepenny bits at the congregated bands of children, who pounced skilfully on this booty. My sister and I soon learned the technique and we had some very profitable periods of loitering outside the church whilst our mother did her shopping.

To return to the Methodist Church, I was persuaded to join the Girls' Life Brigade and, at one meeting, was presented with a uniform of the correct size. I proudly bore home my new acquisition, but Dad took one look at it and said, "That's second-hand and no daughter of mine is wearing other people's cast-offs. We don't know where that's been". My pleas and tears were quite in vain and I was compelled to return the offending garments the following week. My shame and embarrassment must have been palpable, but I was not permitted to continue my membership without a uniform and the rejected items were all that were available. I had been fully prepared in every other way for joining, even to making the necessary vows that I did not fully understand. I chanted, "I promise to abstain from intoxicating liquor" though I puzzled at length over "abstain" "intoxicating" and "liquor" and eventually had recourse to a dictionary, whereupon I realised the significance of my undertaking. I observed my promise throughout my girlhood, student days and early teaching life, but succumbed on my wedding day when, just as we were preparing to depart on our honeymoon, our best man opened the first bottle of champagne we had ever seen. He had selected "Veuve Cliquot" which, at that time, meant nothing to either of us, nor did we respond with the sort of enjoyment that we would today: it was quite a long time before such refinements brought us pleasure.

There were two ways in which the shroud of blackout darkness was illuminated. The moonlit nights were breathtakingly beautiful and the navy blue, velvet sky was richly bejewelled with sparkling stars: but such beauty was, obviously, intermittent. There was also the spectacular red glow in the sky when the coke-ovens were opened at the not too far distant Consett coke-ovens. I never grasped why it was done but, each evening, we would see a vivid, glowing red and huge flames being emitted briefly into the night. Awe-inspiring as these sights were, they were also intimidating, as we realised the encouragement that they would present to any intruding German bomber or reconnaissance plane. So many forms of defence would become impotent during this brief illumination — the barrage balloons glistened bright silver and the tiny anti-aircraft installation, which was briefly located at the end of our road, was inevitably more clearly visible, despite being shrouded in camouflage netting.

The two most important possessions in our sitting room at that time — the offending shotgun having been removed and placed in the safety of the Home Guard stores — were the radio and a world map, pinned to the wall. Dad had bought it in a pack which also contained small national flags on tiny pins: these were regularly and painstakingly applied to the map to delineate our front lines and those of the Germans, Italians and later, the Japanese. Such whoops of joy were heard in the early days if our brave troops were thought to have had any successes and with what disconsolate faces did we readjust the flags if the Axis powers made unwelcome progress.

In the months that followed the declaration of war, the consciousness of hostilities was gradually impinging on us. My father found employment for my sister Clarice's husband as a slotter at Vickers Armstrong, across the Tyne from our home. Mark's work as a lumper (unloading fish from trawlers) had dried up, as the fishing trade was too risky, even before their ships were requisitioned in large numbers for minesweeping duties. We were delighted when Clarice and Mark and their two little boys arrived. They quickly found a house to rent nearby in the Park and so the family was gradually reunited. My brother Stan, already serving in the Naval Reserve, had established his wife and toddler in our former house in Daubney Street. Norah, my sister-in-law, was an amenable soul who usually accepted her husband's arrangements: she continued to live there until, one disastrous night, a German bomb was dropped on houses only a few doors away from No. 10. There were, sadly, some fatalities: especially unnerving was the death of an elderly couple, Mr. and Mrs. Bell in No.16, the house next door to the one that Clarice and her family had recently quit to join us in Blaydon. My brother immediately insisted that Norah and dear little Brian should join the rest of us on Tyneside and we were thrilled to have them with us once more. After a short stay with us, they joined Clarice in her nearby rented house. Because we were all living not far from the huge armaments factory across the river, we were probably no more likely to enjoy immunity from the incursions of German aeroplanes than we would have been in Cleethorpes, but we never encountered quite the devastation wreaked by that air-raid on Cleethorpes and Grimsby, which expedited Norah and Brian's evacuation at that point. Brian was a toddler of only two, but he could recall through to manhood that horrifying metamorphosis in those familiar streets and described it to me not long before his untimely death at the age of 59. There were stories of the intruders having dropped boobytrapped gewgaws designed to entrap the unwary and of the injuries being sustained by children who failed to observe the repeated warnings we were all given about touching such tempting objects after air-raids. Rumours abounded during the war years and one that I recall was on the subject of Lord Haw-Haw, as William Joyce was nicknamed. People in Grimsby claimed that they had heard him issue very localised threats in one of his broadcasts, when he predicted the intention of the Luftwaffe to bomb the Dock Tower and Freeman Street market: I do not think the threat was ever fulfilled.

Bombs came to Blaydon somewhat later. When the siren wailed mournfully, announcing the imminent arrival of enemy aircraft, my mother would hurriedly wake my sister and me, urging us to put on our "air-raid clothes" and then quickly lead us down to the Anderson shelter half-buried in the garden. She coped very well in my father's absence, for he had been transferred to other factories, initially in Crewe, then in Lincoln and afterwards in Peterborough: these moves must have well suited his natural and lifelong wanderlust. One night, her tone was more urgent as she shook us into wakefulness, announcing that poor Newcastle was on fire. Her sense of direction was sound — it was, indeed, in Newcastle that a huge conflagration could be seen, but we later learned that the fire was limited to the food depot which had received a direct hit. It was subsequently bruited abroad that the building had held huge concentrations of cooking fat, which would explain the fury of the flames, but I cannot confirm the truth of that rumour. We felt that our worries would be over after this episode, but it was not to be. The next time we had to take cover, I had a lucky escape, my quick scream saving the other two from sharing my discomfort. I had put one foot inside the shelter to locate the little ladder which led down to the floor, when I felt my foot and shin drenched in ice-cold water. The recent rains had obviously flooded our refuge. We quickly returned to the house, where I was dried and rewarded with my mother's universal comforter — a delicious cup of steaming cocoa. After this adventure, the Anderson shelter was abandoned. We were rescued by the kindly old lady in the adjoining semi-detached house, who invited us to share her shelter, also in her garden, but entirely constructed at ground level. We were so grateful for her company, as she was for ours, for her husband was almost invariably drunk every night and remained in the house, singing "Bonny Mary of Argyll", accompanying himself by dashing the fire-irons on the bulky, high fender in their living room. We were hugely entertained by this unorthodox, harmless old man and his warm-hearted wife who, panicking, screamed at us as we entered her tiny shelter, "Mind me gammy leg". Our not very carefully suppressed sniggers were certainly noticed by our vigilant parent and her reprimands still ring in my ears. It was at this time that the war came close to our door. A bomb was dropped in Blaydon on what was reputed to be a bomb-factory; the consequences of the following explosions caused houses like ours to shake ominously. However, the raid was not over and a stray bomb fell on the entrance to our lovely wood beyond the small field behind our house, its impact continuing the horror of the night. Daylight returned, revealing considerable damage to housing in Blaydon, but little in Axwell Park, though the bomb, which had fallen in soft ground, had created a huge crater. This was afterwards, I am sad to say, the cause of a tragedy which will be mentioned later.

Our schooldays, as well as our nights, were disrupted several times when the whine of the sirens alerted our teachers to guide us to the school shelters, located in the games field behind the buildings. Although we were closely bunched on long forms which ran the whole length of the shelter, the atmosphere was kept cheerful by the valiant efforts of the staff, who occupied us in those cramped and murkily lit conditions with games testing our general knowledge. When the "all clear" sounded, we trooped back to our classrooms and were treated to cups of beef tea, very efficiently prepared in the school kitchen. We all rather enjoyed both the hot drink and the further delay to the restart of lessons.

Before hostilities had such an impact on life in England, May 1940 arrived, with the dreadful events of Dunkirk. Although we were not personally involved with anyone still on French soil at that time, we felt desperate anxiety for the poor, beleaguered troops. However, my brother-in-law, Mark, volunteered to help in the evacuation. As far as I can remember, he did not divulge what part he had played during those gruelling days, but it was well understood that anyone who had become involved in that operation must have been at considerable risk We were all greatly relieved when he returned unscathed, but very subdued and we counted our blessings while, at the same time, mourning the many lost soldiers and sailors.

A restriction entered our lives when we were issued with ration books for food and clothing. The laid-down allocations were strictly observed, but we had the good fortune to have a generous neighbour who provided extra eggs for Mavis and me, although she had to register her hens with the appropriate authorities. Many delicacies evolved from abundantly available soya flour and various essences, from which housewives concocted marzipan and other treats. Oats were used freely in baking and, in my family, we had inviting little cakes made from oats and flavoured with either the ubiquitous almond essence or cocoa. Spam became an integral part of our diet, but we regarded it as a great luxury and my mother enjoyed using the wonderful tins of sausagemeat produced in America. She used to scrape off the fat which enclosed the meat and used it to make very tasty pastry, thus saving her precious fat ration, and adapted the meat to make sausage-rolls and pork pies. Another of her efforts, though, did not meet with the same enthusiasm: one lunchtime she proudly informed us that we could have "bananas" for dessert. As bananas had hardly been seen since the declaration of war, we were full of anticipation, but when we were presented with a plate on which resided an object which vaguely resembled a banana in shape and were encouraged to sample it, we recoiled in horror at its taste. After quickly swallowing the tiny piece we had bitten off, we hesitantly told her that we did not like the "fruit" and she was bitterly disappointed, though she did admit that it was made from mashed parsnips, flavoured with banana essence — a recipe she had found in her *Woman* magazine. The experiment was never repeated. On the other hand, we willingly consumed huge quantities of delicious parkin, given bulk by the oats which seemed to be freely available. This cake was especially good when we came in from sledging on cold winter days and even more when accompanied by hot cocoa or "Vitacup", a wartime instant drink, harbinger of many such products in later, more plentiful days.

Our supplies were always augmented when Dad came home for the week-end from Peterborough. He would call at Uncle Tom's in Boston to collect delicious home-grown tomatoes and, sometimes, strawberries in the summer and an abundance of vegetables in other seasons. "Dig for Victory" was a slogan faithfully observed by so many people and gardens were transformed into vegetable plots all over the country. My father had several rows of potatoes in the field beyond our garden-fence, as well as onions and other vegetables. Mark's cousin had continued with his butcher's shop in Grimsby and would bring us the occasional Christmas turkey and, one year, Clarice received a goose. To eat well demanded ingenuity and industry, but the mothers of the day gave us wonderful meals and the wartime bread was excellent and, at that stage, abundant. Mums even managed to produce a variety of baked cakes for our simple parties, while our elderly neighbour, Mrs. O'Neil, baked every Thursday, as she had always done, and introduced us to her lovely yeasty cake, which we consumed with great pleasure.

I ventured into the "war effort" even while I was still at Primary school, finding myself in the home of the invalid Miss Blackwood, together with a group of classmates. The story of how this all came to pass is clothed in the mists of time, but we congregated in her house in order to knit "comforts" for the troops, my first effort proving to be an abortive try at a balaclava helmet. Having taken it home, I just knitted on and on, so that, when I returned to Miss Blackwood a week later, she suggested that it had better be a scarf! I was full of remorse when I visualised a poor, unsuspecting soldier being presented with that khaki monstrosity for which I was responsible. When Miss Blackwood was housebound by her illness, she plied her sewing-machine and her needles to produce tray-cloths, table-runners, chairbacks and other small domestic textiles no longer available in the shops. When her health permitted, she toiled on foot to my home and, probably, to those of the other girls in the group, to sell her products in order to be able to buy more knitting-wool for the group to use. Such groups cannot have been a rarity. My sister's next-door neighbour established one in her home and, on Thursday evenings, the local ladies met there to produce garments of a rather higher standard than we children were producing. Mrs. Rae, this conscientious housewife, miraculously produced cakes and coffee for her obliging knitters, which they relished as much as all the gossip which was passed around while their needles clicked. My mother told her new friends how much I had enjoyed reading from a very tender age, whereupon

Mrs. Rae offered me access to her books. Thus, I was able to read *Girl of the Limberlust: Owd Bob* and, especially *Anne of Green Gables* and ensuing novels in that particular series. *Little Women* led to the others in that sequence and I counted myself blessed in the warmth and encouragement I received from that very kindly lady.

Another much observed slogan was "Make do and mend", at least in our household. We learned the Tyneside technique of making "hooky" mats and all the old lisle stockings, together with worn-out garments of all kinds, were cut into strips, wound into balls, hooked into the old hessian sacks used as the basic fabric and, finally, placed resplendent on any floor, upstairs or downstairs, where my mother felt there was a need. I would enjoy spending half-an-hour at the frame and adding to the mat. My father made us tools by removing the prongs from old forks and then cutting into the rounded stem to form a hook. His efforts were very creditable.

Old clothes did not always meet with such a fate. A cast-off ladies coat, with some reasonable wear left in the fabric became a very desirable acquisition. My mother was given a dark bottle-green one and delivered the coat to a dressmaker she often used. I was duly measured and, the next week, I had a siren-suit — ideal for our sledging fun when the deep snow came. The memory of my bottle-green suit has stayed with me because, on one occasion, as I trudged uphill tugging our homemade toboggan, I sank into a deep snowdrift and, when the other children, hearing my cries, came both to enjoy my predicament and also to heave me out of my prison, loud was the laughter from us all when we saw that the once virgin, white snow which had enclosed me was suddenly a dark bottle green. However, the suit retained most of its original colour and continued to provide winter warmth for the rest of the season. I felt some apprehension as I trudged home, cold and very wet, leaving my sister behind to continue her sport and wondering what sort of reception there would be. However, I was quickly rubbed down with a warm towel, until I was in a fit state to put on dry clothes and then rewarded with a good chunk of my mother's homemade gingerbread and the inevitable, but highly desirable, cup of cocoa. As I consumed my comforts, she displayed my underwear, now quite colourful also, with bottle-green dye in several places.

CHAPTER
THREE

Grammar School at Last

I started my studies at Blaydon Grammar School in September, 1940 and immediately thought myself in paradise. Although my life was not always plain sailing, for the most part I found it blissful. In our time, it was a very happy, orderly school, full of friendly members of staff and boys and girls. As a very small eleven year old, I could not believe that I was sharing the world of those young men and women called Sixth Formers. Their dignity and size was so impressive. At the Christmas Concert, the males in the group sang as a male voice choir, the like of which I had never witnessed before. I remember their last offering was a parody of a well-known song, "Boiled Beef and Carrots", which impressed me considerably. As well as the concert, we had a "party" which, as far as I remember, consisted merely of dancing, though there might also have been refreshments.

I was very proud to wear the school uniform, though my first gym-slip proved the bane of my life. Every Friday evening, I found it necessary to tack the pleats down because they had disappeared during the week and, after leaving the garment hanging in that condition for at least twenty-four hours, I would dutifully press the pleats with a very hot iron over a very damp cloth. I never won that particular battle and was relieved when we were informed that we could wear pinafore dresses, as the gym-slips became more and more difficult to track down because of wartime shortages. Thus the toil was diminished, though I took immense pride in all aspects of the uniform and especially the two blue gingham dresses that my sister made for me for summer wear. My mother dutifully managed to afford all the items listed on my school list — even to almost the last school blazer available. I became the proud owner of this because I was small enough to fit into it. I thought it the loveliest thing, with its elegant display on the breast pocket of the school badge, sporting the motto, "Urbs sapientio conditur", and the blue binding round the front and lapels.

My feeling is that we were very blessed with the academic staff of the school. As more and more men were called up, including several very gifted young men, presumably because teachers were not in a reserved occupation, we bewailed their departure. I think they were, without exception, very popular with us all, especially Mr. Dand, a superb History teacher, whose lessons were a sheer joy. Gradually, the staff appeared more elderly and there were more ladies among them but, almost without exception, they were just as dedicated and interesting as those who had been compelled to move on. Miss McTaggart, our new

60

historian taught brilliantly, whilst Miss Familton, our dumpy little Latin teacher, who almost sang, "Take out your Latin books" as she bounced through the classroom doorway, always occupied the highest pedestal in my estimation. They all seemed old to us, so I have no idea of her age but, whatever it may have been, she had very modern methods and ideas and even taught us to sing the Hoki-Koki in Latin. I have continued to revere "Gaudeamus igitur", learned from that dear lady. One day, when we were in the 3rd or 4th year, she swept into the classroom in her normal manner and suddenly skidded, landing on her bottom. There was not the slightest titter from any of her pupils, whilst two of the boys rushed out to help her: yes, Fammy was very much loved. The Domestic Science mistress was a different character entirely: very severe and unfriendly, probably because the poor lady had too much to do. Not only did she have a full teaching time-table, but also complete responsibility for the school kitchen and the catering. My memory of the school lunches is that they were enjoyable, as was the beef tea that we were given after an air-raid alert. She controlled the domestic staff well and I remember feeling that I was participating in a different life whenever I saw the appropriately attired school maid, dressed up in her small, lacy pinafore and headband. She was likely to be carrying a tray of tea and cake for the Headmaster, Mr. Williams, or some other member of staff delayed at the end of the school day because of detention duty or even air-raid duties into the night. I think the discipline in the school was so very good that the once weekly detained group was insufficient to half-fill the classroom. I was in that group only once and spent half an hour in deep shame to expiate my crime of having been late three times in one term. It was an unforgivable misdemeanour really, as I lived only a stone's throw from the school: I never risked a repetition of facing such ignominy again. There were other pupils who deserved more severe treatment than I had received, but were clever enough not to be found out: for example, the three girls who waited in the cloakroom for my arrival several mornings, two of them pinning me to the wall while the third ransacked my schoolbag and located my Maths homework, in order to fill in the answers in her duly prepared exercise-book. I was terrified of all three, but I found the tall girl with flaming red hair the most daunting. My habitual lateness was partially due to my hopes of avoiding these onslaughts, but I readily confess to my inherent dilatoriness as being an additional contributory factor to my downfall. The irony of these illicit efforts on the part of the bullies was that I was by no means very exceptional in Mathematics and their homework was as unlikely to be successful as mine, on most occasions. Finally, I fell victim to the far less bullying tactics of Tommy Fairlamb in his one effort at plagiarism. At the beginning of an English lesson in our fourth or fifth year, Miss Morley caused a shudder throughout the class when she icily announced: "I am going to read you an essay which was written for this week's Literature homework, as it appears in Tommy Fairlamb's exercise book". She read two or three paragraphs aloud and then she observed "Your work has made great strides, hasn't it young man? Or has your copying improved? I know who wrote this essay and it was not you. Please tell me how you were able to offer me this work." That was my moment of embarrassment and I blushed as if it had been I who was responsible for this subterfuge. However, my classmate did the honourable thing, thus rescuing me by telling the truth, "I helped myself to her exercise book before you collected the pile from your homework shelf, Miss Morley." I was so relieved that he did not divulge my identity, as I gratefully exchanged a conspiratorial look with my very much admired English teacher. She then announced the inevitable — Tommy was to practise his writing later that week by doing an hour's detention.

Quite early in our days in Axwell Park, my sister Mavis suddenly fell seriously ill and was diagnosed as having diphtheria. An ambulance promptly transported her to the isolation hospital, Norman's Riding, where she seemed to spend an eternity. I was immediately tested for the disease by our family doctor; he rubbed my throat with a huge bud of cotton wool, fastened to a stick. The sample was placed in a large envelope in my presence and the doctor instructed me to take it straight to the Post Office. He also presented me with the disastrous news that I was not to attend school for a week, until I had received notification that I was not infected: but I was immediately to report to the clinic near my school for immunisation. My sympathy was at once transferred from my very sick sister to myself, as I faced being banned from my beloved new school. Thus, I endured my longest absence in the whole of the five years that I was a pupil at Blaydon Grammar School. The other unpalatable consequence for me of my sister's suffering was my severe reaction to the diphtheria injection, my arm swelling up considerably and daily becoming more unbearably painful. However, my throat swab was found to be negative and I was allowed to rejoin my fellow pupils, little grasping how blessed I was to have been spared the dangers of that killer disease. My sister recovered eventually from her ordeal and came home with a few gains and a few setbacks. She had acquired a huge population of unwanted lice in her hair, on which my mother immediately declared war and, as a result, she was able quickly to divest my sister of this colossal infestation. It had also been discovered that Mavis had a slight heart murmur — thought to be a consequence of her illness. She had been allowed to take her most precious doll to the hospital with her, but was refused permission to take it back home, for fear of spreading infection — a huge blow, as the shops were no longer laden with such inviting toys. Her gain from the lengthy hospital stay was a Tyneside accent and familiarity with several local, innocent songs. She entertained the family frequently with her renditions of these, especially with one that began "When ye gan to the pan shop". The rest of us took some time to fathom that "The pan shop" in our language was the pawn shop.

Axwell Park, as I have earlier indicated, struck me as a paradise, an ideal location, where children could grow up safely, even though our country was war-torn and vulnerable. It proved far from secure and blissful for a few families. The first tragedy, shared by the whole grieving community, was the sudden death of a dear little, golden-haired girl, the child of our next-door neighbour, not yet five years old. One sunny afternoon, she was playing on a grass verge, when she inexplicably fell forward. Her long, blond curls spread out on the edge of the grass just as the milk-float was trundling slowly past. Her hair was caught in some way in the wheel of the vehicle and the child was killed outright.

It seemed to us that some kind of curse had descended upon our small community when a little boy from Blaydon came to the park with his school-friend, whose home was near the boating-lake, which the two little boys went to inspect. The visitor to the park walked along what we called the "diving-board" close to the little wooden bridge, slipped and fell into the water. The other boy ran for his mother who discovered the victim, already drowned, standing upright in the lake, his head submerged just below the surface of the water. As both boys were just about of school age, they were much too young to cope with such an accident by themselves. Later, another little boy from Blaydon fell into the bomb crater and was also drowned in the water that had accumulated there. The final accident did not have so heart-rending a sequel: my nephew, Byron, was returning home from school in the bus which ran along our main road and, before he could be deterred, dashed out across the road. In wartime days, traffic was very sparse but the inevitable car was there at the wrong moment: my nephew was quite badly injured and was quickly transported to Newcastle Infirmary. Though, at first, we despaired, fearing the worst, he eventually made a complete recovery, to our great joy and relief.

Yet another small incident disrupted our peaceful existence, but proved of little consequence. One day, my elder sister was about to emerge from her lounge, when she was shocked to encounter one of the boys from the local Naughty Boys' School ransacking her handbag. Clarice could be quite formidable and so took charge of the situation. I do not recall what the precise outcome was, but I am quite certain that my sister came out of the event as victor!

More expected visitors arrived from time to time, my mother actually accommodating two Bevin boys, one of whom was my cousin. They were diverted from National Service in one of the armed Services to assist with the mining of coal, so there were two very grimy young men returning to our house at the end of each working day. They were hard work for my mother, as their clothes were inevitably filthy and all her laundering activities were totally manual, there being no washing-machines in those days — at least, not in our house. I am confident also that there were no pit-head baths at the mine, so the bath was in fairly constant demand. The newcomers fitted into the routine of the house, however, and Ernie, the unknown quantity at first, amused us very much with his north-western vocabulary. He referred to my cousin, his workmate as "me marrer" and the packed meal which Mum supplied daily was "me bait".

Social life was also evocative of a country fighting for survival. We had faith in the protectiveness of the Home Guard — heaven help us! — and, as my father and my brother-in-law had volunteered in the earliest days of the LDV (Local Defence Volunteers), we were always involved in their socials, where sausage and mash was our delight, as were even the feeble efforts of any amateur magicians. Entertaining soldiers temporarily located in our area by offering a meal also produced a little variety in our simple lives.

We found other entertainment, too. Our mainstay was the radio, and especially the BBC Home Service. We also made good use of our three local cinemas and were certainly up to date on the latest films. Several proved quite memorable — Laurence Olivier in *Rebecca*, *Colonel Blimp* with Roger Livesey, *The Road to Morocco* with Bing and Bob, Robert Cummings in *Espionage* and many more. It was in the cinema that we saw shots of the war itself on Pathe news which, with the liberation of Belsen, gave us our first introduction to the horrors of the concentration camps. But the latter was not until 1945 and the war years rolled slowly away in the meantime. During the summer months, many of our school friends would gather together spontaneously and, after homework was completed, we would mount our bicycles and ride for miles into the lovely Durham and impressive Northumbrian countryside. Sometimes we would walk, an activity often preferred because we could talk and even argue more freely. Occasionally, a couple of the boys would lift a turnip or two (known locally as "snannies") from a farmer's field, peel them, cut them into chunks and hand each of us a portion which, incredibly, we enjoyed immensely. In the winter, if Dad was home, he would take Mavis and me out in the dark to skate on a frozen pond. What terrible risks we all innocently took! In the summer holidays, I remember my elder sister leaving her children in the charge of my mother and sister-in-law to cycle with my schoolfriend Avril and me all the way to Whitley Bay, reputed to be an enjoyable holiday venue. The best ingredient of the day proved to be the egg sandwiches I had made before we set out and Avril's mother's delicious cake. The seaside resort, our goal of the day, presented a mournful picture of deserted desolation, dominated by a biting wind from the North. We could not find a single vestige of what my parents had seen there before the war and it did not take us very long to turn tail and cycle back home. Clarice's winter invitation proved more fruitful: she took me once a week to ballroom dancing classes in Newcastle. She always partnered me and I twice disgraced myself while in her care. Stepping the wrong way whilst trying to master the fox-trot, I brought us both crashing to the floor. On a later evening, jumping off the bus when we had returned to our home territory, I fell straight into a very smelly heap of blackened snow. I stank abominably and my sister berated me all the way back to her house because, I think, she was fearful of receiving the sharp end of my mother's tongue for neglecting her charge.

Christmas was made to feel as festive as in pre-war days and we really enjoyed our presents. One gift that

Mavis and I both loved was a whole quarter pound of Spam each to eat without bread! When I was enjoying my first Christmas at the Grammar School, Clarice tracked down for me a now antique copy of Shakespeare's works. I still handle it with great love and respect. Our family entertainment for the holiday consisted of card games or Monopoly as we sat round the table, or a singsong, which I had to lead by playing my accordion. We enjoyed it all, but particularly because of the involvement of our lovely mongrel, Toby, who howled, not quite in unison, of course, whenever I played the instrument.

It was in those days that my love of the theatre was inculcated. Avril and I visited matinees at the Theatre Royal. Newcastle, during the school holidays and I particularly remember Vivien Leigh in *The Skin of our Teeth*, Desert Rats' with Richard Green and Jack Buchanan in *The Second Mrs. Tanqueray*. My first school theatre trip was at the same theatre to see *Macbeth* with Donald Wolfit, a performance which, I think, is best not commented upon. My father initiated me into the joys of opera by taking me to the same theatre for a performance of *La Traviata* and I am so grateful for all these opportunities. I also remember with great satisfaction an afternoon spent with Avril exploring the Keep in Newcastle and can visualise so clearly their exhibit of a small guillotine, fashioned in the Napoleonic era by French prisoners of war, who made good use of the materials provided by their prison food. The bones from the meat they were served were exquisitely and skillfully carved to form the main structure of the execution machine, as well as the tiny figures of the soldiers who guarded it. The cutting materials had also been concocted from their food, the whole being a superb model.

We were fortunate to enjoy a whole series of pets while we were at Axwell Park. Our first dog, Nipper, was purchased on the market in Newcastle and was a poor apology for a white terrier. He was a faithless hound, who would disappear for weeks at a time, to return in due course, stinking foully. We shed many tears on the first such escapade but, eventually, we all lost patience with him and when, on a later occasion, he absconded once more, never to return, we no longer mourned him. For our beautiful black cat, however, we wept bitterly when we discovered her poisoned body: she was awarded a solemn funeral in our front garden. Her tabby successor was duly named Tinker. It was then that we acquired our lovely Toby from the next door neighbour, whose bitch had produced a huge litter. She was so loving, obedient and faithful: a great addition to the family. Meanwhile, my mother had lost her fifty-odd budgerigars in the aviary, slaughtered by a stoat, or so it was thought. My sister and I also brought two chicks back from a holiday with our grandmother in Boston and they grew into fine birds. Disastrously, just as I emerged through the kitchen door, my father was in the process of putting an end to one of them, because it was destined to grace our Sunday table. I screamed, ran upstairs, locked my bedroom door and would not, despite entreaties, quit my sanctuary for the rest of the day. When a roast chicken then appeared on the table, Mavis and I both descended into floods of tears and Mother fruitlessly failed to persuade us to eat any meat that day. Similar refusals were to follow when one of the ducks our mother raised to be duly served up as manna from heaven in that world of strict meat rationing followed the same path. We also kept rabbits, which, I now surmise, were raised for the same purpose, but one night an intruder, this time human, entered our garden and stole our beautiful creatures. All in all, we were not very fortunate with our pets, except for Toby, though no predator attacked my frogs or my sticklebacks: nature took its toll on the latter. The aquaria which I employed for my fish were obtained from the cemetery keeper, a very generous man with the property of others. Many of those glass-covered floral tributes were falling into disrepair and the keeper would habitually remove them from the neglected graves. He gave the glass covers to local children because, when balanced upside down, they made ideal receptacles for pond life.

As I progressed in years, studies and interests, I became enamoured of the singing of Bing Crosby and patiently saved my meagre pocket money until I could buy one of his records. I also had to save the bus-fare into Newcastle to visit the nearest record shop. My elder sister gave me an old gramophone, beside which I spent many happy hours. On one of those shopping trips, I wandered into Woolworths where, in those days, there were counters, divided into separating trays. As the war progressed, it was unusual to see more than two or three of these trays containing any goods for sale. Sometimes, a consignment of combs would appear, to be quickly snapped up by customers, despite the fact that we had learned they would scratch our scalps unmercifully as well, as quickly starting to shed their teeth. As I wandered round a virtually stockless shop, I saw two very young and cheerful-looking paratroopers enjoying some leave. It was late in the war — I think 1944 — and a few days later we heard of the Arnhem landings on the radio and, afterwards, of the dreadful outcome of that invasion. I have thought repeatedly, with deep regret, of those two young men who had probably been enjoying their last days of innocence when I saw them. Later, I cycled to visit my friend Avril in nearby Dunston and, as I passed some farmland, I noticed very bronzed young men working in the fields. Avril's parents told me that they were Italian prisoners of war. I was reprimanded when I returned home for saying how handsome I thought them, when I described the episode. It was wartime and the doctrine was to detest our enemies — not always easy for fifteen year-olds. The war really imposed itself on our consciousness when the residents of the Park woke one morning to find a huge number of army vehicles parked on most of the available empty land. It was very close to Christmas and, as the army personnel had scarcely any facilities, they were invited to enjoy hot baths in some of the houses and provided with a homely Christmas Day, lunch and dinner included. We found these soldiers courteous, entertaining and grateful. I imagine that our leaders were beginning to plan further invasions of the continent and these visitors were harbingers of future events.

When the war finally came to a close, the atmosphere immediately changed. We walked with delight in our hearts, our feet ready to dance with joy as our awareness of the news resurfaced. So, soon after VE (Victory in Europe) Day, my contemporaries and I had another excitement to face — our School Certificate examinations. I confess I found the following days satisfying and exciting and I pay tribute to my school for preparing us so well for these examinations, having been conditioned into the routine of facing the papers with equanimity. However, despite the fact that I had actually enjoyed most of the work at school, there were, for me, dark clouds looming ominously on the horizon. My father's contract with the government ended with the hostilities and all the family decided that a return to Cleethorpes was desirable — at least, all except Mavis and I. Heartrendingly, the only peace we had enjoyed for five years was shattered but two mere teenagers had to accede to the wishes of the family. So, for the first time in all their lives, my parents, sister and brother-in-law managed to put a deposit on a largish terraced house in Cleethorpes and their request for a mortgage was promptly granted. All too soon, therefore, we had to desert our heaven.

CHAPTER
FOUR

Return to Cleethorpes

I was readily accepted into the Sixth Form of Cleethorpes Girls' Grammar School, as I silently deplored the idea of quitting a mixed school for a single-sex institution. However, I must instantly affirm that my new schoolmates were welcoming and friendly, far beyond my expectations, and they found me impressive because I had studied Latin for five years, whereas there, the ones who wished to offer the subject in the Higher School Certificate had to start the subject in the Sixth. It was a new and pleasant sensation to have a feather in my cap. Even more so when, gradually, they all fell by the wayside and I ended by being the only Latin candidate in that year-group. I had an unfair advantage but, in addition, a great love of the subject. Alas, most of that knowledge now eludes me.

Life in my new school was very different from what would have been the case had I stayed in Blaydon. We were treated as young ladies and, as Sixth Formers, we were allocated a room for private study during our free periods. We also took our school lunches in the same room and felt very superior to the younger pupils as a consequence. Our teachers, with one exception, were very kindly and dedicated to their pupils. Their standards were demanding and their teaching was often inspiring, despite their little eccentricities. One of them stored her handkerchief up her knicker-leg, to our great amusement, and the same lady had some entertaining oddities of speech. I still benefit from the teaching of our Headmistress, Miss Daffodil Marigold Fisher, a portly lady with ruddy face and a laugh which was more like a loud exhalation of breath. She taught us, or rather inspired us with, the set books from Chaucer and Shakespeare. I did not need even to revise *Hamlet, The Tempest* or *The Merchant of Venice* for my later degree finals, so well was I instructed in each of these by Miss Fisher. Her treatment of the Prologue to *The Canterbury Tales* and two of the Tales has stimulated my appreciation of Chaucer ever since. Her one weakness was her love of reminiscence so, if we were feeling lazy during an afternoon lesson, someone would ask a question which she knew would engender a desire in Miss Fisher to bring back personal associations with which she would regale us for the rest of the period. We used a similar ploy with the lady with the oddities of speech. We would introduce a line of questioning which led her to use a word with an internal "g", which she seemed unable to pronounce. The efforts we made to get her to say "bungalow" were gargantuan but, if all else failed, we could always engineer a reference by her to "Pitt the Younger".

There was one teacher that we all detested. We had a very uncomplimentary nickname for her (which I will not divulge), but I will admit that her subject was PE and Games. She would drag even the most unwilling of us, brandishing our hockey-sticks, out onto a snow-laden field but, if we were clad in our school berets, scarves and overcoats, we were forced to return to the cloakroom and remove the offending garments. One day, my friend and "twin", June, who was also born on June 12th, 1929, and I decided we could not face the ice-cold east wind, so we concealed ourselves in the gap between the two sets of drawers in the teacher's desk in the Chemistry lab, recently vacated by the last science class of the day. Almost immediately, we were hauled out by the PE mistress, our hideout not being as original and unknown to her as we had hoped. Another member of staff who was unfriendly, but not as daunting, was the Deputy Head. Our beloved Headmistress had, on one occasion, been absent from school for several days and rumour had it that she was gravely ill — not pleasant news to anyone's ears. On one of the mornings of her absence we, the entire school, were hastily summoned to the hall and when the staff and pupils were assembled, full of consternation and fearing bad news about the Head, the Deputy Head swept in and announced portentously, "I have something very serious to tell you all. Someone has stuffed a whole toilet-roll down one of the lavatories and has caused a great problem with the plumbing. That block of toilets cannot be used until the difficulty has been dealt with." A great sigh of relief swept through the hall, followed by a burst of tumultuous laughter, reflecting our newly-found solace in knowing that the Headmistress had not died, as well as our reaction to the ridiculous anti-climax in realising the cause of that woman gathering us all together. I remember our Sixth Form days for the hard work required of us — very often I was engrossed in the work until after midnight, much to my mother's disapproval. However, our daily life also brought us immense fun among our contemporaries, whom I found extremely convivial. Several of us were light-hearted enough on Saturday evenings to attend the weekly dance at a small ballroom called the Cafe Dansant, facing the sea at the end of Cleethorpes Promenade. There, we regarded it as a special honour if one of the "Boys in Blue" from the local RAF aerodrome approached one of us to request the next dance. Their politeness was charming.

The house that the family had bought was becoming gradually more palatable. It had been requisitioned by the army during the war years and servicemen had been housed there. When we first occupied it, it was far from inviting, with dart holes in various doors where a dartboard had been suspended, but the players' aim had not always been accurate. It was difficult to comprehend how the bath had deteriorated so unpleasantly and my parents never discovered the reason for its decrepit condition. It was abysmally encrusted with rust and was totally uninviting to the whole family. Ultimately, my father came up with his kind of solution when he discovered a new kind of paint which claimed to be able to restore the surface of baths. First, he had to spend hours removing the offending rust and, having completed that task to perfection, he then set about painting the interior with three coats of paint, a two-day wait intervening between each application. Once the third coat had been administered, the bath was filled with cold water and left unused for two weeks, as the instructions advocated. We must have been a smelly band by the time that the bath was ready for use! Dad insisted that Mum should be awarded the honour of enjoying the first dip, much to my chagrin, as I felt that, if I remained much longer among the great unwashed I would be cold-shouldered both at school and by the "Boys in Blue" at our Saturday night hop. The bath was duly initiated by mother, but she was mortified to discover that, when she wanted to get out, she was stuck to the sticky paint at the bottom of the tub. Once she had defaced Dad's work, the paint finally hardened, but it was not the most comfortable of surfaces on which to seat oneself. However, we struggled on with our unattractive bathroom for several years until, ultimately, a new suite was installed, creating great relief for all those who had, for years, made use of the resurrected bathtub. By the time that this improvement took place, I was already away in Leicester. I must add that there were many teasing inquiries of my mother as to how much of the paint had adhered to her nether regions, but she ignored these impudences haughtily.

I suppose it was at this stage that I became more aware of the individuality of my mother's colourful idioms and vocabulary She spoke a rich vernacular, some of which I have traced back to Viking expressions. Her word for a long tale or diatribe was "stitherum", which I found in the huge dialect dictionary in the

University library, where its Viking origins were described. My studies in Old Norse led me to accept a similar origin for her verb "orm", meaning "to wriggle". As children, we were frequently told to "stop orming about". The Icelandic texts taught me that "orm" (more usually "serpent") was our word "worm", so I could grasp the origin of that expression. Not all her sayings, however, were so far from modern English. She would say that something "stuck out like chapel hatpegs" and something too small, placed inappropriately on a setting overly large (e.g. a small hat on a large head) looked like "a tomtit on a round of beef". I wonder if she had ever seen such a thing? Her unusual sayings were too many to cite, but I was always puzzled by one of her ready answers when asked by one of her children where she had been: her response was invariably "Eggin' aback o'Doigs". I had always interpreted her answer as meaning that she had visited a fish firm on Grimsby Docks called Doig's to get some eggs, though why the latter should be available there I could not imagine. I just knew her capacity to walk miles in order to stretch the family budget as far as possible. However, though I still have not fathomed "eggin", after listening to a radio programme, I now believe that "doigs" referred to hillsides or banks in Old Icelandic. Some of these expressions emerge occasionally in my own speech and are sometimes acquired by members of my family. I was amused to hear one of my daughters-in-law, despite her Welsh origins, admonishing her firstborn with "Do stop orming about!" Mum's idiosyncratic expressions were so numerous that I remember her speech as being very graphic and often quite amusing. I have never explored the derivation of "sool" a word she employed as a threat of incipient correction if we did not behave and, equally, her warning when she was teasing us, that she would "snickersneeze" us, her finger movements indicating that she was tempted to remove our noses.

Though I loved the caring and affection we received from both our parents, I was gradually hoping, by the time I was sixteen, for wider horizons and a new way of life. My parents were always most accommodating — they allowed my French pen-friend to come to our house for the whole of the 1946 Christmas holiday, and their welcome to Daniel was genuine: they shared their hard-earned festive food and warmth with him, thereby compensating to some extent for the deprivation he had suffered during the German occupation. He will not admit, even today, that he was terribly thin and gaunt as his eighteenth birthday loomed close, and still irritates me by insisting that my mother had boiled the Christmas turkey. He readily submitted to that unfair and prevalent conviction of the French that the English cannot cook. But he truly enjoyed that holiday despite the teasing he received from me, and we were sure that he had put some weight on as a consequence of my mother's liberal, if simple, catering. I admit that I was beastly to him now and again: I assured him that Blaydon Parish Church was far more beautiful than Notre Dame in Paris, though I had never set eyes on the latter any more than he had seen Blaydon. My mother always bought a holly-wreath for my sister

Evelyn's grave and that particular Christmas she persuaded Mavis and me to take it to the cemetery. We were accompanied by Daniel and Mavis's current boy-friend, Maurice. Almost upon leaving the house, I persuaded poor, dear Daniel that the English custom when such duties were performed was for the tallest man in the group to transport the wreath upon his head and the serious young Frenchman walked a few yards performing this task until the three beastly English burst into paroxysms of laughter and Daniel understood that I had played a joke on him. He removed the offending item from his head and reviled me with, "Miss Telma Colam, you have been pulling my leg!" More unkind laughter ensued. My mother and sister both purchased little gifts for Daniel for Christmas Day, Clarice's choice being an unnecessary item of male apparel — suspenders for socks. Daniel wore them when I took him to the dance at our usual haunt to celebrate New Year's Eve. His chorus of the evening, with his strong French accent, "Oh, it ees pulling my whiskers", again led to robust laughter from my friends and me. It is wonderful to recall that, despite these petty torments, Daniel has remained, for sixty years, a loving and generous friend whom I now regard as a brother and his dear wife as a sister. The way that they have both featured in our lives is referred to later.

One of the hopes I had when Daniel was joining us for a fortnight was that my spoken French would blossom, for I feared that the French Oral was the greatest ordeal I would face in the forthcoming HSC examinations the following summer. No such reward was mine — just retribution for my insensitivity to Daniel in several mischievous episodes — but, in any case, it was my lack of confidence and determination that led to our conversations being almost entirely in English. Daniel, on the other hand, deservedly progressed famously.

My pursuit of learning was very enjoyable, as I became increasingly engrossed in the wide range of texts we prepared in English and French, as well as improving our techniques in translation in Chaucer's Canterbury Tales, in the inevitable prose and translations in our French studies and passages of unseens in Latin. The Middle English and Latin exercises I could race through and the French translations were quite manageable. There remained the dreaded prose which, combined with the Oral, seemed to be the great hurdles. The History we studied was European and this continued the work I had done at Blaydon for my School Certificate. I loved all my subjects and counted it a great privilege to be taught so assiduously by the dedicated women who were my teachers. Eventually, those examinations arrived, the first being the French Oral. I couldn't believe that I would have such a pleasant test, the University teacher from Hull proving to be an artist at putting nervous candidates at ease — what a contrast to the dour, sarcastic examiner I had faced in the School Certificate equivalent. It was so comforting when I emerged from that examination to realise that I had not made a complete idiot of myself. Obstacle number one having proved not to be so intolerable, I faced the further examinations with equanimity. When the results were announced by our dear Headmistress as we gathered in her home, I felt a great sense of achievement as, indeed, I had two years prior to this, with the results of that earlier public examination. I hoped that my road would now be clear, as the time to leave for Leicester seemed close, but Miss Fisher instructed me to keep a sense of proportion, feeling that my average was one mark below what was the normal standard for that so necessary scholarship. Ominous forebodings of the Dock Office loomed once again, as I was unwilling, at that stage, to accept a teacher-training grant — I did not feel that my ambitions led me to that career — and was totally opposed to leaving for University expecting my parents to finance me if I had no scholarship to make me independent. They had done enough by supporting me until I was eighteen years old and, though they would have sacrificed their own needs on my behalf, I would not contemplate such a course. In fact, Miss Fisher had concealed the truth from me, as she already knew I had been granted the County Major Scholarship but, I imagine, she thought I should be feeling less euphoric when I attended the interview in Lincoln. I was overjoyed to grasp the news that I could seek those pastures new and know the life of a University student — a dream come true. And there was one other dream in store, the memory of which can still set my heart racing and my head reeling: I was so very soon to meet the love of my life.

A fun feature of that very pleasant summer break came as a consequence of the weekly visit to the dance hall, where I was feeling very carefree and willingly agreed to meet five young men during the following week, each on a different night, of course. One had arranged to meet me on the first evening of the five to take me to a film at the nearby cinema, the Ritz. Over Sunday lunch, I had explained to the family my timetable for the week and I left at 6.20p.m. the following day to meet John. I had not long gone when my sister Mavis heard knocking on our front door. She opened it to find a young man standing there. He asked if he could speak to me, so she asked him who he was. "I am John," he replied. "Oh," responded Mavis. "Have you forgotten you are meeting her at half past six tonight outside the Ritz?" "I have no such arrange-ment," John replied, "I am taking her to the football match on Wednesday." The soul of indiscretion immediately made it clear that she had seen the light and voiced her thoughts, "Now I understand! You are the wrong John for Monday. It's not your turn until Wednesday. It's another John she has a date with tonight!" I was mortified when all of this was recounted to me upon my return from the cinema. The family immediately declared that they would always remember my "five date week". The faithful second John did not fail to collect me for the football match despite my sister's tactlessness, so I was spared the embarrassment of further explanations. This was the last daring behaviour on my part: there was soon to be no reason for such devious planning, for I would have eyes for one alone.

84

Before this happened, a new joy had entered our family life. In the previous October, my sister Clarice had given birth to her third son, Raymond. I adored this new arrival and, once relieved of the mountains of homework and the examinations, much of the summer was spent with this delightful baby. During many a summer's day, I was allowed to stride off with him, seated just below my waist and held firmly by my left arm. We walked, we travelled on buses and I glowed with pride. However, it gradually became a theory among some of my contemporaries that I had furtively produced a son in the previous autumn. I found this a highly amusing rumour, as did the rest of my family. It is true that, over the last year, my figure had become rather less sylph-like than I would have wished, for my mother had insisted that, since I must work "all hours that God sends", as she put it, then I had to be built up nightly and she almost force-fed me with either onion gruel or Blakey's oatmeal before she went to bed. There can be no doubt, however, that this summer with Raymond awoke in me the desire to have baby boys of my own, and we shall come to that later.

CHAPTER
FIVE

October, 1947

After an interview with Dr. Bryan, my timetable for the coming year was investigated and I was quite surprised to discover that the provision of time for private study was very generous compared with the Sixth Form norm. There were several lectures a week, however, as well as two weekly seminars, one of which was with Professor Humphreys, a most gentle and kindly man, and the other with Dr. Arthur Symonds Collins, whose encouragement was a great blessing to me. I felt I was in the presence of great intellects when I was in their company, but I was also in awe of my fellow students, all of whom, I was convinced, were utterly brilliant. I could never grasp how I had been selected to join them as an undergraduate.

I was determined to compensate for my weaknesses by becoming an industrious and conscientious student: I always rushed to find a seat at a table in the library as soon as my lecture was over. However, during the evenings, after the meal taken in the main building which, in its earlier days had been a lunatic asylum, we would assemble in the rooms of those girls with whom, by this time, we had become friendly. Thus it was that I came to know a young lady called Pauline who seemed to me to be a wordly wise woman, even though she was of a similar age to me; she promptly informed me that there was a dance hall in central Leicester, the Palais de Danse, because I had already told her of my attachment to the Cafe Dansant in Cleethorpes. She proposed a visit to the Leicester counterpart that first Saturday night. I willingly accompanied her and was quite impressed with what I considered to be the immense size of the establishment. Imagine my surprise when, quite unexpectedly, I was approached by the young man who had been entertaining his group of friends in the Dean's queue a few days earlier. As we danced, I found him to be nicely spoken and courteous; already, my first impression was being modified. The evening passed quickly and, as Pauline and I returned by bus to University Road, I thought to myself that I would have enjoyed a second dance with that charming but still nameless young man. It was Pauline who provided me with one detail; she had heard that he was a Czech. My head swam with this knowledge. Because of its intriguing name, which I had learned from reading placards outside newsagents when I was ten, I had always imagined that Czechoslovakia would be a magical place; now a native of that country had danced with me that evening.

Later in the following week, Pauline and I decided that we would sample the pleasures of the Palais once again, so that I consequently practised my first deceit on a fellow student who had invited me to dance with him repeatedly during my first visit to our chosen venue and had pursued me relentlessly during the following week. I confess I was not at all attracted to this young man, so that when he approached me to ask whether I was intending to visit the Palais again, I shamelessly told him that it was very unlikely. Once in the dance hall for the second Saturday running, I scanned the crowd in search of the Little Czech, as I had heard him referred to by another student who was also quite obviously smitten with him. It was not long before he joined me and we spent most of that evening dancing together. He made polite conversation, asking me about Cleethorpes. Thinking him very odd when he asked me if there were many dart boards in my home town, I could only reply that there were several booths along the promenade where the holidaymakers could throw darts at the boards and win a prize if they scored a bull's eye. He looked as perplexed at my response as I had been by his question. It finally dawned on both of us that the noise of the music had distorted my hearing when he posed that initial inquiry: we enjoyed unravelling the misunderstanding when he had in fact asked about dance halls.

It became patently obvious that I would have a new chaperone to accompany me back to College Hall that night. As we reached the front door, he quickly brushed my cheek with an inexpert kiss and dashed off into the darkness. The following week furnished me with another scrap of information: I learned that his name was Fred. Excitement filled the air that week among the newly arrived students I knew — on Friday, October 31st, we were invited to the Freshers' Social. The evening began with an entertainment, after which the dancing started. The persistent, unwelcome attentions of the student I had sought to avoid for another entire week led to his next ploy. He was booking as many as five dances ahead with me and I was feeling more and more dejected when Fred, who had participated in the concert, finally approached me to ask for the next dance. Forlornly, I explained my plight but, undismayed, he countered with assurance that he would reserve the sixth dance. I reeled with joy when it proved to be the last waltz; by the end of that, we both sensed, after dancing cheek to cheek, something very powerful was overwhelming both of us. Fred said, "I'll wait for you outside the girls' cloakroom" and hurried to collect his coat. The forsaken would-be beau accosted him as he did this and dramatically declared, "I suppose the best man has won." He certainly had.

We walked back from the hall in the Wyggeston Boys' School where the evening had been spent along a wide pathway bordering Victoria Park and called Mayor's Walk, when at last I heard those dreaded words, "I still do not know your name". Inwardly cringing, I revealed the name I had found it hard not to reproach my mother for choosing for me and which I had always loathed — "Thelma", I tentatively admitted. "Oh, I don't like that. Have you got another one?" was his response. I knew then and there that this was the young man for me. When I told him my second name was Margaret, he assured me that was what he would call me — perhaps varied to Maggie on some occasions. The kiss on October 31st was a great deal more ardent than that first perfunctory attempt had been. Our relationship would assuredly flourish.

As I was walking on clouds in the following days, it is difficult to recall how frequently we met, but we certainly took lunches together in the college refectory, where we could even suffer the loathsome odour of whale steaks, so absorbed were we in each other, whilst some braver souls were courageous enough to tackle that uninviting dish. We normally selected the more innocuous macaroni cheese, even though it was formed into a patty and coated in breadcrumbs before being deep fried.

Sadly, out of the blue, my blissful state was abruptly shattered when a fellow student gleefully announced to me one evening that her new boyfriend had confided in her that my beloved had the foulest vocabulary of all the men in Hall. After my detestation of drunkenness, I most loathed swearing, having heard too much of it in my early days at home, though the adults never resorted to obscenities which she claimed Fred employed and which were totally unknown to me. I passed a sleepless night during which I concluded that I would find Fred incompatible, in view of my new knowledge of him. We met as arranged the following day to go together to the refectory, but I was too distressed to speak to him, let alone to kiss him. A silent and minimal meal ensued. Totally wretched, we walked outside and found ourselves once more on Mayor's Walk, where, not long before, I had ashamedly confessed my first name. When he asked me why I was suddenly so unhappy, I explained that I was afraid our affair had to end because I found that what I had learned of his abominable habit was too repulsive for me to accept. Fred tearfully vowed immediate renunciation of his foul language if I would relent. Of course, I at once retracted my threat: I loved him so much and found his distress heart-rending.

The joy returned into our lives and so many happy days followed. Wednesday afternoons on Knighton fields became memorable because, for the first time, but certainly not the last, my boyfriend involved me in helping with catering — afternoon teas were provided for the University hockey team, of which Fred was a member, and their visiting opponents. I think I remember making sandwiches, sparsely filled with rationed fillings or sandwich spread out of a small jar and somehow there were small cakes provided — not yet made by my ever willing hands. On those Wednesday afternoons when there was no hockey, we made for the "Prairie", a small mixed common room, little more than a wide landing, an ideal trysting location for wintry afternoons. If we had a few pennies to spare, either on the free Wednesday or on Saturdays, we would walk into Leicester to save the bus fare and regale ourselves with Brucciani's espresso coffee and a Kunzle cake or a toasted teacake and tea at another small cafe, the name of which now eludes me. Nearby, there was a shop window with a wonderful display of leather handbags, one of which I really coveted. Unknown to me, Fred had made a mental note of the bag I admired so much. We also drooled over trays of engagement rings in a jeweller's window. The name of this establishment I clearly recall — "Lumbers", and it became our dream to celebrate our love for each other one distant day with one of their diamond and sapphire rings.

As the weeks progressed, our conversations frequently consisted of stories about our earlier days and soon Fred was relating the details of his history. He invited me for tea in the common room of his Hall of Residence and turned the serving of beans on toast into a prestigious ceremony. Whilst he was "cooking" our meal, he left me to look through his family album and so I set eyes for the first time on photographs of his beautiful mother and equally beautiful sisters, as well as pictures of his wonderfully handsome father — the latter encouraging me to recognise what my constantly grinning boy would one day achieve in elegance and dignity.

Fred returned with his offering and I was soon filled with embarrassment as one of my baked beans fell on to a page of his album. He had returned to the kitchen for some reason, so I was able to remove the offending smear before he returned, thus enabling me to allay some of my shame.

After our meal, Fred turned the pages of the book, explaining the photographs and telling me the names of the people. Innocently, I asked him where his family was at that moment. So it was that I learned of the early death of his father when Fred was only a few months old and of the fate of his mother and sisters in a concentration camp in 1942.

This information appalled me; it was impossible to say anything. I did not wish to probe beyond these facts at that juncture. Other details emerged gradually as Fred invited me to accompany him when he was to receive his official naturalisation papers. Inevitably, I was puzzled by the contrast between the tragic end of each member of his family, his survival and his ability to lead a happy go lucky life. How had he been transformed into this devil-may-care youth? When, eventually, I voiced my bewilderment, it was then he related the story of his departure from Czechoslovakia and of his rescue by Philip Austin. A typical, patriotic young product of wartime Britain: a surge of pride swept through me as I heard of this superb achievement by a compassionate Englishman — for thus I judged him to be. I was convinced at that time that all my fellow countrymen were replete with tolerance, courage and good will, with an eagerness to accept all those people who were in danger or need. A green eighteen year old, I had so much to learn! My reaction to his story was to say to Fred, "You must be so proud of this man and feel a tremendous obligation to him." My blood ran cold as I heard his reply, "I could get him put in prison, if I wanted to". Who was this person with whom I had become so intimately involved? I was filled with indignation at his seeming ingratitude, but I was too distressed to divulge my feelings. However, Fred continued at once to explain why he had made that half-threat, explaining the unscrupulous misdemeanours of that shameless paedophile — in those days, called homosexuals by most innocent and ill-informed young folk and by the majority of older people also. I also learned from that cruelly bereaved lad that he had never told anyone of his recurring ordeals over some eight years until that day when he was confiding in me. Not only did I adore Fred, but, from that moment on, I felt the awakening of an amazing maternal solicitude for him. His way of coping with this offensive treatment was obviously by adopting an irresponsible attitude to work and play and this led to a tendency to undervalue himself and his undoubted potential.

Not long after these revelations, we were saying "Goodnight", outside my hostel when, out of the blue, I froze when I heard Fred say, "I can't really ask any girl to wait for me. I have five more years of study after this." Boldly and without hesitation I said, "I will willingly wait." So it was that we considered ourselves unofficially engaged, ringless as I was and destined so to be for a further eighteen months or so. Nevertheless, we were indivisibly united by lasting and dedicated love. It was the consequence of this conversation that led to our frequent visits to that jeweller's window in Leicester.

My memories of that first term are chiefly concentrated on the two of us, but I also entered another good and lasting friendship with a fellow English student, Win. We always attended lectures with each other and shared the same seminars. I recall how we laughed together on Sunday mornings and tunelessly sang the cockney songs my friend had taught me, as we washed our "smalls" in the hand-basins in the ablutions room and then put them to dry in the crowded drying room, where earlier birds had long preceded us. I went once with Win to her preferred Anglican church but promptly returned to the small Methodist church where the services closely resembled those in the church I attended in Cleethorpes. Before very long, Fred said he felt he should find a religion, having of necessity had no opportunity of contacting anyone of the faith into which he had been born. He said he had found it to be a cruel faith, though he did not elucidate that statement further. I suspect that his opinion thus expressed did not derive from any profound thought or knowledge, for he has frequently vowed that his family was not at all devout. I asked him if he would like to try Methodism and he accepted the suggestion with alacrity. We attended the evening services held in a large central Leicester church, but occasionally visited a Baptist Church which boasted a fiery, tub-thumping preacher who was gripping and positive in his message. He repeatedly would refer to some temptation or other or a heinous sin and after these darkly expressed words he would chorus, "It is the fly in the ointment, men and women, the fly in the ointment." We were tempted to steal a sly grin to each other at this constant repetition. With such shared experiences, our lives became more and more welded together.

Fred went to Hull one Wednesday afternoon to play chess at the University, thus missing an introduction to my mother and father on the only occasion that they both visited together. They had come on a coach trip to see me and I enjoyed showing them round my college.

95

They were very much lacking in assurance and, for once, followed me around like wary sheep; their visit was a great treat for me, however. The alarm clock that Dad had bought me before I left Cleethorpes had been broken by the college cleaner who cleaned the bedroom I shared with four other girls, so my father had generously bought me a new watch, of which I was inordinately proud; what is more, his largesse extended to the gift of a ten shilling note as a result of which I felt exceedingly affluent. Both my parents were anxious to know about this boyfriend I had written about and I, of course, was agog to tell them. When Dad heard that he was a Czech refugee, he, quite a small man, seemed to swell apoplectically and furiously pronounced his verdict: "You don't want him — a cruel continental. They make chattels of their wives." I could always hold my own with my father, much as I loved him, so that I responded immediately with, "Dad, if ever a man made a chattel of his wife, it was you." Catching my mother's eye, we both burst into uproarious laughter and Dad's intolerant opinions were never voiced again. However, it was apparent when he later set eyes on Fred in Cleethorpes, that his reaction was totally reversed.

The reason I was sharing a bedroom/dormitory with four other girls was because the fourth of the new strips of hostel rooms had not been completed. The bedroom we occupied had been that of one of the Attenborough boys, when his father had been appointed the previous year as Principal of University College. I found the other people who occupied that room very compatible but a difficulty arose for me in November when I discovered that Fred's birthday was December 1st. Meagre as my spending power was, I mustered enough money to buy wool and a pattern for what in later years became known as a tank top, but, in 1947, was considered a fashionable garment called a pullover. It qualified as the height of fashion if it was knitted in a Fair Isle pattern. I was, however, faced with the need to knit it after all my studies of the day were completed and my room-mates desired lights out at ten o'clock, which was normally the time when I was at liberty to pursue my hobby. I solved my problem by memorising the pattern in advance and placing the different coloured balls of wool in a logical order so that I could work away in hours of darkness. Fred was very pleased with my offering. At that stage, it dawned on me that he had not acquired new clothing for a long time and his wardrobe was in a very sorry state. He possessed two second hand suits, which he explained to me had been sent by a cousin of his mother who lived in New York. One suit was too small and the other too large. I later discovered that his shirts, a motley collection, were from the same source and sported very frayed collars. I volunteered to wash his socks and underwear when I tackled my own laundry on Sunday mornings with the result that I discovered that his socks were handknitted in very thick, harsh wool, and sweat-encrusted. All my work had to be done by hand — washing-machines were to emerge in later, more affluent times. The water exuded by those far from fragrant socks bore a strong reminder in colour to the gravy served with our college food; I discovered, moreover, that they were riddled with holes. In due course, the larger suit suffered an ignominious fate when, one evening, we sat on a bench on the large lawn facing the façade of the main college building. Unaware of my misjudgement, inadvertently, I sat partly on the sagging upper leg of his baggy trousers. As he moved towards me, we heard the ominous sound of ripping material. His knee and sizeable lengths of his upper and lower leg emerged through the gaping rent. He was faced with returning to Netherclose on the cycle he had borrowed for the evening, displaying a virtually unclad leg for all to see. The following morning, several people hastened to tell me that they thought Fred looked very nice in his "new suit". Totally mystified, I anxiously awaited his appearance. He did, indeed, look more spruce than usual but it was immediately apparent to me that he was clad in borrowed plumes; Fred confessed at once that his kind friend "Hoppy" had come to his aid, at least temporarily. It was fortunate that I was able to enhance his appearance a little by the addition of the Fair Isle sweater.

A further activity, this time in the dark, took place towards the end of that term. We loved to attend the Saturday night hop in the Inner Hall but, finding our resources very depleted (was it yet another Kunzle cake?), we danced to the music from the hall above in the garden, where we had free rein. The music was produced entirely by gramophone records and we thought it great fun to dance to the Bing Crosby recording of "Dancing in the Dark", always a great favourite of mine.

Beginning to espouse the ideals which have continued into our later years, we wanted to assist people in greater need than ourselves. The only thing that we could give was some of our blood at that time, so we attended Leicester Royal Infirmary for several appointments to give transfusions. Ultimately, it was suggested that I should abandon that duty, as they were encountering difficulty in taking even half a pint of my blood and, after one or two more visits, on returning to hostel, I had vomited and then fainted. I was pretty disgusted with my feeble contribution.

Whether we liked it or not, the end of term loomed closer and closer and, ultimately, we had to accept the inevitability of separation, when I would board the train bound for Sheffield, whilst Fred worked briefly in the Leicester Sorting Office before taking a train from the LMS station for his nauseating visit to Liverpool, where Philip Austin's widowed mother resided. My school friend, June, was awaiting my arrival on the station in Sheffield, where she was attending a teacher training college. We were taking the opportunity to enjoy a swift exchange of news as she accompanied me to the other station, where I was to join the train to Cleethorpes. Her college had shorter vacations than the universities but, in a week or so, she would also be heading back home. June was anxious to tell me of her new conquest — an ex-Serviceman called Alan Coleman, whom she admired particularly because, in her eyes, he resembled my father and his surname closely resembled ours — Colam. Dad was Dad to me and I found her enthusiasm for his manly beauty a little odd. Having

99

digested her news, I then proudly announced that Fred and I were "unofficially" engaged. She responded in her normal forthright, Lincolnshire manner, with "Your parents won't allow it." I quietly pointed out to her that the choice was not theirs. The subject was not pursued any further.

Fred had met another Alan, a student who lodged in Middlemead, where the men from Fred's Hall also ate. There they took breakfast and evening meals together whilst, curiously enough, Alan and I often seemed to fall into easy conversation near the library or in the Crush Hall. Alan was a History undergraduate who was in the same year as me, whereas Fred was still catching us up and preoccupied with his Inter studies — the irritating consequence of his Sixth Form indolence. Although this acquaintance was quite casual in those early days, it later developed into one of our closest and most lasting friendships, beautifully in keeping with our lives and with a development in Alan's life in the autumn of 1948. A lovely young girl arrived in Leicester at the beginning of that term; in my eyes, at least, she resembled Judy Garland both in looks and vivacity. She promptly won Alan's lasting devotion; Eileen, that young lady, shared our lodgings when she was in her first year and Win and I were in our second, and it was thus that our friendship with that happy pair was cemented. We spent countless memorable times as a foursome and were deeply saddened by Alan's death in January, '06.

To return to Christmas, 1947 and my arrival home: I still, after so many years, experience a warm glow as I recall that first breakfast of my homecoming, when I was eating with my mother for company. She was eager to know how the situation was developing with Fred, whilst I was determined to reveal to her the profound sympathy I felt for him because of his lost family and his dependence upon the Austins in Caldy Road. I told her what I knew of Philip's sexual proclivities and of Fred's struggles to keep him at bay. My mother immediately observed that, like me, she did not fully understand the implications of what I had related to her. She did, however, grasp that the contact that he was forced into with Philip was so distasteful that she spontaneously reacted to my disclosures with her habitual vehemence. "You needn't think he is going back there again for future vacations. He is to come here. I don't much like the sound of that bossy mother of Philip Austin's, either." That was so like her — she had never set eyes on him at that stage but, immediately, on hearing the story of his difficulties and of the fate of his mother and sisters, she displayed her natural instincts to protect and support the vulnerable. I also think she was pleased to envisage the acquisition of a second son, which she had long wished for. I was jubilant at her reaction, regarding it as the best Christmas present I could wish to receive. Dad was away at sea when this conversation took place but, thinking of his earlier prejudice, I asked her how he would react to her decision. With great alacrity, she assured me, "We can sort him out, can't we?"

It did not take my mother long to recount to my elder sister what she had learned from me and immediately they were both his ardent allies, wondering what they could send Fred for Christmas; their eagerness to do something for him accelerated when, a few days later, a parcel arrived from him. He had received a delivery from his mother's cousin in New York, which included a large pack of delicious maple crunch biscuits and other desirable supplies to people who were still enduring stringent rationing. He sent the biscuits and a packet of orange pekoe tea for the Colams and Appleyards and he had also raised enough money, (probably Post Office earnings), to buy me a very smart, grey mottled fountain pen, quite an acquisition in those post war days: it gave me good service until 1952. My sister and mother bought him some much needed socks after I described the hideous ones I washed for him. They must have parted with some of their precious clothing coupons to provide these little treats. He had said to me some weeks prior to this that he longed for some family life and it was a delightful thought that his wish would soon be fulfilled.

That Christmas break seemed interminable but, finally, the day dawned when I could take the train to return for our longed for reunion in Leicester. The new term first made me aware of missing faces — Pauline was no longer in evidence and others had been persuaded that they were better advised to adopt the general degree course rather than to continue with honours, which had been their preference. I had held on to my honours studies, I guess by the skin of my teeth, and I was delighted to continue along the path I had chosen. I still worried about my security in the

English Department for a few more weeks, but was comforted by the encouragement from Dr. Collins, who recognised my increasing skill in the history of the language studies for which I received his guidance in tutorials. This later led to my selection of that area as my "special" eighth course, the other seven being obligatory.

The second term passed serenely, without any outstanding events. I was persuaded by Fred, on one occasion, to attend a French Circle meeting, where I met a junior lecturer, Adrien Favre, (known to the more impudent young students as Charlie Favour) who spotted a likely couple of baby-sitters in Fred and me. We readily agreed to look after his daughter, Francoise, for our reward was a pan of delicious hot chocolate prepared with French finesse by Charlie's wife, Paulette and the opportunity to work together in comfort. Our friendship with him lasted many years and continues to provide us with precious memories. I was not cut out, however, for spending an evening where everyone was confidently chatting in fluent French, so I never accepted further invitations to the Cercle Francais, despite my having succeeded in A level French along with my English, History and Latin.

Fred spent some time probing my tastes in music and was somewhat nonplussed, I fear, when I enthused about Bing Crosby. He asked what I felt about classical music; I readily admitted that my knowledge of instrumental music was limited to a little Chopin, Liszt, Strauss, Beethoven (Minuet in G), and the first movement of Tchaikowsky's piano concerto in B flat minor but that, with my father's encouragement, I had developed a taste for Grand Opera. Dad first took me to a performance of *La Traviata* and I later attended performances of *Faust* and *Carmen* when I was a Sixth Former in Cleethorpes. Fred confessed his lack of interest in opera but went on to talk of his love of orchestral music He told me that there was soon to be a concert performed by the Halle Orchestra with Sir John Barbirolli at the de Montfort Hall and suggested we reserved promenade places for that occasion. Fortunately, I agreed, for I found the experience quite memorable, despite the discomfort of standing so long. My unschooled tastes happily enjoyed *Eine Kleine Nachtmusik* and Don Gillis's *Symphony No.5 1/2 for Fun*. The contortions Sir John indulged in as he conducted that piece were quite memorable. I remember also my introduction to Wagner when they played the Overture to *The Mastersingers* — very rousing.

As the days of that Spring term passed, my excitement increased, encouraged by imaginings of what it would it be like to take Fred home to Cleethorpes to meet my family. We had discovered that if we could accept a lengthy day of travel, by doing the journey in a series of service buses, we could travel much more cheaply compared with the train. That first bus adventure introduced us to some Leicester and Lincolnshire landscapes which would become very familiar over the next few years. To me, several of the place names were captivating — Kirby Bellars and Croxton Kerrial, for example, whilst Fred was lost in admiration for an abundance of picturesque village churches. We spotted curiously clipped tall cupressus in front of an important-looking building in Melton Mowbray and the memory of a comic strip in The Daily Mirror, displaying "Schmoos", was stirred by those oddly deformed creations of the topiarist. In Grantham, we alighted from the bus to await the arrival of the Lincoln bus. We were impressed by the statue of Sir Isaac Newton, but the spectacle of the day was the towering beauty of Lincoln Cathedral. We finally boarded the Grimsby bus and relaxed as we travelled the last lap. We quickly caught a trolley bus to Cleethorpes, where it stopped very conveniently, leaving us a short walk to my parents' home.

We were shyly, but happily, received by my welcoming family and my sister's children looked relieved — they must have wondered what a Czech would resemble. Only Dad was missing from the group — still out at sea — engineer on a trawler. He appeared a few days after our arrival, entered the living room sheepishly and his face registered an instant transformation as he set eyes on his future son-in-law for the first time. His relief was lovely to behold and augured a future attitude of total approval. It was not many hours later when he was proudly displaying his books to Fred — without admitting that he had never completely mastered the more advanced sections on Mathematics. However, what pleased me above all was everyone's delight in welcoming an addition to the family. The situation became even more satisfactory when both of us were taken on as temporary staff at the Income Tax

Office. Our meagre pay enabled us to insist that we supplemented my mother's housekeeping money by each giving her ten shillings weekly. She had, at first, protested vehemently, but we were adamant that we were not going to be a burden, as we had guessed that there was not too much spare cash in my mother's purse. By this time, Mavis was serving her apprenticeship in tailoring and dressmaking and contributing five shillings a week from her starvation-level salary. Despite the limited means in the home, the table was always generously laden at mealtimes with good nourishing food. There was frequently a good helping of delicious fresh fish, which was provided from my brother-in-law's free allowance from his work as a lumper: he unloaded the catch from the holds of trawlers in the small hours of the morning. Consequently, we had to creep very quietly in the house during the day, whilst he was catching up with his sleep.

Mother saved her pennies by walking a good two miles two or three times weekly to Freeman Street market from which she returned pushing Raymond's pram, well laden with the baby and a goodly array of fine locally-grown vegetables and fruit. Our home was a healthy and spotlessly clean house with a happy atmosphere most of the time, despite the penetrating odour of Dad's home-rolled cigarettes, Clarice's Craven A and Mark's very smelly pipe. On occasions, the overfilled ashtrays were accidentally spilled or my father carelessly missed his ashtray on a stand and flicked ash on to the hearth-rug, bringing icy comments from my mother and, now and again, I was known to utter my own disapproval. When I later succumbed to the use of the disgusting weed, I grew to be ashamed of those admonitions I had expressed, knowing that my father loved me very much. I should add that, after the purchase of food, the next priority in our household affairs was the regular delivery of coal for the open fires downstairs, one of which was located in my parents' living room and the other in the kitchen/living room of my elder sister — her family had a warm room, but we all benefited from the hot water supplied by the back boiler behind that fire. The coal was also the fuel for the built-in "copper" in the back scullery, regularly fired to provide a large quantity of piping hot water for the weekly laundry. Some of the water was brought up to boiling point and thus the white linens were always a perfect colour as they hung drying on the clothes-line, strung across the tiny yard for the day, but collected in before nightfall.

On Sunday evenings, Fred and I attended evening service at Mill Road Methodist Church when we were in Cleethorpes and, on rare Saturdays, visited my old haunt, the Cafe Dansant, for old times' sake. I had made one visit there during the previous Christmas break, but was immediately accosted by the young man whom Mavis had named "the wrong John" in my sixth form days. When I told him of my new attachment, he said ruefully, "Just as I feared", and he abandoned his pursuit forthwith. We enjoyed our break from Leicester and walked miles just to glory in our own company, once the day's work was over and the evening meal consumed. My freedom, however, was abruptly curtailed once my mother beckoned me out of the room with a peremptory look on her face that first Sunday night before we set out for church. Displaying great indignation, she demanded to know whether I was aware that Fred's one remaining suit had a jacket pinned together with an abundance of large safety pins. As I had eyes for him alone, and was drawn only to his dancing blue eyes and ever ready smile, I had never noticed the need for repairs My hawk-eyed mother told me in no uncertain terms that I had better do something about the offending garment. Soon, I was spending hours seated at Mum's elderly treadle sewing machine every evening and weekend repairing, not only the jacket, but also darning the less gaping holes in several pairs of the thick ugly socks. Every night, I heard my father drily observing, "You have done more mending for that lad in the last couple of weeks than your mother has done for me in all the years we have been married." "So what?," I thought, as I daydreamed about the purchases we would make for him in Leicester with the money we had saved from sewing new collars which I had cut out from the tails of his shirts to replace the frayed originals. I also supplemented the collection of new socks he had received at Christmas by spending Tax Office earnings.

Once back in Leicester, we found a blue sports jacket for forty-five shillings and some coarse pin-striped flannels costing only £1.10 shillings in an army surplus shop. Our remaining hoard, at my insistence — a consequence of years of my father's indoctrination that footwear should always be of the very best quality —

was finally spreed on a pair of strong brown leather shoes and these, devouring more than £3.00, gave years of stalwart service after their relegation from Sunday best. How I longed to buy him a lovely new blue shirt, one of the recently introduced "drip-dry" variety, but that had to be delayed until I had some new resources from my pitiful earnings at Butt's Green Harvest Camp, where we worked for six weeks in July and August. After leaving the camp in mid-August, 1948, we had decided to spend our accumulated money in London, where we planned as many theatre visits as we could afford: we hoped to spend as little as possible on accommodation. When we stepped off the coach, we spotted a phone and, in those days, the telephone directories were always intact and reliable. We found the number of the YWCA, where I hoped to find an inexpensive room; I received a satisfactory quote from a rather severe sounding lady, whereupon I responded with, "OK I'll come at once." "Don't you say OK to me, young lady," she snarled in reply, to which my instant reaction was to crash the phone down, turning to Fred and exploding with, "I am not going to stay there! They are obviously very authoritarian." We quickly decided to seek advice from Win, who was at home, fortunately, together with her eldest sister. The latter was able to recommend a small, reasonable and respectable hotel in Streatham and she provided us with its number. We were lucky to discover that they had two single rooms available cheaply, so we accepted with alacrity and made our way to the hotel in order to deposit our cases, so leaving us unencumbered for the rest of our stay. We were supplied with a front door key, so were free to return at our leisure. Our luck held out as far as our theatre ambitions were concerned as, by queueing for the cheapest seats before each performance, we were able to enjoy a matinee and an evening show daily: so we saw *Oklahoma*, *Annie Get Your Gun*, *School for Scandal* with Vivien Leigh and Laurence Olivier, and a play called *Crime Passionel* which has not proved memorable to me. We were invited that first evening to the family meal at Win's home and very much relished the wit and the laughter it produced at that family gathering. For the remaining days of our stay, Fred was pleased to introduce me to the food at Lyons' Corner House and Wimpey Bars. I had hoarded enough money to buy Fred the much coveted blue shirt and a couple of text books on my list from College, as well as our single train fares to Cleethorpes after our mini-holiday was over. All these expenses were covered by the accumulation of our one shilling and six pence per hour, for which we had toiled at Butt's Green.

Fred had really surprised and thrilled me on my birthday in June by giving me the lovely leather handbag I had so long admired in the shop in Granby Street. After the fountain pen at Christmas here was a further demonstration of his generosity.

Quite a few weeks before the end of that Summer Term, the attention of many of the four hundred and fifty students who formed the complement of the Junior Common Room was drawn to the activities of four lecturers. They struck the new undergraduates as mature people but can only have been in their twenties, in fact. It was quite apparent that these four had become two couples in those early months. Mr. Wilson, a lecturer in the German Department, was clearly a suitor for the hand of Miss Gullen, my beloved lecturer in the history of the language course. Mr. Evans chose a fellow historian for his romantic attentions: the lively and very gifted Dr. Ann Roberts — later known as Babette Evans. Many of the students were thrilled to learn of their marriages after the mini break. Is that where the title "Whitsun Weddings" sprang from? Philip Larkin was the dour junior librarian at that time and assuredly a fellow member of the Senior Common Room. I longed for a similar outcome for Monica Jones, another youthful English lecturer, and one of my idols, but little did my friends and I know of her secret attachment to the no doubt brilliant but, to those like me, the sour Philip Larkin. Leicester in 1947-1948 was certainly the place where love-affairs flourished.

After our treats in London, we economised on further spending on the hotel and took the midnight train from King's Cross. Our final destination was Cleethorpes, but we had resolved to break our journey at Boston, to extend Fred's acquaintance with my relatives by visiting Brown's Road to see my Grandmother and my mother's sister, Auntie Ethel. We finally called on my more recently acquired aunt — my Uncle Harold had married Florence after he was demobbed, having spent a considerable part of the war years in the Middle East. I had previously met Florence when she and Harold had spent a few days at my parents' house during my Sixth Form days. My Uncle wanted to show off his bride-to-be to us all, but he made a special fuss of me, as I had kept up a regular correspondence with him for a good few years. Florence and I became friends at once and that relationship endured until she died in 2006. That summer, we had given her no warning of our intention to call, but we found her at home and she was delighted that we had come. I gathered that her first meeting with Fred had been extremely cordial, but I fell fast asleep as soon as I sat down in her living room — an inevitable consequence of my sleepless night on the train. They had to wake me up so that we did not miss our train to Cleethorpes but, fortunately, I did not have to face another night-time journey.

Back at home, we were once more employed in the Income Tax Office and the rest of that summer passed serenely. Fred had succeeded in his Inter examinations, so he returned to Leicester able to start his French Honours course, whilst I resumed my English studies.

Win and I had not really enjoyed life in Hall, so we chose to sample approved lodgings, thus entering the domain of the redoubtable Mrs. Catcheside. We survived the first term with her but demanded a change for the following term, her parsimonious strictures and regulations being more than our love of freedom could bear, along with the rebellious reactions of our stomachs in response to her indigestible food. Her insistence on lights out at 10 o'clock we found a great impediment to our essay writing and the immense amount of reading we were expected to tackle, so that our work was suffering. We, therefore, insisted upon a transfer to other accommodation, perhaps out of the frying pan! We joined two other girls already at Mrs. Jeffries where, like the other pair, we shared a double room which was very spacious. We very speedily learned that Mrs. J. had taken an instant dislike to my friend and me. Her obvious preference for the other two students was a constant source of amusement to all four of us. It proved difficult to conceal our laughter each morning as the first pair arrived for breakfast. Our landlady would peep round the door and serve the more cosseted pair with lovely lean rashers of bacon, whereas Win and I were always destined to consume cheap, fatty streaky, if we could stomach it. Fred was in digs not far from mine, but his accommodation was arranged only for men and provided no facilities for the washing of clothes. Mrs. J. decreed that any washing by hand that we wished to do had to be tackled on Sunday mornings only and it had to be pegged out on the line stretched across the small backyard As soon as I knew Fred had a laundry problem, I immediately offered to do what small amount of washing he had. The following Sunday, I washed the two shirts he had brought me together with my own clothes and hung them all on the line. It was not very long before the ire of Mrs. Jeffries descended upon me — she stormed into our sitting room and vehemently instructed me to remove "that man's shirts" from her line. I pointed out that they were dripping wet and that I had nowhere else to dry them, but she swept out to grab the offending items and, returning, threw them at me. I asked her why she was so perturbed by their presence and she shouted that I would have the neighbours talking about her, which astounded all of us, as we were all aware that she was living with a man who was not her husband and she made no bones about hanging out his washing at other times in the week. Already, we were longing for another change of location, though we succeeded in enduring that term and one more in the premises of that demon, after which all four of us joyfully escaped her clutches. Whilst we were still housed with her, she astonished me by offering some clothing coupons, which were highly prized in that era of rationing. Gleefully, I took an early opportunity to visit C&A's where, having selected an item of apparel, I went to the till, clutching my coupons and was promptly informed that they were no longer required, as clothes were no longer rationed. What a spiteful woman she continued to be!

By this time, I was proudly wearing my wonderful engagement ring — a sapphire flanked by two diamonds. We had also acquired the first trophy for our "bottom drawer", for we had been presented with an oval silver-plated shallow dish — a gift from the jeweller from whom we had bought our ring. It is still a precious memento in our home today.

We had both settled down to our studies, Fred having the admirable Professor Sykes, as well as me, breathing down his neck, both of us stressing that his irresponsible attitudes of yore were no longer permitted. His ability was early identified by Professor Sykes who was already predicting that he was capable of achieving a First, if he could combine ability with conscientiousness. My admiration for the great man, the Prof, wavered when my fiance informed me that he had been advised by his mentor to spend less time with that female student with whom he was so obviously enamoured. That was one piece of professional caution that was totally ignored. The weeks raced by and soon we were enjoying the Christmas vacation back in Cleethorpes. Easter saw us catching a ferry to the Isle of Man (to Philip Austin's aunts), where we had our opportunity to explore that beautiful island and to enjoy the superb meals produced by Edith, who had always kept house for her sister Nell, a retired teacher. The latter treated us to many instructive conversations, often tinged with her idiosyncratic, humourous observations. Her most entertaining comment, to my mind, was, "The trouble with Americans is that they have zip fasteners on everything except their mouths", original, though, in my opinion, not really true of the many Americans I later met and grew to love.

Our holiday with Edith and Nell led me to two wonderful experiences and another which was very nearly fatal. On one of our many walks, I was befriended by a baby lamb which agreed to my lifting him (or her) whilst Fred snapped a photograph of the pair of us. This picture is reverentially placed in one of our youthful albums and when I look at it I recall the euphoric state the delightful experience had catapulted me into. Another stroll took us to the small village church and its churchyard which we searched thoroughly. Imagine my incredulous excitement when I came upon a large upright stone, obviously of considerable age, which had been clearly inscribed with Runic symbols. Instantly, I scrabbled in my handbag to unearth a slip of paper and a pen in order to transcribe the text to take back to college for a full investigation of my trophy. I have no memory of the results of my research nor of the whereabouts of that valued scrap of paper, so long a treasure of mine. The third unforgettable episode, which could so easily have been disastrous, was entirely a consequence of my own stupid lack of observation, which filled Fred with terrible alarm. I saw a little rabbit running along a narrow twisting path and, so enchanted was I in pursuing it, that I had failed to notice that the path clung precariously to the very high cliff, of which I suddenly became aware. Looking down, I saw immense, brutal-looking rocks being lashed ferociously by angry foam-edged waves. At that moment, Fred regained the power of speech, as he yelled, "Get down on all fours and don't move." I was only too pleased to do as he commanded and soon realised that he was advancing towards me, crawling on hands and knees. It seemed to take ages for him to reach me but arrive he did, firmly instructing me not to look down. He backed slowly and guided me at the same time. At last, we breathed sighs of relief as we reached safer ground and the ensuing embrace and kiss were quite memorable. One day, towards the end of our stay in Lewaigue, Edith and Nell treated us to a bus tour around their lovely island, when I was fortunate to share a seat with Nell — a very erudite lady whose conversation was always worth the candle. On that occasion, she pointed out much of interest in the landscape and interspersed these comments with an account of her adherence to theosophy. She told me of her deep belief in astrology and of her skill in working out horoscopes. She explained her assessment of me now that she had acquired detailed knowledge of the time and date of my birth and its geographical location. She claimed to know that I was typical of my sign — Gemini — and the reason for that was because I must have had many previous existences and one expiates one failing of the sign in each existence. The most astonishing information she passed on to me that afternoon was that, at the moment her nephew, Phillip Austin, was born, she had worked out his chart and knew he would, one day, be put in prison. Knowing Fred's history, she recommended the works of Louis Golding, especially *Magnolia Street*, in order that I might learn something of the Jewish way of life. I had to neglect that suggestion until after my graduation, but then I discovered some real treats. Back home in Cleethorpes, we were again employed in the Income Tax Office, but the final assurance from my newly acquired aunts that we would be welcome to visit them again was a happy conclusion to our first stay with Edith and Nell.

Once again in Leicester for the summer term, studies were our uppermost concern as we prepared for the end of year examinations. We were both successful and were soon setting off from Leicester on a train which took us to Wisbech where, in a nearby village, Leverington, we were to spend the first six weeks of the summer vacation in an NUS harvest camp. After a few

117

days strawberry picking, we quickly acquired what the local children called "the strawberry walk" and grew accustomed to their chanting this as we painfully toiled back to camp. We laughed in unison at noon when a stenorian voice with a broad Cambridgeshire accent owned by our foreman bellowed *Mark yer rows*, the signal for lunch break. Hastily, we each bundled together an armful of straw to indicate the spots where, an hour later, we would recommence our picking. In due course, we were transferred to raspberry picking, a very frustrating occupation for our hours of piecework, the crop being sparse that year. Next, we had to face torture by gooseberry bushes, whose long thorns tore at our hands and arms, spilling our bright red blood. We were moved later to the redcurrants which, again, was a meagre, unprofitable crop, so that, once more, we engaged in a thankless task. We realised we were not destined to make our fortunes in that area. It was time to harvest the blackcurrants, so a makeshift bridge had been thrown across a shallow ditch to provide easy access to these bushes. One day, very soon after we were directed to this new area, Fred sneezed violently as he was almost halfway over the bridge; snatching a handkerchief from his trouser pockets, he forgot that he had wrapped in it his newly acquired tiny denture which he had returned to collect from his Leicester dentist the previous day. He had found that intimate new possession uncomfortable and had cured the pain in his usual predictable way. Speedily raising the handkerchief to his nose to intercept another incipient sneeze, Fred saw his new denture hurtle through the air

118

and down to a thick bed of nettles in the ditch below. We both loudly bewailed the loss, but one of the overseas students, having witnessed everything and failing to recognize those vicious English weeds, leapt into their midst in spite of being bare-legged and, on impact, performed a wild war dance but, at the same time, located and rescued the errant denture. Though covered in stings, he phlegmatically returned his booty to Fred and offered not a single word of reproach or self-pity. After a couple of weeks spent fruit picking, I was approached by the camp organiser and his wife the head cook: the latter had been deserted by her assistant cook and she stressed her need for a replacement. Her husband went on to explain that he had noticed my engagement ring and had surmised that probably I was able to cook. He hoped that I would be prepared to fill the vacancy on a salary of three pounds a week! I accepted with alacrity, because I had come to loathe toiling among plants and bushes when they were laden with cold morning dew, whereas his offer would satisfy my growing taste for catering. The only disadvantage of this change of status was that I would be deprived of Fred's company during the day, though I supposed the evenings would prove even sweeter. I found that new occupation in the small haven of the camp kitchen a very instructive experience, as I learned how that sparsely equipped place was made to function smoothly and how one organised the production of eighty hearty cooked breakfasts and served them in good time for the campers to board the lorry which was to transport them to the work area of the day. After the main party

119

was on its way, it fell to me to prepare a variety of sandwich fillings, using the various ingredients decreed by my boss; each day, half a dozen students were retained for the first part of the morning to be on fatigues, their task being to assemble trays of sandwiches, midday meals for their comrades on the land. My regular and reliable pay gave me a comfortable, prosperous peace of mind by the time it came round to closing the camp at the end of the season.

The return to Cleethorpes presented Fred with an unexpected and unique experience when, through the good offices of my brother, who was still at the level of mate on a trawler, he was able to secure a job on that ship. The pay offered seemed to us colossal and he joyfully accompanied my brother on board as "trimmer-below". Most of his time on that trip was spent in the bowels of the vessel in the coal-hold, where his task was solely to shovel coal, thus freeing its access down to the fireman who shovelled it into the furnace beneath the boiler. He passed hours in a very restricted space, not only sweating profusely, breathing in coal dust, but also enduring a ravenous hunger. Describing the experience later, he emphasized the cook's glorious meals twice daily at breakfast-time and evening when the invariable menu was freshly caught fish together with delicious crisp chips. No one cooks fish and chips better than those experienced in this finest art of Grimsby. The "magnificent" results of his arduous toil for ten days on Dogger Bank were two-fold: I was honoured with the chore of shampooing his dusty mop of hair six times before the coal dust was no longer in residence and, with great pride and anticipation, he was able to collect £20 from the trawler firm's office on the docks the following day. How affluent we were! Just as well, since the enforced separation from each other loomed ominously near, when Fred would be in need of all his resources to pay for his journey to St. Brieuc in Brittany. There, he was destined to spend the following academic year as an assistant in the Ecole Normal — affirmed as essential by his professor, a man who was an avowed supporter of the highest standards in education. How we dreaded that impending, inevitable separation. We made the most of the remaining days and returned to Leicester by bus in time for his departure from the LMS station. As soon as we had kissed goodbye, I swiftly turned, finding myself incapable of looking back, my eyes streaming with tears, as I hurried towards the "flat" that Miss Forster had finally agreed that Win and I could rent for our finals year. We would have been denied this permission had it not been for the kindly intervention of our dear Professor Humphreys, who had practised his gift of persuasion on that formidable lady, as some of her students judged her. By a happy coincidence, the bedsit kitchen was next door to his own house. Having met with nothing but opposition from Miss Forster, despite letters of support for our plans from our fathers, we had then thrown ourselves on the mercy of our Prof. In his normal, gentle voice, he had promised he would have a quiet word with the women's warden and, to our delight, he had succeeded in the argument.

121

Thus liberated from grumpy landladies, our newly found freedom enabled us to create our own domestic routine and expenditure and we were able to benefit from the resulting peace and quiet in our new environment to enjoy our intensive studies in preparation for finals in the following June. I found myself lonely without Fred, but we compensated a little by producing our own catering and occasionally in entertaining compatible friends. Win was a good companion with a lively sense of humour. I cannot remember which one of us made the preposterous suggestion that we should invite Miss Forster to tea but, once the idea was shared, we both decided that it was something we would like to do so that we could demonstrate to her what responsible lives we were leading. We planned to serve the great luxury of those days — toasted teacakes — which Win prepared, lavishly spreading them with our tiny butter ration. Win swept into our bedsitting room with a great flourish, causing the teacakes to roll onto the floor. Fortunately, as the treasure fell to the floor behind the the settee on which Miss Forster was sitting, I was able to keep her interest as I told of my intention to go to France to visit Fred, whom I grandly referred to as my fiance. I warned her that the phone in our room might ring, as I was expecting a confirmation of my travel bookings. Actually, I had deliberately arranged this call in the hope that our guest would be duly impressed. In the meantime, Win had dropped to her knees and replaced the buns on the plate, then set about making her second grand entrance whilst I fervently hoped that she

122

had given the treasures a quick dust over before she ceremoniously offered them to our visitor. The phone then rang and, as I repeated the information the travel agent was giving me, I was wondering if Miss Forster was being impressed with my grown-up conversation. After the call, I explained to her that I was to go to Saint Brieuc, where Fred was accommodated in the Ecole Normal in which he was employed as an assistant and, for me, he had arranged a lodging in the home of an elderly couple where the husband was a retired businessman of English origin and his wife was French. Mr. and Mrs. Stamp ran a tiny non-conformist church and provided me with the warmest of welcomes. Was Miss Forster impressed? I think she probably accepted that we were capable of looking after ourselves.

CHAPTER
SIX

Christmas in Paris

Not much work was done during that vacation, despite the weighty collection of books I had carted with me and although I had set out with the best of intentions. Fred still had classes at the Ecole Normale, where I continued with my studies whilst he was in a classroom and, like him, I very much enjoyed the delicious meals prepared at lunchtimes and in the evenings by the chef with whom, typically, Fred had forged a firm friendship. On the days we travelled to Rennes, where Fred kept abreast of his studies, the chef would cook us a quick steak, as the rest of the school had already completed their evening meal. My presence at the table on normal days caused a stir, as I was the only female present, so that I had to survive the lengthy stares that Frenchmen are prone to, as well as the muted chorus of "ohs" and "ahs" from the students. The teachers and surveillants flattered me shamelessly at the table, something I very much enjoyed and I also remember a most amusing accident to the Prof de Philosophie, M. Rolland. At the end of the meal one evening, he strode from the table and marched in military fashion towards the door, where he turned to face me, clicked his heels and saluted, saying in English, "Free French Officer", turned about quickly, forgetting that the door was still closed and walked straight into it. He finally left the dining room, staggering with a most unmilitary gait.

Although our reunion was the principal reward of my expedition, we celebrated Fred's twenty-first birthday belatedly. With great pride, I had bought him a pair of Bedford cord trousers to complement the brown jacket he had purchased with some of his summer earnings. How elegant he looked in his coffee and cream outfit from the jacket pocket of which he would proudly produce the cigarette case my sister had sent him to mark his milestone birthday. He would then, ostentatiously, light a cigarette with the lighter my parents had asked me to deliver to him.

The end of his school term eventually arrived, whereupon we took a train to Paris and sampled the Metro for the first time in our lives, as we made our way to a small dingy hotel off the Boul'Mich near the Luxembourg. The hotel had been recommended to me by a fellow Leicester undergraduate and Fred had reserved our rooms in advance. I reacted with great indignation to the suggestion from the proprietress, who tried to persuade us to share one double room, obviously hoping to increase her profits by letting the room she wanted us to abandon to two more people. Firmly rejecting her idea, although she assured us that in Paris all such arrangements were acceptable whether we were married or not, we insisted on taking the rooms we had booked. After we had located our rooms, I was in desperate need of a toilet and Fred assisted me in my search for one. "Here you are," he cheerfully announced but, on opening the door, I was confronted by a so-called toilet which was simply a hole in the floor. Explosively rejecting this find, I felt I was being hurled into the seamy side of an alien world as I exclaimed "If you think I am using that, Fred Austin, you are very much mistaken." A more traditional convenience was promptly discovered and peace reigned once more. How those rudimentary facilities seem prehistoric when we measure them by the luxury of the en-suites we now regard as normal, even though they have a French name!

We left our hotel to explore its immediate surroundings and were on the lookout for somewhere reasonably priced where we could eat a palatable meal. Fred had hoarded his earnings from the Ecole Normale, which enabled us to eat daily in economical restaurants. We bought croissants for breakfasts, as there was no food served in our hotel. The following day we walked miles, as we found the rue de Rivoli, the Opera, Boulevard Hausman, the Champs Elysees with its impressive Arc de Triomphe, the Place de la Bastille and many other historical attractions. It was difficult to grasp how many landmarks we had seen as day after day we visited art galleries, Montmartre and Sacre Coeur, the Louvre, Notre Dame, the Conciergerie and the intimidating Eiffel Tower.

Theatres also played a stimulating part in our holiday. At the Comedie Francaise we enjoyed performances of *Phedre* and *Cyrano de Bergerac*, and at the Theatre des Elysees, a not very successful production of *Hamlet*, even though the title role was played by Jean Louis Barrault. We found the staging of Laertes' leap into Ophelia's grave and Hamlet's subsequent jump into the hole hilarious, as a trap door was lifted by a stagehand to accommodate the interment and the following demonstrations of devotion.

It is amazing how many incidents from this fortnight stand out in my memory after sixty years. My Christmas present from Fred was a small brown suede handbag, which we still have; it cost far more than he could really afford, but I had admired it in an elegant shop on the Boulevard Hausman. I still feel a tremor of guilt at my eagerness to possess the lovely thing, although Fred has continued, over these many years, to take great pleasure in purchasing further elegant bags. We searched on Christmas Day for a restaurant serving turkey — compulsory for anyone brought up by my mother. Having succeeded in our hunt, we were introduced to the delicious chestnut stuffing served with the turkey, the like of which we have never tasted again. And how we both laughed when we discovered that Fred's order of "pommes purees" for dessert turned out to be potato rather than his anticipated apple. No wonder the waiter gave us a strange look when he took the order for dessert. Needless to say, it was consumed, as it had to be paid for! Our Christmas lunch became even more memorable when a violinist came to our table to serenade us. We had already started our day with a special treat: on Christmas Eve we had bought two hard boiled eggs in a bar and from an upmarket patisserie we invested in 100 grams of exquisite petit fours, each one different from the others. When I went to my room, I placed the eggs on the radiator in a bizarre approach to my mother's obligatory Christmas Day cooked breakfast. The following morning, we consumed the tepid eggs then, ceremoniously using his penknife, Fred cut each tiny petit four in half, so that we could both taste all of them. After our wonderful lunch, we walked to the Palais de Chaillot to enjoy a Wagner concert, magnificently performed by a French orchestra of supreme talent. Fred was enchanted.

Another shopping spree was indulged in a day or two later at the Galeries Lafayette, where I had admired blue bras — never once seen in those utility days in England. I decided on one of these and the young lady assistant advised me to try it on before I bought it. She conducted me to a makeshift "changing room" — a space between some high pieces of furniture. As I was about to remove the bra when I had decided that it was entirely satisfactory, I looked up to witness a French peeping Tom, one of the young male assistants. I was steadily becoming more and more disdainful of those immoral French! Hastily, I assured myself that the bra was a perfect fit and, since the young man had swiftly scuttled away when he saw me staring at him, I was enabled to overcome my embarrassment, pay for my purchase and escape with another prize.

Prior to my departure from Leicester, I had contacted Daniel to tell him of our plans to visit Paris. Promptly replying, he wrote to say that we were invited for dinner at the family home in Rue Dagorno. I was taken aback to be climbing a rickety wooden staircase which led to the first floor of the shabby block of flats where the parents' home was situated. We became oblivious of our surroundings as soon as our knock was answered and we were received very hospitably. Daniel's mother had prepared a delicious meal and the entire family displayed their pleasure in having Fred's fluent French to help the conversation along, as we consumed the food with relish. In spite of myself, I fell to debating silently as to where I would have slept if my father had allowed me to accept their kind invitation in 1946, since Daniel's bed was in the room where we were eating and his younger sister slept in her parent's room. I have no recollection of a bathroom and the communal toilet was outside on the corridor. The next matter to surprise us was the comment by Daniel's father when we both refused his offer of wine, saying that we preferred water. Monsieur Gault assured us that water was intended for horses and wine for people. He showed no sign of offence at our rejection of his offer, to our great relief.

As the years have passed, I have frequently rejoiced when contemplating the prosperous and contented life that Daniel has created for himself since he qualified as a doctor. He was not, however, quite as popular with us the night after that reunion with him when, after our words of farewell, he had persuaded us to meet him for a cinema visit to see "Au Balcon" and afterwards he guided us into the nightclub "Mimi Pinson", where we wickedly succumbed to his urging us to drink something alcoholic — quite beyond our experience. I was severely castigated by my methodist conscience for the rest of the evening. We had never entered a nightclub before, nor have we since, as it proved to have little attraction for us. As time ticked on, we kept pointing out to Daniel that it was getting perilously close to the departure of our last metro train, but he insisted that there was a later one. Unwillingly, we acquiesced to his pleas to stay longer, only to discover disconsolately that we had indeed missed the last train, which had left at the time we had seen on the timetable. We were thus compelled to part with some of our dwindling store of francs as we took a taxi to the hotel Berthelot, feeling both impoverished and indignant.

A further hospitable invitation, however, provided us with a substantial and delectable meal on New Year's Eve, when we went to the home of M. Rolland, the teacher of philosophy in St. Brieuc (Free French Officers!), whose permanent home was a far more spacious and luxurious apartment than the tiny Gault flat. A fellow guest was Rene, a young surveillant from St. Brieuc who, by degrees, consumed a vast quantity of wine, some of which he eventually spilt on the beautiful white damask cloth with which Madame had adorned her table. In a slurred voice, Rene displayed his grasp of English with "Oh! I 'ave made a festoon of myself!" Further histrionics gripped us when M. Rolland was asked by his wife to carve the magnificent joint of beef. Soldier to the marrow, he produced a bayonet and ostentatiously stabbed the joint, alarming his poor wife, for she feared for her valuable serving dish. Fortunately, she found it was still intact, but that did not prevent her from giving vent explosively to her justifiable indignation. He had a lucky escape, as her serene nature reappeared swiftly. When this genial hostess served her dessert, she presented us with an entirely new delight, which she informed us was creme de marrons, which she had made herself. Once we were married and settled in our two attics, I struggled repeatedly to produce this delectable chestnut puree but always faced failure. I was very pleased to find cans of this delicacy in French shops on later visits, although the mass-produced contents never equalled the quality of our first tasting that New Year's Eve.

As mentioned earlier, we enjoyed several theatre visits, as well as long sessions in the Louvre and a variety of art galleries for a few days until, finally, we had to return to St. Brieuc in time for my departure from St. Malo and onwards to Leicester. The end of June, 1950 seemed unbearably distant, despite the ominous approach of those final examinations to be faced in the early part of that month. After a swift visit to my family in Cleethorpes, I returned to Leicester to look forward to five months of concentrated study, happily punctuated by the arrival of regular letters from Fred.

CHAPTER
SEVEN

My Finals Year

We had agreed to continue our practice of writing to each other daily, but to post our letters every three days in order to effect the economies impecunious students were bound to embrace. Win and I had a very contented relationship and enjoyed finding ways of reducing our housekeeping bills. We discovered one health food which proved inexpensive and very much to our taste — a nut rissole mix, which we reconstituted, cooked and relished for breakfast: we found this very sustaining, especially in cold weather. This find enabled us to hold back on our egg ration until we were possessed of a ravenous hunger at the very late end of our evening's work, when we loved to feast on a fried egg and its accompanying fried bread: we were not well schooled in healthy eating in those far off days. As the weeks snailed slowly by, Alan Martindale and I took to comforting each other, for I was prepared to listen to his reports of his beloved Eileen, now a student in Matlock Teacher Training College and he would endure my news in the same vein about my dear one in St. Brieuc. We were both impressed by the knowledge that the previously irresponsible boy, Fred Austin, had

132

become mature and ambitious and was taking the first part of a French University Licence — the equivalent of our BA. When Fred obtained his BA later, he discovered that he was qualified for an exemption, so that the certificate he had achieved in Rennes and his first class BA meant that he would only require two more certificates to give him his full Licence. Soon, he was thinking of another year in France in order to acquire the further qualification once his English studies were complete. That adventure was now envisaged for 1953 and appeared to me quite nebulous.

Although I was engrossed in revision, I found time to apply to the NUS for a cook's job in a harvest camp and Win agreed to be my assistant cook. We felt that four weeks would be long enough in that employment. By return of post, our positions in Leverington were confirmed: we were to open the camp, together with an organiser called Keith. After this successful negotiation, a disaster soon followed, when Win dropped something on the cloakroom floor alongside the clothes rack: she leaned down to retrieve the lost item but failed to notice a half-concealed fencing foil which pierced the white of one of her eyes and, as she straightened up, I could see blood ominously trickling down her cheek. We raced to the Leicester Royal Infirmary where she was immediately and efficiently treated, as she courageously endured the stitching of the cut. We left the hospital with poor Win generously bandaged, so that half of her head was covered. She was obviously greatly relieved that her sight was unimpaired by this unfortunate accident but, for the next few days, it

133

proved impossible for her to read with only one eye unbandaged. Consequently, revision faltered, as I read to her to compensate for her misfortune. Fortunately, she had not spent the Christmas vacation gallivanting in France, so she was reasonably prepared in some of the texts. Eventually, she was liberated from the bondage of the dressings, so that we were both able to pursue our pet subjects independently, which we did well into the small hours of many a morning. We continued to enjoy our midnight feasts, however, for as long as our rations lasted. June arrived with amazing rapidity and the exams were soon upon us: a very different ordeal from that faced by undergraduates of today. Those eight exams were the only source of assessment for our three years of study. We faced eight three hour papers, which followed one after the other pell mell, morning and afternoon, although we enjoyed a free afternoon on the fourth day. For those of us who had selected the language option, the final paper was on the fifth morning; it had been a demanding course, during which we had studied Old Norse, Gothic and Old Germanic — texts and grammar.

In the ensuing days of liberation, our first treat as a group was a visit to The Royal Shakespeare Theatre for a performance of *Much Ado about Nothing* — one of our plays set for intensive study. We were feeling we could find ourselves easily entertained by anything extraordinary that caught our eyes so, soon after our arrival in Stratford, when we saw one of our fellow students — a very proper young lady — fall from a boat being inexpertly rowed by one of the male members of our year, we gave vent to loud and mischievous laughter. Both occupants of the boat discovered, when she had been hauled out of the river, that one of her shoes had remained in the water, but her companion gallantly suffered a dripping consequence when he entered the Avon and rescued her shoe. That gave rise to more hilarity. Very soon after that episode, we were all seated in the theatre balcony, agog to behold the performance of one of our set plays. It is quite true to say that there was appreciative laughter as we listened to the witty exchanges between Beatrice and Benedict, but the overriding response from our group was a loud groan from most of us when it was illustrated that we had failed to recognise the context question in the Shakespeare exam.

Once all our studies were over, Win and I rushed into the preparations for a party with our female friends from college, to celebrate the end of the examinations and to mark my 21st birthday, which had fallen on one of those toilsome days of six hours of examinations. We first tackled decorating the two tiers of birthday cake which my mother had baked for me with some of the contents of a huge box of catering marzipan, given to us by the flirtatious young man who occupied the bedsit adjacent to ours and who constantly reminded us that he was a traveller in cake decorations.

This admission had given rise to many jibes from us, but he always responded in a tolerant manner. He admitted that the box containing the marzipan had been attacked by a verminous intruder; but the contents were unadulterated, so we welcomed his

135

generosity. Nevertheless, we cut off a large margin of paste around the entire block and still retained more than we really needed. As we had so long been restricted in all kinds of food, we thought it would be a rare post-war treat if we were to cover each tier of the cake lavishly. We then went on to cover the almond paste with royal icing and aired our knowledge of *Beowulf* by painting in runic quotations from the text of the poem, which displayed the inevitable doom and gloom of Anglo-Saxon poetry. They proved to be prophetic as far as that cake was concerned. Win worked her socks off to make my party a success, although I did experience one painful accident at her hands a day or so before the party, when she removed a tier of her much vaunted lemon chiffon cake from the oven. She tilted the tin, whereupon the cake escaped and fell into and below the neckline of my low cut blouse. Whilst I found it very uncomfortable, I also thought the accident very funny but Win grew very irritated by my habit of later describing the event frequently to other people. Before our guests arrived, we had prepared a selection of artistic sandwiches — the height of fashion in those far off days — and our final task was to place four pillars on the bottom tier of the birthday cake and carefully stand the upper tier on top. This masterpiece was to be brought into the room after the other food had been consumed. It was at that point that the dismal warnings of the Anglo-Saxons were fulfilled. We had tempted providence by being reckless with the layer of marzipan and, as the cake was ceremoniously produced towards the end of the party, the top tier parted company from its companion below. Never mind, it tasted fine and the escaped section was rescued and placed carefully in a tin so that Fred could enjoy it when he returned from St. Brieuc to join us in Leverington.

Despite the fact that I had been granted a place in the Education Department for the following year to take the Diploma in Education qualification — given that I would be awarded a degree when the results were divulged — I did not feel cut out for teaching. I was concerned about the chances of my finding what I considered would prove to be a more compatible career, so I applied to the University Appointments Board for an interview. I had recently rejected an offer of a civil service job in the Inland Revenue — my vacation experiences in Grimsby not having engendered ambitions in that direction. The day that Win and I were due in Leverington I had an early interview in Nottingham with the Appointments people. My heart was set on journalism but, after I had been put through various tests, I was advised that I was too sensitive for that profession and would not withstand the horrific experiences I would, of necessity, encounter. The interviewer told me that I was more suited to working with people and he advocated personnel work. He promised to pursue this on my behalf and, later, I received a letter from Marks & Spencer, offering me a training in London, lasting six months and leading to my becoming a Personnel Manager. Needless to say, the separation from Fred for a further six months was more than I could bear: I rejected the offer. The

Education Department it would have to be in September. Win and I had left our nice little apartment, being too impoverished to pay the retainer the landlady demanded. We risked finding an alternative home until nearer September, when our course would start and my scholarship would continue. Win would receive a Teacher Training Grant, which was freely available at that time.

CHAPTER
EIGHT

Cooks for a Month

We took a series of trains that June day after the visit to Nottingham and, when we reached Wisbech, we were collected at the railway station by a mature student who informed us that he was the Camp Organiser, about to join us in Leverington. When we reached the camp, we discovered bare huts, with wooden bunks and nothing else, while the kitchen was devoid of any equipment, save for the huge coke-fired built-in cooker and, in a small extension, a capacious cupboard which was totally empty. As the three of us looked at each other forlornly, a large car raced into the area between the huts and the kitchen: a burly man with a stentorian voice emerged from the car and told us to pile in with our luggage. He explained that we were to spend the night in the much larger camp of which he was the Organiser and then he would transport us back to Leverington the following morning, when all our necessities would be delivered. On the way, this man explained that his cook was cooking a meal for us and they had made a temporary dormitory for Win and me, with beds already made up. We were overwhelmed with what we considered to be marvellous service, until we located this "dormitory": there were three beds located between rows of concrete sinks where, apparently, soft fruits were washed in great quantities. Each sink had a cold water tap and these were to provide our "en suite" comfort. I am unable to recall the whereabouts of a toilet block in that place. Shortly, we were summoned to the evening meal. We learned that the cook was a newly-arrived Finnish student, who was accompanied by her boy-friend and were relieved to hear that food was imminent. As we arrived at the table, we were greeted by the cook who apologised to us and admitted that she could only prepare Finnish food. We were delighted to be encountering a new cuisine and were astonished to be served beans on toast — never a gourmet meal for my friend and me. We suppressed our laughter whilst determining that our students would receive more lavish treatment that this poor girl appeared capable of.

We had had a long day, so retired quite early to our splendid accommodation, where we were quickly joined by the cook, obviously weary from the arduous toil of the kitchen. She undressed rapidly and snuggled into her sleeping-bag. Immediately, Win and I were alarmed to hear her calling, "Josef! Josef!" Win's immediate response was, "If Josef is coming, I am not staying!", which was also my unspoken reaction. Josef, however, was apparently intercepted by the two Organisers, who refused to let him join his lady. After all that, we enjoyed a peaceful rest and rose early to endure an icy wash in the fruit-sink of our choice. A substantial

140

English breakfast, cooked by the Senior Organiser, was produced and we then returned to our own camp.

Pell-mell, supplies of all kinds arrived: bedding, tents for the men — as the huts were to be totally a female preserve — and masses of kitchen equipment which had, unfortunately, been lavishly greased to protect it during the previous winter. So, as fuel had arrived, we hastily built a fire in the stove to ensure a good supply of hot water for washing everything. When it became necessary to turn on the kitchen taps, the water proved to be foul-smelling and a disgusting blackish colour. Keith, our Organiser, was displaying a characteristic which became very familiar to us in the following weeks: as soon as work was required, he retreated from the camp, so it fell to my lot to climb up and look into the water-storage tank, where I was horrified to see a large number of dead birds, floating on the surface. There followed one of the most gruesome tasks I have ever faced, as I removed the poor bodies from the tank. Meanwhile, Win was running the water and, as the tank refilled, we had clear, wholesome water available. We made sure, for several days, however, that all water to be consumed or used in cooking was well and truly boiled in the large black kettles with which we had been abundantly supplied. We toiled to clean away the grease and, as Keith had still not returned with soap (no washing-up liquid being available in those days), the work lasted interminably.

The next shock followed. A large lorry, bearing the name "Danish Bacon Co." arrived and the driver immediately began to unload an enormous quantity of

141

provisions, which had been ordered by someone in the NUS head-office. Imagine our horror when the bacon for about 80 people was presented to us as a whole side, the tea was contained in an unopened wooden chest, the salt in a large hessian sack, as was the sugar, and another unforgettable item: an enormous tin of mustard powder! There were bottles upon bottles of vinegar, a huge sack of flour and, horror of horrors, 500 grade D duck eggs. The latter, I refused to accept, as I had heard my mother frequently say that many people had been poisoned by eating these. The future bossy teacher/mother emerged prematurely, as I insisted that he remove the offending eggs and threatened the poor driver with hell and damnation if they were not immediately replaced by hens' eggs, accompanied by many other foods which Win and I deemed to be essential. Very quickly after the van's departure, a very elegant gentleman from the firm arrived and recorded our further order, which was completed the same day. The sack of salt was replaced by packets which would not get damp so easily and we were ultimately relieved to see that an acceptable meal could be provided the following day, when the students were due to arrive. All this took place in the absence of the man who was supposed to be running the camp. Imagine our indignation when, eventually, he returned, but still without soap! He was firmly despatched to acquire some. Surrounded by sacks and cartons, we hastily set about cleaning the huge storage-cupboard so that the food could be packed away. As we were working, there arrived a small group of little local boys. They were agog when they saw the size of the containers and, in their lovely Cambridge lilt, they asked what we would do with all that salt and mustard. I asked them if they liked mustard pie and salt pudding? They admitted that they had never tasted either, so I invited them to return the following day when we would have made both for them to sample. They kept the appointment and one little lad acted as their spokesman, saying, "My Mum reckons that you were pulling our legs!" Win and I had hastily bought chocolate bars in the village and I told them that their first taste of our cooking had to be accepted with their eyes closed and their hands open in front of them. They were not to open their eyes until I said, "Now!" Once they viewed their treasure, they readily thanked us for "our baking" and rushed home with their prizes, almost seeming to fear that they would be confiscated if they delayed their departure. They visited us quite frequently afterwards, but always made their stay quite brief. Lovely kids!

Finally, their presence was supplanted by an unashamed Keith, who had the nerve to announce that he was hungry and dying for a cup of tea. Had the duck eggs not been removed, they might have been used as missiles. We told him he had to fulfil his role of chief fireman and assiduously tend to the needs of the cooker. We learned, next morning, that he did not rise early enough to relight the fire and it proved to be my first chore every morning, which meant I had to set my alarm 15 minutes earlier than my normal contract duties required. I wonder if any woman was fool enough to marry him?

143

The influx of 80 students quickly arrived and we were delighted to meet the large Finnish contingent. They spoke good English and displayed an abundance of cheerful good nature. Whilst they settled down to daily toil in the strawberry fields, returning with rather bent backs at the end of their working day, they were quickly followed by a troupe of local boys, shouting "They've got the strawberry walk." Win and I raced to provide sandwich fillings and bread straight after breakfast, to be used by the conscripted group of students, whose first duty of the day was to produce sandwiches for the lunches of those industrious fruit-pickers and then to peel potatoes for the evening meal. After this chore, we raced to produce evening meals for the whole complement of the camp. We always provided a substantial main course and an old-fashioned pudding or pie. Jamie Oliver would have totally approved of our menus, which displayed an abundant variety of vegetables and fruits, kindly donated by our friendly farmer. These were incredible bonuses, as we had to produce three meals daily, seven days a week, on the allowance of 15 shillings (75 pence) per week, per person. The problem of the huge side of bacon was quickly solved by a medical student accustomed to dissection: he neatly produced a mountain of sliced bacon, which we successfully preserved in an ice-box, before the maggots eventually arrived: the ice-blocks were regularly delivered, as was the bread, milk, fish and meat. We were always ready to retire early, but since their main beverage of the day had been tea, we willingly provided hot cocoa before we took to our beds. We even stretched to Horlicks on some nights because, along with the enormous tin of cocoa, we received an unimaginably large container of Horlicks. The representative from the firm who brought this gave me a white jug, with a metal gadget inside, which could be used to froth up the drinks. It is still in my possession, but could not be really useful for 80 students.

We soon became acquainted with all the students, whom we addressed by their first names. There was, however, a plethora of "Joes", whom we ingeniously called Irish Joe, Persian Joe, Chinese Joe and Girl Jo. I remember them all so well: I have a clear mental picture of Irish Joe running stark naked from the men's showers when I left my bed to berate some of the men who had been swimming and were singing at the top of their voices at 5.30a.m.: "If you were the only girl in the world!" He received an earful of my Lincolnshire acidity, to which he gently responded, "Sorry, Miss!" Persian Joe was a handsome, but far too familiar young man, who constantly made improper suggestions to me, his most frequent one being an invitation to take a shower with him. How I yearned for Fred's return from France to protect me! Chinese Joe was a large, almost obese man, whom the Organiser had invited illicitly and who enjoyed many privileges free of charge. He shared Keith's office as a dormitory, but we were far too innocent in those days to conjecture about their relationship. I disliked the man intensely because he gorged on our food without contributing a penny, never did a scrap of work and would enter my kitchen and help himself to any food he took a liking to. I retain only a faint memory of the young lady who shared the name Jo. A youthful South African, called Peter Pretorius, was also rather forward in his advances until a more recently arrived student earmarked him as her conquest: she spoke incessantly in ridiculous baby talk, announcing every morning that she, "Patty", and her Peterkin were going to earn some "bwite pennies". She was not our favourite person but, very soon, the infection of her infantile language spread mockingly to several students whilst other creative members of the camp sang their parody of the National Anthem — "Send him Pretorius". I wonder what became of the incredible couple? We served our main meals through a hatch which gave on to the large barn where the students congregated, so that it served as a refectory as well as a common room. The hungry mass would queue in the disciplined manner we had become drilled in during the war, whilst we would ladle out healthy portions. One of the Finnish boys yelled at us every night, "No peas", whether there were peas or not, and his other constant cry was, "Sugar is poison!" It was from the same hatch that we served their substantial cooked breakfasts each morning, as we waded through our mountain of sliced bacon: but never a solitary grade D duck egg was permitted to soil anyone's plate. All the washing up was tackled by the team that was on jankers that day, after which they would assist with the "spud bashing". We hoped that both teams could complete their chores within the hour, so that they could be transported to the work site by lorry.

146

Finally, the day dawned when Fred was to arrive in Peterborough on a train from Southampton and my loneliness would at last evaporate. I had a lift into Wisbech, where I found a hairdresser to shampoo and set my hair. The day was of such significance that I had decided to indulge in that extravagance and I can still visualise every part of it. As I sat under the hair-dryer, I remember reading a magazine article which explained why the Australian cricketers out-played the English. It claimed that the Australians had been able to consume large steaks from childhood, whilst the poor English had suffered the torments of meat rationing throughout the war. I believed this for many years, especially when I read the Neville Shute book which described the little old English lady who, a little after receiving a food parcel from down under, died of malnutrition. A post mortem revealed that all her stomach contents consisted of dried fruits only and these had been in the gift parcel.

After the hairdo, I made my way to Wisbech station, where I took a train for Peterborough. There, I quickly located the platform where Fred's train was to arrive. Almost at once, my heart somersaulted — he was approaching me. He remembers what I said to this day: "I saw a grin followed by Fred." Life began afresh for us that day and we have never again been apart for so long. Clouds lifted, work proved less onerous, for there was a true gentleman around now who tended the kitchen fire every morning and pottered around in the kitchen before leaving for fruit picking each day with his fellow workers. He was in need of earnings, though

147

he had harboured a good share of his meagre French salary to tide him over.

The last week or so passed blissfully and, soon, we would be leaving for Cleethorpes, whilst Win would travel home to Southwark. Two replacement cooks arrived to overlap with us for three days and it became immediately evident that they regarded those three days as theirs to relax in. I very soon disabused them of that conviction by pointing out to them that they were already being paid and so should do as much work as Win and I were doing. Thus, they were press-ganged into doing a fair share of the labour. Win and I planned to produce a "grand banquet" for our final offering on our last duty evening, so we insisted that these newcomers on the penultimate evening of our joint contract tackled the catering, thus enabling us to accept the invitation from many of the students to join them at the village pub for half an hour before dinner. Grudgingly they agreed and when we all returned for the meal we found that nothing was ready and, ultimately, we were kept waiting for their undercooked food for almost a further two hours. Impetuous as ever, I was tempted to return to the kitchen, but was restrained by the indignant assembly.

The following day was hectic, as we busily produced our seven course meal. Fred and the camp organiser made themselves paper bow ties which they pinned to their white vests, so that they could perform the services of waiters — an added touch of fun for the event. Some of the art students produced menus for the tables, as well as a large card each for the two cooks. I still have one of the menus and my card, "From a grateful and appreciative camp". All of the campers had signed the cards and one very nice mature student who had constantly assured me, each time we served a fish meal, that he abhorred fish, signed himself "Eric Jamieson B. Cod" awarding himself this qualification whilst, like us, he awaited his finals results. I have very happy memories of the lovely people we spent part of that summer with. At the end of the meal, as everyone toasted Win and me with their cups of coffee, we were both presented with five pound notes — a farewell gift from our fellow students. It was hard to believe they could afford to muster so much between them as, at that time, it was more than our week's wages.

It was quite sad to leave these pleasant, carefree folk, but we were looking forward to seeing my family and to enjoying a less onerous timetable. We had shared quite a good proportion of the birthday cake which I had brought to Leverington, but the family enjoyed devouring the rest of it and they were ably assisted in the process by Fred, who really relished cake in those days — particularly the home made varieties. Once back home, I became more aware of the imminence of the date for my finals results.

CHAPTER
NINE

Training to Teach

My degree result arrived during Fred's absence and I was, I must confess, disappointed in my Lower Second, for I was immediately convinced that I would be the only member of my year to receive so lowly a result. Later, I was astounded to discover that most of my contemporaries were in the selfsame category or even lower, with Thirds, and an unfortunate few with fails. Many a modern politician would opine that those students were not as bright as their counterparts are today or that their teachers were not as gifted as those of the twenty-first century. I aggressively assert that these wiseacres were not there at the time, so that they have no right to pronounce their prejudices in this way. What they will never accept is that standards were much higher in those days and the quantity of work was much more demanding. Before they entered the various departments, the selection process was rigorous and many who started their courses were rejected during their first term, whilst others were asked to leave at the end of their first year, and this not usually because they had not put in sufficient effort. It must also be pointed out that I was a member of a large contingent from working class homes, students who had received their Secondary education in the excellent Grammar Schools of that era. These memories do not merit a scoffing disbelief from people who were not even born in 1950. There was no coursework counting towards the exam, but a mass of essays containing genuine individual research and thought. All of this work was not taken into account in our final grading, but was intended to prepare us for the countless essays we would have to write in answer to the unseen questions which would appear on the examination papers. The work we did was demanding and was a guide for the academic staff to know whether or not we were achieving a standard which justified our remaining on our chosen course. Needless to say, we did not have an all-consuming social life, nor did we have enough money to seek out luxury and diversions, just the "hops" on Saturday nights which were organised by the students' entertainments committee, who provided the music by borrowing records from friends or using the growing collection purchased with the minute charges for the evening, and then remaining the property of the Students' Union.

In great contentment, Fred and I enjoyed our walks by the sea and along the golf links for a few more weeks, though we also took on holiday jobs to pay our way and to retain a nest egg for future needs in Leicester. Finally, we took our familiar buses to our new commitments. I went to Bulwer Road, where I was to share with Win a converted doctor's surgery and waiting room, an extension at the back of a terraced house of a lovely widowed lady. We had to cope with cooking in a narrow little passageway which led from our "front" door to our back door. This space housed a tiny Baby Belling cooker, identical to the one in our kitchen of the previous year, though it was not so securely placed on an orange box. We had no conveniently running water in this little area but there was a small handbasin in the little storage room off our living room which had been the doctor's dispensary, where we could draw water and also do some washing of crocks and clothes. We had to walk through the landlady's kitchen, dining room and upstairs to the first floor whenever we needed the toilet and we were permitted to take a bath once a week. However, we were very happy there and made the best of this inconvenient accommodation. Fred joined us for evening meals as well as Sunday lunches, because he was in digs with a Polish family who provided him with a small bedroom and breakfast only. In our diminutive living room, previously the doctor's surgery, there was a table and four chairs, as well as two easy chairs, so we could entertain. We remember the Sunday when Fred brought a young Frenchman, who was an assistant in a Leicester school to share our meal. Fred had become acquainted with him at the Cercle Francais. He puzzled me when he asked if I knew "Ashby saus" — south? I told him that I had never been there, my response likewise confusing him. He repeated his question painstakingly and, between us, we realised that he was asking me about HP Sauce. He also induced laughter when he asked Fred about St. Brieuc, enquiring: "Was your boss a jolly boss?"

Win and I were, by this time, involved in our education studies and, frankly, I was detesting every moment of it. Without telling a soul, I took myself to the Leicester Employment Office and asked if they had any vacancies. The first person who interviewed me asked about my age, qualifications and experience. I could mention only my vacation jobs — Income Tax office and cook in a harvest camp. She thumbed through a box of cards and told me that the only vaguely appropriate job she could offer was that of a manageress in a bakery. I readily agreed to accept, but she asked me to wait while she investigated further, soon returning and ushering me into a small, private office, where a formidable, portly lady towered over her desk and glowered at me. Imagine the reception this virago would receive from a 21-year old graduate of today, when she gave vent to the following tirade: "You are a very silly girl to contemplate working in a bakery after the success you have so far achieved in your young life. Forget all about this nonsense and go back to College to complete your Teacher-Training course." I practically crawled back to the bus-stop, my face glowing with blushes, but I confess I was rejoicing inside, as I reminded myself afresh of how delightful the daily contact with Fred and Win was. I would have to coerce myself into enjoying the pedantry of "Bully" Bantock, as well as the droning of the other tutors.

There dawned the day when we would-be teachers had to go on school practice for ten weeks. Having been allocated a place in a girls' secondary modern school in Central Leicester, it was with some trepidation that I entered the building for the first time at the beginning of the Spring Term. I was immediately cordially greeted by a lady well into middle age and found myself responding to her warmth. She became my stalwart support during those intimidating days and inducted me into the skills of her selfless commitment to the less academically able pupils of the school, unkindly, but not maliciously, labelled "the dull and backward group" in those days. She was a very gifted lady, I learned, and I found her example inspiring. I taught several other classes, where I was able to cover much of the work for which I had received guidance in the Education Department. I produced my own projects, including a production of the scene in *A Midsummer Night's Dream* when the workmen were rehearsing in the wood and Bottom acquired his ass's head, much abridged, of course. I chose this option because I discovered in the cupboard which contained theatrical costumes, a ready-made headpiece for Bottom. With another group, we produced booklets entitled "A Brief History of English Literature", both projects being well received by my tutor. Having gained in confidence as the term progressed, I was finally sad to leave my newly-found friends at Willow Mead, but now recognised that the life of a teacher could offer rewards.

The outcome of these contacts led me later to accept the offer of a post in an even more unfortunately situated girls' secondary modern, not far from the city centre. I was persuaded to take on the "special needs"

154

class, having been tempted by the carrot promised that, as soon as my College course was complete, I would be salaried whilst I visited other such groups for observation. Even these few weeks on full pay were a considerable advance over living on my scholarship. The end of term arrived and Win and I were parted after four years of precious friendship, but Fred and I were now both on holiday. During my education year, I had worked as a Saturday-girl in Woolworths and, at the end of my final term, I invested these earnings in a 1930 BSA three-wheeler which, we felt, promised easier means of getting to Lincolnshire. Unfortunately, Fred failed his first driving-test because he had relied on a couple of lessons from Adrien Favre, the Lecturer with whom we had been friendly for a long time. Forlornly, we took our usual string of buses back to my home and our casual work. After a few weeks elapsed, Fred took a train back to Leicester to take a second driving-test: absent-minded as ever, he turned up for the test a day late. I remember only too clearly my indignation when he returned with a very hang-dog expression, but had to accept that a further delay was our fate.

Eventually, the summer passed and Fred was destined to become a more dedicated student than he had ever been, with finals looming the following June. I returned to my school long before he was back in College so, once again, he was able to work casually. I took over my "special class" and very soon felt surrounded by a ring of fire. A distant and unsupportive headmistress left me to fend for myself, though her deputy, who shared the same surname, was a totally different kettle of fish. The elderly teacher who had controlled that type of class since the 1930's had, I subsequently learned, resigned from that particular post in the school because the current group of "educationally subnormal", as they were labelled, 28 in number, had proved to be beyond her control, displaying a plethora of behaviour problems, as well as extreme learning difficulties. I knew nothing of this when I had blithely accepted the appointment, as I envisaged a group similar to the one I had become familiar with on school practice. A further complication tortured me when the Local Authority announced its willingness to pay an additional £18 a year by making posts like mine a post of special responsibility. The lady in question, who had passed so many years with earlier groups, set about me in the Staff Room and only after a stream of bitter recriminations about my "award", did she listen to my assurances that, as a probationer, I was not entitled to the allowance. Nevertheless, she never took to me, nor did I to her.

As the weeks passed, I endured many tortures: on an almost daily basis, I was being bitten quite viciously by a very unpleasant 11-year old. In addition, she bewildered me by constantly informing me that her father was still on holiday in the Isle of Wight. Finally, it occurred to me to relate this information to Fred and add that the family must have more money than her grubby appearance and clothes full of holes indicated. My dear fiance laughed uproariously and explained the true meaning of this "holiday" in the context. Feeling sorry for her, I wrote in a letter to my mother an account of her pathetic, ragged and unlaundered clothing, a characteristic shared by several others in my group. Spontaneously sympathetic, Mum took herself to Grimsby market and bought a large quantity of second-hand clothing which she posted to me and which was rapturously received by a number of the girls. I allowed them to select whatever they wanted, but compelled the daughter of the gaolbird to leave these clean clothes in the cloakroom and trained her to change from her normal garb each morning. Thus, I was able to launder her "school" clothes each week-end and I persevered with training her in the art of neck and hand washing in the cloakroom basins adjacent to our classroom before she put on her clean clothing. Despite my efforts, she continued untamed and I had finally had enough of her vicious bites. The headmistress had refused to believe my complaints so, ultimately, after one of her usual attacks, I deserted my classroom, briefly and hurried to the Head's study to display the teethmarks and saliva on the back of my hand. Her response, unsympathetic as ever, was to announce to me that she was suffering from the smell of cigarette smoke, where someone had used her phone and smoked. I grasped her implication that I was the main suspect, but, as I smoked only three cigarettes a day, I don't know whether or not I was the culprit. I received no help with my vicious pupil problem.

CHAPTER
TEN

Wedding Preparations

My friend, Lorna, and I would buy ten cigarettes between us, three for each of us and two each for our fiances. The friendship which sprang up between us was one of the loveliest I have ever known. Lorna was a very gifted Music teacher, as well as a knowledgeable cook, as a consequence of the excellent domestic science teaching she had received at the Alderman Newton school where she had been a pupil and also from her home background, having a mother who produced first-rate meals and a butcher father, who made sure that his family was well supplied with the best of his wares. Fred and I were always delighted to be invited to eat with her family. Another matter which brought Lorna and me together was our fast-approaching weddings, destined to take place for Lorna and Eric on July 1st and, for us, on August 2nd. We planned our trousseaux together, and compared our achievements in making our wedding dresses and the garments for our honeymoons. We even made our underwear and our night apparel and were prepared to spend time embroidering some items. I was living in the house with our same landlady, having relinquished our previous flat, where the rent was too high for one person. Mrs. Gisborne had offered me a bedroom in the main part of the house — much more conveniently situated for the bathroom. I had the use of her kitchen, so I was able to invite Fred to share my food, which I served in the adjacent dining room. Once our meals were over, Fred retreated to his own digs or the College library, whilst I joined Mrs. G. in her living room, where she guided me through my dressmaking, my goal being ten dresses for the honeymoon, the underwear and, finally, the wedding-dress and veil, which I was inspired to copy from a beautiful picture, published in Vogue magazine. I bought the pattern and many an evening was dedicated to this major production, under the perfectionist control of my mentor. The numerous button-loops on the placket, from the neck to below the waist and for several inches up the tight-fitting sleeves in this Elizabethan style dress, had to be made from the dress material, a simple off-white brocade. Every one of the vast number I produced, either frayed uselessly or was vigorously rejected by Mrs. G. as not fine enough. I really despaired of succeeding with them but, with her assiduous assistance, perfect examples were eventually produced. The day dresses were completed very efficiently and economically, as reasonably-priced fabrics could be purchased in Lewis's. Excellent in quality, they were easy to cut and sew and were quite to my taste at that time, with waffle cottons, piques, poplins and seersuckers, almost all in plain colours, although I recall one cheerful Horrocks' cotton, with strong patterns in contrasting colours. A sundress was

159

made out of sale material, which cost under £1 for three yards and I was still wearing it seven or eight years later! I found the first gossamer thin nylon to come on the post-war market in Marshall and Snelgrove's and, from a length of pale blue, I made a beautiful night-dress and negligee, carefully adorned with Chantilly lace. I was present in the same shop when their first consignment of nylon tulle arrived and I gladly invested in that for my veil. Mrs. G. found a string of pearls which she no longer required and, together, we made a headdress out of not-very-easily manipulated millinery and fuse wire, making a fairish copy of the pearl headdress I admired in my prized Vogue magazine.

Late in the term, I was leaving Bulwer Road to take my morning bus, when I found, addressed to me, a card in the letterbox. A surge of ecstasy swept though me as I read its message, written by Fred's professor: it asked me to congratulate Fred on Prof. Sykes's behalf, for his achievement — a first-class Honours degree. There was a memorable and totally unexpected drawing by this scholarly man of the fun figure at the time — Mr. Chad, who was depicted with a very wide grin, peering over the wall. Caution fled. I took my usual bus, but jumped off at its second stop to race up to the Czyrkos' house in St. Albans Road. My importunate knocks on the front door were promptly answered and I astonished that good lady by unceremoniously dashing upstairs to Fred's bedsit and finding him still asleep. I jumped on him, shouting, "You've got a first! You've got a first!" After a few hugs and kisses, I realised I was going to be very late for school. Rushing back to the bus stop, I knew I was in for a very sour reception, but nothing could remove the joy I felt that day. I took the mid-morning break, which I had long been denied, in order to tell my colleagues — above all, my dear friend Lorna — our great news. Fred and I agreed that we could not have received a better wedding present.

Confidentially, as our wedding day was approaching, Lorna pointed out to me that, if I wanted to avoid an immediate pregnancy once we were married, I would have to take evasive action. She instructed me to visit a certain doctor who would explain my needs. I was completely astounded by all of this new information, but did exactly what my friend decreed. How ironical this all proved to be when, ultimately, the baby that we so much longed for did not arrive in the usual way. After the end of term, it was time to return to Cleethorpes, not long before the long-awaited day of our wedding dawned. Laden with wedding presents, including a lovely trolley cloth from Professor and Mrs. Humphreys and a marriage-guidance book from Prof. Sykes, I returned to Cleethorpes, where Win joined me to help with the final, hectic preparations. My mother had selected the hotel for our reception and Fred and I had previously arranged with Herbert Lindley for the ceremony at Mill Road. This very handsome and inspiring minister had become a friend and we had been several times to his house for supper. Some time before the wedding was imminent, Fred had decided to be baptised in the Methodist church and, with just the three of us present, Herbert had performed this service. I was thrilled that Fred had reached this decision but, just as Herbert administered the water on Fred's brow, a huge flash of lightning illuminated the building, swiftly followed by a clap of thunder. I momentarily asked myself if God was displaying his wrath when Fred was rejecting his more ancient religion. Fortunately, the tension was removed almost immediately, as Herbert made a joking reference to the event.

Having attended an interview at London University for a post-graduate degree, which he had immediately rejected, Fred returned late in the evening before the wedding, bringing our best man, Abie, in the 1932 Hillman Minx that was our recent acquisition. I had been obliged to meet Mrs. Austin from her train and and bring her to the house, where she behaved in a supercilious manner towards my parents, who were treating her hospitably. Vengeance was sweet the next day, when I saw my mother looking most elegant and that woman in a most unattractive dress, with a gaping hole under her arm. The two men and Mrs. A. went to their rooms, booked at Darley's Hotel, Mrs. A. taking the opportunity to say that, "Her family are not really of our class," to which Fred responded by, "Don't be such a snob!" Abie, on the other hand, presented Fred with a bottle of Veuve Cliquot champagne as an additional wedding present.

The next morning, at an earlier than arranged time, a taxi-driver friend of the family, Len Burton, arrived to transport Mavis, Win, little Lynne, and Raymond, the 6-year-old page-boy, in his beribboned taxi, then returning to pick up my father and me. Because he was early, he had time to drive me ceremoniously along the Promenade, where I was embarrassed by the stares of the numerous trippers as we passed them by. I was met at the door of the church by Herbert and the bridesmaids, who all busied themselves with arranging my exceedingly long veil. The congregation sang heartily and Herbert was superb — he told us during his brief homily that we should never go to sleep without a reconciliation after any disagreement — advice to which we have, on the whole, adhered, though I have on a few occasions sulked and turned my back on him. Fred has never been so petty, but he is blessed with a sunny disposition which, like me, most people find enchanting.

Herbert refused our invitation to the reception, as it was at Darley's Hotel — not at all an appropriate venue for a dedicated Methodist to enter, in view of the sale of alcohol. We enjoyed greeting family and friends before the meal and took pride in our bridesmaids and little page-boy. On the steps of the church, while photographs were being taken, the smallest attendant, Lynne, who had fresh sweet peas clipped into her hair, had a bee settle on one, but Win and Mavis managed to flick it off before any harm was done. Fred was, in the meantime, mortified, when he noticed the collection of holes in the dress of that snobbish woman, who considered herself to be so superior to my family. The reception was held in the hotel where Fred, Abie and Mrs. Austin had spent the night. We were so happy as we received the good wishes from family and friends and were quite satisfied with the meal that my mother had decided upon, despite my elder sister's criticisms, as she disparagingly opined that the lettuce in the salad was totally unwashed. I was upset for my mother as I overheard her complaints, since we were both proud of the arrangements Mum had made, in spite of the fact that she had to provide two wedding receptions in four and a half months on a rather limited income. My parents had even subsidised Mavis's purchase of the lovely lace that she had chosen for her wedding dress, which displayed their generosity further, because they well knew how restricted Mavis was in her earnings. The fact that they were prepared to finance so much for our meal for almost 100 people displayed their committed approach to their children and I felt deep gratitude for all they did. I also remember with great affection the short, hesitant speech my father made when he declared that he was so proud of Fred's first class degree and he hoped that he had provided Fred with a first class wife. You would have to ask Fred whether Dad's hopes have been fulfilled.

Having bought us a china tea-service, a product so difficult to acquire at that time, as the manufacturers were pressurised into exporting the bulk of their products in order to revive our economy, Abie also added that bottle of Veuve Cliquot, which we opened and offered to anyone who had the good fortune to be in his bedroom at that point. I smile when I have champagne nowadays, for that taste at Darleys was our initiation and I remember our comments to each other once we were in our car and driving off on our honeymoon that it seemed to us that it tasted like vinegar. We have acquired more discerning taste-buds in later years, after quitting our life of total abstinence. Another reminder of the first hour of our honeymoon occurs as we picture ourselves climbing out of our car, once we were well and truly out of sight of our guests, in order to remove the string of tin cans that my mischievous Aunt Ruby had tied to our car. She also organised a group of the fit and able to rock the car vigorously before we were able to make our escape. We really did enjoy our wedding day, despite the fact that, as we left the immediate vicinity, we faced a veritable cloudburst as we drove up to York, where we were to spend two nights at the Chase Hotel.

CHAPTER
ELEVEN

Adventures on Honeymoon

We felt very grand that evening when, after a refreshing walk, we entered the hotel dining room and ordered our meal, which consisted of dishes regarded as great luxuries in those days. We selected melon, served with a dish of ground ginger and another of sugar, followed by Maryland chicken — quite an expensive meat in those distant days. The memory of the dessert has completely faded with the passage of time but we felt we were raised a few rungs on the social ladder by being able to choose such a feast.

The following day, we drove to Knaresborough to inspect Old Mother Shipton's cave and the petrifying well and, after lunch, we travelled back to York and learnt something of its central area. The name of the street named Whipma Whopma Gate intrigued us, though we have failed to discover its derivation in the intervening years. As we left York the following day, the rain was not so heavy as it had been on our travels from Cleethorpes, but the road was greasy from the drizzle which continued. Before we reached the Scottish

166

border, Fred negotiated a sudden swerve to the left but could not know that there was a concealed hazard to face — the camber sloped the wrong way, so that the car slithered to the wrong side of the road, its front mudguard mounting a lengthy, strong wire attached to numerous fencing posts. Luckily, our vehicle came to an immediate halt. Stomachs heaved as we looked through the wired-off edge of the road and saw, to our right, a very steep drop. For a moment we were stunned, as we felt that our married life looked destined for a premature end when, in no time at all, out of what had appeared to be a deserted wilderness, a hand appeared at a window and began to drum insistently on the glass. I opened the window and was greeted by the peremptory voice of a very military-looking gentleman, who ordered me to alight and then instructed Fred to follow me through the same exit. As we emerged, we saw three more men, who were obviously subservient to the first man. "Now, Men," the organising "officer" asserted. "We'll have this car off that wire in a jiffy." And so they did. After thanking our rescuers profusely, and enjoying their cordial handshakes and good wishes, we were once more heading for Edinburgh, the cars of that era being more substantially built than the products of today.

Our journey took us through Hawick, which gave me considerable pleasure, as I had long been initiated into the accepted pronunciation of that town's name — "Hoyk" — according to my Tyneside friends. We were booked in at the Roxburgh, recommended in the invaluable AA book given to members: the nightly

167

charge, believe it or not, was eight shillings and six pence for bed and breakfast. In those days, it struck me as an extremely gloomy establishment, with few of the modern amenities expected by the clients of present days. We did not have en suites in any of the hotel rooms we occupied, merely hand-basins in the bedrooms and communal bathrooms on the corridors; and every wall in the building sported ugly heavily patterned wallpaper and a crowd of framed portraits of dour-looking celebrities. However, to us, it seemed very superior in the service it offered to its guests. I was particularly impressed by the conscientiousness of our chamber-maid, who turned back the bed each night and tastefully spread out our nightclothes. She made much of the blue nylon negligee I had made, so, at least, my labours had impressed two persons.

We were able to see much of the city and spent a good deal of time exploring the castle, the gardens and Holyrood Palace. The floral clock was very impressive, we thought, and although we enjoyed visiting various elegant shops, the rule had to be "We can look but we cannot touch!" How pleased we were to discover that Sam Wannamaker was appearing in one of the theatres, so we booked seats for the evening performance. Unfortunately, neither of us can recall what the play was, but it has left a memory of a successful extravagance. We left Edinburgh after a two-night stay at the Roxburgh, which has now become a more prestigious hotel with several stars. We drove through increasingly impressive landscapes and finally reached Fort William, where we had reserved our room at the

168

Highland Hotel, to join a house party organised by Poly Holidays: this included full board and several interesting days out. We saw castles, Loch Lomond, Inverness, where, for the first time in our lives, we encountered fresh salmon, with which, on that first acquaintance, we were not particularly impressed, preferring the ever-fresh supplies of newly-landed white fish served at 70, Harrington Street, Cleethorpes and cooked skilfully by my mother or my elder sister. The evening meal at the Highland was the high point of the day because, daringly, on the first night, we had risked ordering venison — a plunge in the dark for us — and this became our choice for every subsequent evening, such a luxury after the dearth in the meat provisions of wartime and post-war Britain. One day, when there was no tour arranged, entertainment was organised by the selection of a guest brains-trust team, who successfully copied the Home Service programme: one of the audience asked what had been used to fill the extremely hard mattresses which, like us, most of the guests had found very uncomfortable. The final opinion of the team was that the beds had been stuffed with heather. That evening, there was a dance in the hotel, which we were very pleased to attend. Unfortunately, in the Highland Fling — a dance quite new to us — a fellow-guest inadvertently flung out his arm and I staggered after receiving a harsh blow under my chin. My gallant new husband was tempted to return the compliment but, stunned as I was, I succeeded in dissuading him. The following morning, the final full day of our stay, we decided to take a walk, as no activity

169

was arranged until after lunch. I had so enjoyed sporting all the new dresses I had made and was wearing the final one of my collection, which was quite out of keeping with the stout pair of shoes I had bought in Edinburgh to contend with the damp of a rather discouraging Scottish August. However, I scorned my coat as we set off on our adventure. When we were some considerable distance from the hotel, inevitably down came the rain and my Knight in Shining Armour swiftly removed his sports jacket and enveloped me in it, as we hurriedly retraced our steps. He has continued, for many a long year, to be thus attentive — to the envy of many onlookers. That final night, the two spinster ladies, with whom we shared our table throughout our stay, presented us with a little package containing a small glass dish with a thistle design on its base. We expressed our surprise and pleasure at this gift and still treasure it. All along, we were convinced that they were totally unaware of our being honeymooners, but they assured us that evening that they had guessed that we were newly-weds at the very first meal. Apparently, the courier had subtly conveyed our status every time there was a coach trip by inquiring, "Is little Mrs. Austin there at the back?" So much for our imagined success!

We set off the following morning to Dunston, where Avril's parents still lived: we were to spend our last night away in their house. Irritatingly, we were delayed on that journey by a series of punctures, although there was always a rescuer near at hand to help us with the car. We were somewhat horrified by one, who told Fred to lie on his back by the car to assist in the repair. As all our clothes were precious, our concern was natural. That evening, after unloading our suitcase at the Smith's house, we drove up to Whickham, where Avril and her husband George were renting accommodation. We were truly feasted in the Smith family tradition, but we concluded our stay the following morning.

We reached Cleethorpes without further mishap and, very soon, Fred was working for Nickersons, loading and unloading sacks of freshly-harvested corn, as a result of which he suffered the first affliction of our marriage. His skin was very badly invaded by insects, hitherto unknown to us, but called "harvest-bugs" by the locals, who explained that they were tiny creatures which burrow under the skin and cause a mass of ugly, red swellings. He really experienced considerable discomfort, but refused to stop working, so eager was he to earn a nest-egg before he re-entered the life of a student to study education in his final year at the University. I found a temporary job in the Cafe Dansant — the old Saturday night haunt of my 6th Form years. There, I was the most incompetent waitress the establishment could ever have known, providing clients with their laden plates of fish, chips and bread and butter, together with a tray holding teapot, sugar and milk and saucers with spoons, but often forgetting to provide cups. I rushed to one table when they beckoned and, before they could speak, I exclaimed, "Two coffees, please!" I think many of my customers must have reported my failings to the management, as my duties were transferred to the small area where I was known as the still-room girl, filling teapots and

171

cups of coffee. Of course, I no longer received any tips, but that really made no difference because, if clients had left me something, other waitresses managed to purloin it before I got there. I was not a success in that field, but, when no meal-service was required, I was directed to go outside and clean the huge windows. Once again, I betrayed total ineptitude as I toiled and the harassment from one of the instrumentalists in the small band, who repeatedly requested a date with me, added to my embarrassment until, finally, in pure irritation, I told him of the "dream man" I had married that summer. I was promptly liberated from his attentions. My last job at the Cafe was serving in the tiny shop located near the entrance. Primarily, I sold chocolate bars and cigarettes. Once more, I was plagued by a total stranger, well-spoken and smartly dressed, who ambled up to the counter and furtively announced that he was quite penniless, hoping that I would give him a packet of cigarettes free of charge. I went cold with horror, there being no support nearby, yet I mustered enough courage to brush aside his preposterous demand, whereupon I solved the problem: being a smoker myself, I fished for my handbag and produced from it a few of my own cigarettes, which he readily accepted and then beat a hasty retreat.

CHAPTER
TWELVE

Newly Weds in Leicester

Soon, the end of the vacation approached and we prepared for our return to Leicester, where my landlady had agreed to reserve for us her two attics, which she termed her upstairs flat. We packed our treasured wedding presents in the car on the day of departure and made a halting journey back to face the rigours of the new academic year — Fred in the Education Department and I with the dread of those insufferable weeks with that impossible group of miscreants. Sad news greeted us that day when we returned to Bulwer Road, where we learned that Mrs. Gisborne was seriously ill in Leicester Royal Infirmary. She suffered terribly from an unspecified cancer and never returned to her house. The result was that Fred and I were the only residents in the property and, with our landlady's permission, we set about redecorating the front attic. This room became our living room and the refurbishing simply consisted of painting over the unattractive wallpaper, which we then covered with one width of stripey paper, going up the one wall, over the sloping ceiling and down the other side. We believed our parsimonious endeavours to be very smart and, therefore, prepared for the inspection by guests. We assiduously cleaned our domain each Friday evening, proudly polishing our fine new tea service, which we had purchased with the money sent as a wedding present by Jack and Lolek, Fred's cousins in America. How we applied our elbow-grease to the chrome Morphy Richards toaster, given to us by Adrian Favre, and the prestigious five-pint electric kettle, bought by my elder sister and her husband! A square carpet, provided by Mrs. G. was heavily worn and soiled by previous occupants, so we ingeniously turned it upside down and appreciated its haircord effect, which reflected the taste of those days. Our washing-up facilities were rudimentary — at the top of our staircase, there were two upended orange boxes and an enamel bowl. Warm water came from either the bathroom or from the kettle which had boiled. One night, I was carefully washing our dishes whilst Fred dried them, when I saw something which, with my short-sighted eyes, I thought to be fluttering on the stairs up to our flat. I went down a couple of steps and leapt back up screaming when I realised it was a mouse. In a flash, I was in our living room, perched on the table, whilst Fred was pursuing the fleet-footed creature. Utterly terrified, from that moment onwards, I was ever vigilant on the stairs and in the kitchen where we had been granted permission to use the cooker and any of the crocks and equipment we required. We always tried to use our meagre property in preference, but there was one occasion when I needed a larger jug than any we possessed: I spotted one in Mrs. Gisborne's "kitchenette", a green tallish cupboard with glass doors. As I removed this jug, I saw a dead mouse curled up at the bottom. Fortunately, I had the presence of mind to thrust the jug straight back on the shelf before I slammed the cupboard door, emitting my usual scream.

Fred and I had saved our summer earnings and, almost immediately, having found the flock mattress provided on the bed to be uncomfortable and damp, we spreed what seemed to us a fortune on a good quality Dunlopillo mattress, which lasted us from 1952 to 1993, and, even then, we transported it to our newly-acquired holiday home in France to be used in a guest bedroom. We felt we were living in great luxury, with a more comfortable bed and the fine cotton sheets which I had bought and the thick, warm blankets, our wedding present from Edith and Nell, the Isle of Man aunts.

My tortures continued with the class that I had to call mine. They managed to do horrible things. A large girl of almost 14 would regularly urinate on the classroom floor if attention was drawn to her; one or two others defecated, one morning break, on the floor of the adjacent cloakroom and then rubbed the PE clothing of others in that disgusting mess. The caretaker had to shovel up the offending items and hurl them into the school furnace. Then, the biting vixen took to dipping her fingers into an inkwell and smearing ink all over her face and arms, so negating all my efforts to encourage her in better hygiene habits. A few started a new activity, which was most disturbing and which they pursued for several weeks. Three or four of them had taken to going into town in the lunch-hour and stealing in the British Home Stores. This was reported to the Head, who then decreed that I was to spend my entire lunch hour with them in the classroom, in addition to the morning breaks, which she had already inflicted on me. This new ruling further alienated that nasty group at my expense, so they took to waiting for my departure at the end of the afternoon and following close behind me as I walked to my bus-stop in town, shouting, "Green-faced pig!" repeatedly in unison. I found this to be totally demoralising and, as I stumbled towards a seat on the bus, I was blinded by tears. Generally, I found myself seated alongside an elderly bachelor, who encouraged me to share my problem with him and observed, "My dear, you must change your job or else you will soon be very ill." I toiled on, dreading each day, though there were some delightful interludes to compensate. When we were sewing, we sang some of the simple hymns I had been taught in Sunday School and, with Christmas in the offing, I wrapped little gifts for them. Their Christmas/leaving gifts to me were somewhat bizarre: for example, a British Rail teacup, still with tea leaves in the bottom and, from another source, a bunch of completely dead flowers, obviously thrown away by one of the stall-holders on Leicester market. One very corpulent pupil enjoyed having to spend the break in the classroom, for she sat in comfort, devouring a large penny bag of the previous day's doughnuts from a shop facing the school. One day, overwhelmed by a sudden surge of generosity, she ambled towards me with one of her treasures in her hand, saying, "'ere you are, Miss." Reluctantly, I accepted her well-meant gift somewhat gingerly but, after I delayed a few minutes, the donor shouted, "Eat it with your coffee, Miss!" I was compelled to oblige, though its pool of gory-looking jam made me cringe. Being closely observed by a number of pairs of eyes, I waded through the unpalatable gift politely, concluding with "Thank you, Mavis, that was delicious," whereupon she leapt from her seat and proffered another offensive weapon. I accepted in order to acknowledge a well-meant gift, but explained that I would have to eat it later, as I had no appetite left at that time. She beamed, bless her.

My indelible memories, however, of High Cross School occurred after our marriage in the summer vacation. The Biter showed herself to be knowledgeable about married life, describing things expressed with obscenities which were new to me. One evening, I asked Fred what one of them meant and he responded, "I don't want you ever to use that word again," but he did reveal its meaning. The torments of the shouting group continued, as did the disgusting talk of the Biter. The only compensation was my friendship with Lorna and it was lovely to know that, after a few weeks of married life, she and Eric had decided to abandon birth control and to hope for a pregnancy. As ever, she was more knowledgeable than me and explained how quickly she would know if she was pregnant. She described how rabbits were used in the testing process: they were injected with the woman's urine. Completely baffled, I asked if their reactions by screaming would indicate a positive result, whereas they would remain silent if the result was negative. That story was often used to tease me, especially by my husband.

My bachelor neighbour on the bus continued to encourage me to escape from this unbearable life, but relief was soon to come. Feeling rebellious, during one school lunch hour, I ignored the severe regulations imposed by the Headmistress and walked in to the nearby city centre to indulge myself with a short spell of window-gazing. As I ambled along, a lady approached me and said sympathetically, "Whatever is the matter, Mrs. Austin?" I was being addressed by the Primary School Inspector, who had previously persuaded me to teach a night-school group of her Nursery Assistants, a band of pleasant young ladies whom it was a joy to teach after the trials of my days in school. I poured out my woes to her, whereupon she suggested that I accompany her to her office, where she commented that my present full-time post was patently making me ill. She advised me to resign immediately, though I would have to continue until the end of term. She advocated my taking a job in one of her primary schools, where there was a vacancy arising in January for a reception class teacher. She assured me that I would find my new life blissful after all my recent ugly experiences. I took the plunge and agreed to transfer when I was legitimately free to do so. Those final weeks seemed interminable, but there were a few disconsolate little faces whom I was reluctant to quit despite the horrors which continued relentlessly.

After the Christmas holiday, we were pleased to learn that Eileen — now Mrs. Martindale — was employed in a Leicester school and Alan was fulfilling his obligations to his country by doing his national service as an aircraftsman; they would be able to visit us in our "elegant" surroundings. Eileen was very lonely when Alan was posted to the East Coast to assist in the rescue work required after the disastrous floods from the spring tides of 1953. She joined us for a meal one night and we were all three surprised to hear the front door bell ringing. Fred went down to investigate and found a very grimy and exhausted Alan on the doorstep. He summoned the energy to climb all those stairs and, very soon, was holding his young bride in his arms. Cuddles completed, he confessed to being desperately hungry and cold. We immediately recommended a luxurious hot bath and, since there were no left-overs from our "feast", we scraped together a quick meal, using bacon that Mum had sent from my father's triple ration, eggs and tinned tomatoes for the ravenous airman, now clean and shiny bright, as was his normal wont. He made short work of any food that was put in front of him and we were all delighted to know that he no longer had to face those terrible scenes on the coast.

As we settled round the diminutive and decrepit electric fire for a chat, Alan surprised me by asking if I could do him a favour. I responded willingly enough, until he said he wished to borrow some money, as they were hoping to buy a caravan in Stafford, there being no married quarters for the use of National Servicemen. I had often pulled his leg, before their

179

wedding and ours, when we chatted in College, our soulmates being far away in France or Matlock. He was very money-conscious and always told me how much he had saved each week. Though I saved never a sou most weeks, I would always claim superiority by quoting a higher sum if he asked me what I had put aside. When he made this request for aid, and I knew only too well that I had nothing left, I felt unwilling to admit my mischievous behaviour and responded with another lie: "I am sorry, Alan, but our money is rather tied up at the moment." I never confessed the truth. They still acquired their caravan somehow and we happily accepted invitations there on several occasions.

By that time, I had quit that first job and settled in at Harrison Road. I thus had the pleasure of my friend Joyce's company, because she was working at the Secondary School adjacent to our building. When people saw us together, they assumed we were sisters, for we were both small, dark girls and loved wearing our full-skirted, homemade pink dresses. Joyce and her husband John, a fellow student from College, had previously occupied the attic flat which we now lived in. They had moved up to better accommodation since they were both on teaching salaries by this time. We had lovely times with them: there was always much laughter when we were together. On one occasion, we went out into the countryside to enjoy a picnic and considered ourselves really stylish as we spread a tablecloth in a clearing in the Chamwood Forest and then set out our food in dishes. We must have been very naive, since we realised that we had to be very careful where these

180

things were placed and also where we sat on the ground, the clearing having previously been occupied by cows. As we were about to tuck in, we saw some of these ambling towards us. Hastily we packed away food and ourselves — bear in mind that our 1932 Hillman had no boot — and there we cowered until the curiosity of the animals was satisfied, whereupon they leisurely strolled away again. We finally managed to consume our picnic, tortured by a cold, blustery English summer wind. Our fare was simple but the company was first-rate, all the more lovingly remembered when, almost two years later, we faced the tragic news that John had died, as a consequence of a blow on the temple by a cricket ball. Nobly, he had joined in a staff/pupil cricket match — I say "nobly" because John had never had much taste for sport. When we received the announcement of his death, we had just become established in our own house and it was this which made us realise how precious each day was. Our plans were reversed and we decided to try immediately for a baby — but that is a long story for later.

So, it was in early January that I met my darling little five year-olds, who were so loving and obedient. The boy to whom I was most attached — though one should not have favourites — was called Tommy. He was so mature and intelligent that I furtively began to teach him to read, despite the current decree that that should not be done in reception class. His reading skills developed at a colossal pace, leaving me satisfied with my misdemeanour, as that child was obviously ready to master the books we used. Tommy was good fun to have around: I learned of his close relationship with his father, who took him on weekend adventures in the side-car of his motorcycle. The boy recounted his experiences of these jaunts with great animation. Another little lad, named Kenneth, who had won my heart with a tiny nosegay he had picked from someone's garden on the way to school, trailed after me all day, demanding, "Do like my fwowers, Misaustin?" One day, he had found in the toybox three bricks which would form a bridge. He constructed one and then found a small Dinky car which he intended to push under the bridge. Master Tommy was avidly vetting this operation and swiftly assured Kenneth that the car was too big and would not go under the bridge. "Shurrup!" countered Kenneth. Tommy's warnings were repeated several times and Kenneth's repulses continued, despite the fact that the bridge fell down with every attempt. Finally, Tommy turned to me, sighing deeply and saying mournfully, "I am afraid that Kenneth is like Winnie the Poo — a boy of very little brain!" I recall only one naughty child among the 30-odd children and he, Adrian, was never a nuisance in school. His problem was that he could not resist letting down car tyres as he walked to school. Several of us on the staff had lengthy discussions with this sweet-looking little boy but, as far as I remember, we failed to deter him from further interference with vehicles — he was subsequently interviewed by the police.

My two terms in this school coincided with the frantic preparations in all sectors of the population in this country for the celebrations designed to mark the

Queen's coronation. At school, the children learned patriotic songs, "Soldiers of the Queen" being the particular favourite with my class. Each child made and painted a Union Jack and we were all impressed with the achievements of the top class; these artists came round every classroom to display their "Crown Jewels". Once they left our room, one of my little boys, Bruce, declared that he was very worried in case those big children didn't get the crown to London in time for the ceremony. The day we were breaking up for the extra holiday, the entire school, staff and children, marched round and round the playground, waving our flags and singing our newly-learned songs. It was so lovely to be with them and a striking contrast to my experiences in the first four terms of my teaching career. When we re-opened after the holiday, my dear little Tommy appeared, heavily bandaged around the head. "Whatever has happened, Tommy?" I anxiously enquired. In his special voice, which came to the fore when he was feeling very brave, he explained, "Mrs. Austin, I nearly knocked that Midland Red bus stop off the map when I smashed into it on my bike." I hope that little boy grew into a healthy man and fulfilled all the promise he displayed at the age of five. Later, we took our pupils to a cinema in the centre of the city to see the film of the coronation and, throughout, my eyes streamed with tears, so much did the enthusiastic cheering and clapping of these little children move me. They could not contain their joy when they saw the red uniforms of the soldiers.

One morning, as I was closing the register, I noticed that one of the diamonds was missing from my engagement ring. Throwing caution to the winds, I rushed to the phone and was permitted by the Headmistress to telephone the jeweller to ask if my ring could be repaired. I was kindly informed that I could bring it in for the work to be done and I delivered it on my way home from school. The following morning, when I was dealing with the register again, the errant diamond fell out of the blotting paper. Once more, there was a dash to the phone and the jeweller assured me that they would wait for me to deliver the rescued jewel. The following break, one of my little boys, as he returned to the classroom, offered me a piece of glass, adding, "Ere y'are, Miss Austin. I've found you half a diamond in the playground". Evidently, the children had eavesdropped on my conversation with the sympathetic Head, who came into the classroom to congratulate me on my find, with the result that the children knew all about my misadventures.

Not long before we had to leave Bulwer Road, our dear, kind landlady had succumbed to the cancer and her grasping sister was already prowling round the house. She swiftly gave us notice to vacate our little flat, but we were fortunate to find a superior one nearby for a similar rent. We left a forwarding address and that dreadful woman quickly pursued us, accusing us of stealing the mattress and pillows from the bed that we had slept in. Burning with indignation, I wrote to Mrs. G's daughter, deploring her aunt's actions and assuring Margaret that the Dunlopillo mattress and pillows were

184

our property and the bed had been left intact with the uncomfortable flock mattress and the lumpy old pillows. I was so deeply offended by this charge of theft that I still resent deeply that woman's accusations.

Our new landlady was a delightful spinster, whose comment about Fred I have long relished: she observed that my husband was, "Such a nice, typically English boy". With his perfect English and his love of cricket, nevertheless, there was one recurring mispronunciation in his speech — a lisping "somesing" — which most people assumed to be a speech defect. It really amused me and I was inclined to mimic him whenever he used the word. Finally, quite out of character, and in the presence of my mother that following summer, he grabbed me, put me across his knee and spanked my bottom, which my mother found very entertaining. When, at last, I was liberated, I said, "Right, Fred Austin, that is the first time you have administered corporal punishment and, be warned, that is the last time! I will divorce you if ever you offer violence again." He never has. He diligently sought to eliminate his speech defect and very quickly achieved success, so I was no longer tempted to mock him.

The summer term passed swiftly and happily, as we enjoyed the many celebrations for the coronation. For the first time, we saw television at a friend's house and the fireworks in Victoria Park that evening were spectacular, though not at all like the displays of today. The most memorable was the grand finale — a set piece which brilliantly contained a large illumination exhibiting the head and shoulders of our young queen. I can still visualise it over 50 years later.

When the summer term finally ended, I forlornly said goodbye to that school, the staff and the lovely children. On the bus back into the city, the ball of wool from my knitting fell out of my bag, rolled along the bus floor and out along the road. Immediately, the helpful bus-conductor hauled the wool in and passed it to me to rewind quickly: that kind man retrieved it all, but I had to endure his stream of flippant comments as he did so. Miraculously, the yarn was still usable so, once again, I was saved from expense, making it a memorable day for the retrieval of diamond and wool.

One painful duty was marring our delight in our new home — the fact that we had to confess to our delightful landlady that we would be vacating the accommodation at the end of term, since we had decided to spend the following academic year in France: this would allow Fred to complete the "Licence" which he had started in Rennes. He had already been appointed for the following September as Assistant in a boys' school in Toulouse. We finally informed the landlady, who reacted as graciously as ever, bless her. So, we soon bade farewell to the city where we had known utter contentment for six wonderful years.

Our first ensuing journey took us, predictably, back to Cleethorpes to find the usual casual work in order to finance our drive to Toulouse in late September. We took a two-week holiday at the beginning of our stay, when we were joined by my sister Mavis and her husband, Steve. Our clothing and our primitive supplies were strapped in a roomy cabin trunk on the luggage rack on the back of the car. Our daily cooked breakfast was prepared on a single-ring petrol stove, but we particularly relished lunches in cheap little restaurants or not very high-grade hotels. In those days, still plagued with shortages, the sole main course on offer in all the establishments we patronised was roast beef and Yorkshire pudding, the quality of which varied immensely. Being children of the war years, we consumed whatever was available with gusto. One episode stands out in my memory — a consequence of our stop in Torquay. We walked down the steps to the beach, my companions all bearing towels and swimsuits. I, the unwilling participant, was appointed guardian of the belongings. Earlier, Mavis, a keen and talented swimmer, having been forbidden to change on the almost deserted beach by her husband, had not confided this restriction to me. As the menfolk ran down to the sea, my sister began to cry. She admitted his decree, whereupon I indignantly held a large towel round her, having persuaded her to stand close to the sea-wall and urged her to dress herself hastily in her swimsuit. She then raced happily to the water's edge. Eventually, they returned to me and not a word was uttered about her defiance. The following day, as the two of us sat on the back seat of the car, I again realised that she was in floods of tears. Making no secret of what was exchanged between us, I learned that, since they had come out of the sea on the previous day, Steve had not spoken one word to her. The family temper

187

surged in me and I launched into my brother-in-law in no uncertain terms. He was not accustomed to a female virago and Fred, ever the peace-maker, held his tongue. However, fairly quickly, their relationship returned to normal and I suspect that both were really pleased with the return of the happy atmosphere.

We enjoyed the rest of our holiday, now rapidly nearing its end, and stopped, on the last day, in a tiny cafe, where Steve, feeling less generous than I had been the night before when we stopped at a "posh" hotel for an expensive meal on which I spent my last few pounds, bought us each a cup of coffee and a slice of toast. Once back in Cleethorpes, we joined the family in Harrington Street, whilst the other two returned to their accommodation in Steve's parents' home. Fred was free to work for a lemonade firm, delivering its wares to cafes and shops with their lorry. He distinguished himself at the end of Cleethorpes Promenade one day, whilst executing a U-turn to return to his base. He turned too quickly and soon realised that several crates containing empty bottles had fallen onto the road, where a lot of the bottles had shattered on impact. As usual, he was able, with the help of Ken, my nephew, who had been employed as his assistant, to rectify everything and his insecure load went unspotted by anyone in authority. Another, more significant, event took place on one of these delivery tours. Ken had spotted an attractive girl working in one of the cafes and, each tine they called there with a delivery, the two young people managed to have a conversation. One day, the latter was delaying Fred more than he could accept, so he took the bull by the horns, deciding on their behalf that they would meet at about 6 that evening for their first date: they have now been married for almost 50 years. The matchmaker succeeded, as he has continued to do with most things, apart from loading lemonade crates safely and erecting shelves which have often proved very insecure.

CHAPTER
THIRTEEN

Peritonitis is No Joke

As days passed quickly, we began to pack away the few belongings we planned to leave at my mother's, on the landing under the second floor staircase, which led up to the two attic bedrooms. Our Dunlopillo mattress, two Ercol chairs and a Long John occasional table, the only furniture we had, so far, accumulated, were left there. The only bulky item to travel with us, apart from our trunk, was my precious portable electric sewing-machine, for which I had budgeted in my first year of teaching. So it was that Fred drove our elderly car down to Folkestone, where we spent one night in a hotel and boarded the ferry for Boulogne the following morning. Once on French soil, we were astounded by the number of small, thriving restaurants serving Sunday lunches to the many eager clients. Fred was delighted to make his selection of kidneys for his main course: whatever I chose was eaten with equal relish. We then took the Route Nationale down to Pontoise, where we spent the first night in France. There were no motorways, obviously, so our journey to Toulouse took four days, with the next stop at Chateauroux, where the waiter's response to our order of an omelette was a haughty sniff and a disgusted "C'est tout?", since we were economising after our expensive lunch in Boulogne. On the third day, we drove on to Bergerac. Our brief stay there remains imprinted on my memory, partly because I was permitted the extravagance of *langoustines à l'americaine*, together with *un quart de vin blanc*, but, less happily, the succeeding encounter with a mouse, which removed some of my euphoria. The next day, we finally reached our primitive student flat in Toulouse and set about making our bed, into which we gratefully sank, exhausted by that endless negotiation of French roads.

The following day, we strolled into Toulouse and enjoyed buying some provisions on the street-market, as well as picking up groceries in Monoprix. Fred had to go to school the next day, leaving me with little to do, but I quickly acquired a means of earning a few francs by giving English lessons to a German teenager, who was staying with a very well-to-do family, occupying a large, impressive apartment. I was also invited to teach a mature lady, who was anxious to improve her spoken English. I found both my pupils very congenial and always had little jewels to entertain Fred with after each lesson. I remember the German girl telling me in her halting English of the horror she had experienced at dinner the previous evening, when she was served with, for the first and, probably, the last time, "the foot of a little pork". The married lady confided that she had been "cambriolated" four times. However, she stirred me deeply by her descriptions of events that she had witnessed, on more than one occasion, during those terrible years of German occupation. Graphically, she related how she saw Jews, old and young alike, resident in her street, being dragged cruelly out of their homes during the hours of darkness, the little children weeping with shock and terror as they were marched away amid jeering shouts from their heartless captors and some of her fellow residents. Horrified as I was, I felt relief surge through me, recalling the way Fred had been spared a similar fate.

Homesick as I was, those days dragged wearily along. One late afternoon, as we strolled past a few shops, we stopped to gaze at the wares in one shop-window, where I noticed a packet of McVitie's Chocolate Digestive biscuits and, with a surge of nostalgia, I dissolved into floods of tears, even though I recognised that the French price was exorbitant. However, my kind husband found a packet of French biscuits which he hoped would quell the pangs of homesickness. His kindness was superb but the biscuits did not measure up to their English counterpart.

Our occupation of the flat was to be terminated four weeks after our arrival, but my stay was abbreviated by the onset of my peritonitis. After three weeks there, having taught the German girl during the morning, I walked, as usual, through the courtyard of the house where she was staying, stepping gingerly as ever because of the amount of kitchen waste in buckets — a permanent hazard — when my eyes lit upon a dead mouse littering the pathway in front of me, whereupon I made a speedy escape. I wondered if I would ever dare to return for another lesson with Sibylla, but I was not destined to see her again. As we ate our lunch in the flat, I admitted to Fred that I did not feel well enough to continue with the meal. He put my indisposition down to homesickness and urged me to consume the food, including the Brussels sprouts, our vegetable of the day. Having emptied my plate, I felt even worse, so Fred decided I had indigestion and pressured me into drinking his mix of bicarbonate of soda and water. He then rushed off to his school, whilst I feebly struggled with the washing up. When I had finished that chore, I collapsed in agony onto our bed — but not for long. The only available lavatory was outside our flat, on the corridor, and I raced towards it, swaying drunkenly. Once inside, I was violently sick and suffering unbelievable pain. I staggered back to bed, still assailed by gripping spasms. Soon, I repeated the procedure back at the toilet and then back to bed. The pains were rapidly growing more and more severe and, every time I struggled with them, I knew that death was a strong possibility, so I urged myself to fight back each time that I was tempted to succumb. That interminable afternoon dragged on and Fred did not reappear until 6 o'clock. He took one look at me and raced downstairs to seek the advice of the concierge about finding a doctor. Having failed with the first two recommended medics, he succeeded in persuading the third, a Polish doctor, to come immediately: rapidly, the doctor examined me, repeatedly saying, as I groaned and writhed, *Ne pleurez pas, ma petite!* He was sure that I needed a surgeon at once and explained to Fred that he could not recommend the post-war conditions in the local hospital, suggesting instead a clinique, to which Fred readily agreed. They supported me downstairs and into our car, in which I was quickly transported to the Clinique, the doctor having undertaken to telephone the office and warn them of our imminent arrival. Once there, I was examined and prepared for surgery. The operation took place at ten o'clock that night and, back to my single room, still anaesthetised, I was plagued by visions of the dead mouse seen that morning. It seemed to be dive-bombing me. Fred remembers that, as I was returning to consciousness, I asked him where the baby was. No baby was available, but, on my bedside table, was an enamel dish which had my lengthy, perforated appendix on it. The staff at the Clinique were astounded when I refused to accept it, pickled in a test-tube, to preserve for posterity. Because of its length and evidence of disease, they considered it to be quite a trophy. I ventured to assert that I would donate this remarkable English treasure to France.

The ensuing three days involved further torture. I was denied all fluids by mouth, with the exception of one teaspoonful of water every four hours, and I was even barred from brushing my teeth, lest I should be tempted to swallow any additional water. My dressing was replaced daily and it was in raising my head from the pillow one day, that I saw a large safety-pin inserted into my interior, holding a tube. Little wonder that any movement on my part produced a searing pain. After three parching days, I was asked if I would like a coffee the following morning. Delighted to have my favourite beverage offered, I waited, filled with great anticipation. Beaming, the nurse strode into the room with a large, steaming bowl, proudly announcing "I have brought you tea, because you are English." Hopes dashed, I rapidly rejected this "cup that cheers". After she had gone, we discovered that she had made tea on a half-and-half basis, filling the top half with hot milk. Fred soon appeared and, coming to my aid, tipped the offending concoction down the basin and, furtively, replaced it with water from a jug. I felt that I was returning to the real world. Not long after this, my surgeon came to see me and proudly told me that he had just removed an enormous tumour from a woman's uterus. *Attendez! Je vais la chercher pour vous la montrer*, he declared. What a grotesque object it proved to be! When would I escape these ordeals? That evening, my first meal was brought in: my starter was a leaf artichoke, which totally mystified me. Fred scornfully observed, "I don't particularly like them, but you pull off the leaves and dip them in the vinaigrette." Initially, I was not very impressed, but worse was to follow. A large, luscious steak was served and I salivated at the prospect of tasting a serving of meat which was larger than any I had ever seen. Cutting off a chunk, I squealed with horror as a flood of bright red blood oozed onto my plate. I simply could not face eating it, but Fred consumed it with gusto and had the incredible nerve to accept another steak which the nurse kindly brought in for him. How I yearned to return to our own catering, stick-in-the-mud that I was, as long as there were no Brussels sprouts. Times and tastes have developed and I would consume that steak with pleasure today.

CHAPTER
FOURTEEN

Our House in Lardenne

Eventually, the long-desired day dawned and I was permitted to leave, but not to return to the scene of my dangerous ordeal. Fred drove me to the village holiday home belonging to the friend of M. Favre, the French lecturer in Leicester. We were to occupy the house free of charge, the owner requiring as our rent my services once a week at his College de Commerce in Toulouse. The house, a less demanding residence in many ways, no huge staircase to mount and possessing two good-size bedrooms, meant that we could sleep in one and concoct a sort of lounge in the other. The difficulties were that there was little heating in the winter — a tiny stove, fired by boules (compressed coal-dust) in the large kitchen and an open fireplace in the lounge/bedroom upstairs. The stove kept me warmer on winter evenings when I rested my feet on top and, sometimes, we endured the smoke which poured out of the badly designed chimney upstairs, in order to create the illusion of warmth upstairs. Off that room, there was a cubby-hole with a primitive basin which had a plughole in the bottom and no water supply whatever. Jugs of water had to be carried upstairs and the waste water then carried away. We took to visiting the public baths once a week to preserve some level of cleanliness. The other difficulty with our so-called lounge was that its walls were covered with a hideous, heavily patterned wallpaper, even the doors being similarly disguised. Sometimes, late at night, we had a real struggle to locate the door.

The kitchen was by no means well equipped. A large floor-to-ceiling cupboard was adequate: we were able to store groceries and our pots and pans there. A roomy ice-box graced one corner and the ice-man called with long ice-blocks twice weekly. As the door of this contraption refused to remain closed, we very quickly dispensed with the ice-man's services. We placed perishables in the box, but had to consume them quickly. In another corner was a large, shallow sink, which sported the only tap supplying running water in the entire house. Washday was not easy but, having bought a zinc bath, I was able to fill it with water and bring it to the boil on the small cooker with its two gas-rings. Thus, my whites remained bright and clean and there was ample space for hanging out on the lines outside. Miraculously, I avoided scalds as the water was thrown away. How I coped with the drying when the snow came, I simply cannot remember. Fred says that he fixed a line in the kitchen, which eludes my memory, but I do know that the laundry was dutifully done, ironed with a series of flat-irons which we had to heat on the gas-rings, though it meant that I became acquainted with iron-mould, unfortunately. Underneath the little rings there was a minute oven, about which I learned an alarming fact once we were safely back in England: Fred confessed that he had opened the oven door once he had helped me upstairs on the day of our arrival and a mouse dashed out. His secret was closely guarded, because he knew that I would insist on moving if I had known the truth. However, he was kind enough to ask me not to go down in the cellar for the boules because, he admitted, he had seen mice down there.

We were soon invaded by two cats belonging to our next-door neighbour, which must have provided some protection from further vermin. One of the cats, obviously pregnant, kindly produced her offspring in the small cupboard in our lounge, where I stored our sparse supply of household linens. Once her babies arrived, the mother cat deftly transported her kittens to their home next door; the other cat continued to haunt our premises and quite enjoyed himself, for example on the day when he grabbed the corned beef from our insecure ice-box and consumed it with relish. So much for the Cornish pasties I had intended to make! My method for cooking pasties, both savoury and fruit-filled, was my own invention: we had a deep pan we used for cooking chips, but I dared to experiment by putting the pasties in the deep boiling oil very soon after moving to the house. The results were delicious though, I imagine, our more time-worn stomachs might rebel against their richness if we were to reproduce them today.

It was at about this time, that we discovered the British Council library and there we learned that there was also an American Library. The latter we found an absolute treasure and we devoured American novels and short stories in great quantities. Fred was studying American literature in preparation for a Certificate in his Licence and I was able to occupy myself by enjoying reading on those two interminable evenings I spent alone while Fred was earning extra francs in the Universite du Soir in Toulouse. One or other of his students would provide him with some error-ridden English which he used to entertain me with when eventually he returned home. The outstanding example I recall was the following sentence in one piece of written work: "If I do not make out, this boy will overgo myself!" We had an alternative source of feeble entertainment when we rented a decrepit old radio, which crackled away through the 9 o'clock news from the BBC and "Round the Horn", which came before the news. We could never get reception for anything else! Once we had heard, through the good offices of the French Professor we had met at the American Library, that M. Renard, the Minister, had found me a post in Auch, we felt that, in January, we would be more prosperous. In due course, we were able to buy six beautiful table knives, accompanying dessert knives, and a chrome crumb-sweeper, which adorns our kitchen to this day, albeit with some small damage inflicted by Master Jack Austin. A further indulgence was a meal in a Vietnamese restaurant which proved to be a dismal choice: we particularly scorned our selection from their dessert menu which offered *gateau de riz* — no more than a slab of cold, dry rice pudding. The menu did not live up to normal French standards.

January came soon enough and I was transported to Lardenne station at an unearthly hour, to join my little Micheline rail-car. I found my school easily and met the Surveillante-Generale, one Madame Sadoul, who explained the timetable she had arranged for me. I was introduced to my lovely colleagues, Mme. Causse and another teacher of English, the wife of a doctor, whose name escapes me. They were my great comfort after various onslaughts I had to face from Mme. Sadoul. I took my lunch twice a week with Mme. Causse in a small restaurant where several teachers from other schools congregated. I remember with pleasure the pork chops and the Toulouse sausages — a vast improvement on the Vietnamese restaurant, as well as on the one school meal that I took on my first day there. On that occasion, I was horrified when I, an almost total abstaining Methodist, observed schoolgirls pouring wine into their glasses and diluting it with water. I was delighted to avoid further commitments to that refectory, where the loud chatter was not particularly welcome after my early rising, my train journey and a full morning with large classes. The great compensation, however, was on the train journey as, on spring and summer mornings, I witnessed the most vivid sunrises imaginable. I also cherish a memorable comment from a French soldier, as he walked through the train. He halted in true military style, clicked his heels and warmed my heart with the words,

201

Mademoiselle, je n'ai jamais vu de beauté comme la votre, My memory retains another remark uttered by a Spaniard who dined at our restaurant. He nodded confidingly to Mme. Causse and said *Bonita*, as he pointed to me. My colleague explained that I was the English Assistant and, apparently, he denied that it could be so, as I was a little dark-haired woman, whereas English females had to be very tall and have bright red hair. My rejoinder to Mme. Causse was, "Oh, no! He is thinking of Scottish females."

In due course, we were very pleased to have a visit from Adrian Favre, our friend from Leicester. He had arranged my job with M. Billieres, enabling us to occupy the rent-free house. When Fred was in school one day, Charlie, as we still called him furtively, confided in me that his divorce from Paulette was complete, their daughter Francoise now residing with her mother in Grenoble, and admitted his great joy in having met an English lady whom he hoped soon to marry. The story of their meeting was as comical as many other Adrian Favre adventures: having decided to take up riding lessons, he became acquainted with the school's owner/instructor called Joan and, very quickly, had fallen in love with her. Contact suddenly flourished when Adrian fell from his mount during a lesson and sustained a broken arm. Joan drove him to the hospital where he received prompt treatment, and this was a heaven-sent opportunity to declare their love for each other. He was still relying on a sling when he came to us in Lardenne.

Adrian had readily accepted an invitation for the three of us to visit an old friend. He was able to take advantage of Fred's willingness to drive him to Agen — about 60 kilometres away — where the friend had a veterinary practice. On our arrival, we were ecstatically greeted by an enormous chien des Pyrenees, of whom his master really approved for, as we were told, that huge creature cost nothing to feed: he made a daily round of several butchers' shops in the town, where he was warmly welcomed and lavishly fed. Was this a reflection on the supposed parsimony of French country folk?

A delectable meal was finally served and, as we ate with gusto, our enjoyment was suddenly interrupted when the vet's wife jumped up, yelling frantically. One of their numerous hens had offered her daily performance, having fluttered into the room through the open window, by laying an egg in the lady's handbag. Fred and I found this hilarious, especially as it was accompanied by a stream of invective from the irate housewife. If it was a daily performance, why was the handbag left open, we wondered.

Before Adrian was due to leave, one morning, while Fred was at school, he asked me if I could advise him about birth control, as neither he nor Joan wanted children. Once again, this dear man had flabbergasted me so, after a brief hesitation, I took the bull by the horns and told him all I knew about the subject — meagre as my knowledge was. With most other people, I would have been terribly embarrassed but, because it was Adrian, I did not even blush.

CHAPTER
FIFTEEN

Easter in Spain

Another visitor to Lardenne was my College friend, Win. It was a great pleasure to have her with us and we, all three, planned a trip to Spain. Soon, liberated from school for the Easter holidays, we set off on our journey through the Pyrenees to the Spanish frontier. The old car did us proud as we toiled up steep mountain roads, bordered by walls of snow on either side, just as the snow-plough had left them. Once at the frontier, we found a spot to park the car, having decided to walk over the border and take a train to Barcelona to enjoy a far cheaper journey than we could have done by car. We carried our suit-cases through the customs-post and past the Spanish frontier guards into Spain. We promptly found an incredibly cheap hotel, with the necessary rooms available, and were served with a memorable meal. Win suggested some wine and selected one of their bargain bottles. We enjoyed our food but Fred, a non-drinker in those days, because of his terrible experience with Philip Austin's alcohol, eventually decided to try half a glass of wine. I, daringly, took a full glass and Win coped with the remainder of the bottle. It was a blessing that Fred was not driving the following day, as he spent most of the train journey being ill in the toilet; he was very pleased to alight from the train to walk briskly down the Ramblas and reach the Pension that had been recommended by our Spanish friend in Toulouse for its reasonable tariff. The owner conducted us to our rooms, pointing out the toilet on the way — an imminent necessity for Fred once more. The said toilet was a monstrosity: bulbous, cream in colour, with large cabbage-type roses decorating the outside. Thinking myself free to express whatever opinion I formed, I said, "Oh, my Gawd! (Win's habitual exclamation) Queen Elizabeth must have stayed here!" The Spaniard was standing close to me and he broke in with, "Do you speak English?" Totally mortified, I inwardly asked myself when I would learn to keep my big mouth shut? Normally, Fred would respond with, "Never!" Later, when we examined the toilet more closely, we spotted the text "Made in Manchester". How could they?

Fred remained quite poorly for the rest of that day and retired to bed. Our room had a balcony overlooking the Ramblas and Win joined me there, a prime viewing place to watch the Easter procession of penitence. Some walked, dragging colossal chains, whilst others were self-flagellating and one man dragged an enormous cross. We were duly impressed with all we witnessed, but gradually became distracted by two young men on the adjacent balcony, who were making inviting noises and gestures. In our discussion of that performance, either Win or I said, "Romeo". Their faces registered instant approval, but the ever-vigilant Fred leapt from the bed, firmly and protectively guiding the two of us back into the bedroom and tightly closing the windows.

Soon, we were able to contact Juan, the nephew of Dr. Vinas, who had instructed the young man to help us. Juan made various suggestions of interesting things to see — La Sagrada Familia, El Pueblo, the Santa Maria and other attractions, for, during the day, he was busy at the hospital. He regarded the long Spanish evenings as his responsibility and, along with a fellow medical student, walked and walked us, demonstrating the activities that Spaniards enjoyed. We felt perfectly secure at all times, both in Barcelona, on our day-trip to Tarragona, as well as on a visit to Gerona (Juan's home), where we were intrigued to see farmers being charged a toll as they entered a gateway to the city, with their wagons laden with produce for the markets. The outings illustrated the traditional feudal life in places such as these in the days of Franco, whose portrait was dutifully displayed everywhere. We were quite shocked to see policemen with large hand-guns holstered over their hips. When we again saw La Sagrada Familla in the 21st Century, we were amazed to discover, 50 years on, how little progress had been made in the meantime. We realised, however, that the greatest difference was in the hazards of walking the streets, as soon as Fred was robbed within our first hour in Barcelona in 2004. The regime was harsh in 1954, but the people were more honest.

We had decided to take the ferry to Majorca in order to have a change of scenery for a few days and when we told Juan and his friend, they agreed that it was a good plan. The owner of the pension suggested that we placed our luggage in the reception area, in readiness for an afternoon departure, so that our rooms could be prepared for a further letting until our return and we would be free to spend the morning unencumbered. After lunch, we returned to the hotel to collect our belongings. They were no longer there. In great consternation, we informed the owner, who explained that two men had said that they had been asked to collect them on our behalf. Whatever could we do? Our host assured us that they had not long set off and were seen to be heading in the direction of the docks. Our heels took wing as we raced after the "thieves". Almost at the berth, we spotted first our cases and then recognised our porters — Juan and his friend, as always, being attentive to our needs. They had told the man at the hotel who they were, but he was obviously not listening. Overwhelmed with relief, we told them how much we appreciated their help and, before we separated, we arranged a reunion on our return from the island break.

Once on board, whilst Fred appropriated some seats and a table in the bar, since we were travelling steerage, Win and I explored the deck. We were promptly joined by two amorous young men, who proceeded to serenade us with their guitars. Unused to such flattering treatment, we were charmed into loitering. There suddenly descended upon us an irate Fred who, grasping us both firmly by the scruff of the neck, marched us down to the seats he'd reserved. The only means of resting during that interminable night was by placing our heads on the table, but relaxation for me was not on the cards, as a consequence of my greed. We had bought a large quantity of strawberries, which we devoured on arrival at the table. My reward was a bout of vomiting after this over-indulgence. I was not restored by sleep and I, for one, was delighted to step off that ship in the morning. As soon as we stood on the quayside, we were surrounded by a host of men who clamoured for our custom conducting a Dutch auction with their accommodation. Eventually, Fred called me over to explain that he had the offer of two rooms with breakfast and dinner for an incredibly low price. Unfortunately, I was in the process of accepting an identical offer from a very young man. When he was told that I had to join my husband, he countered with, "Let him go to their hotel and you come to mine!" Fred saw my quandary and ushered me back to the man who had been accepted and who had offered transport to his establishment, included in the price. It was a far cry from today's inflated prices and over-booking. We found ourselves in a clean little pension, with two small rooms already prepared and enjoyed breakfast on arrival, when we were served with the lightest brioche-type rolls we had ever tasted and excellent coffee. Once we had washed and arranged our luggage, we set off to explore Palma but, almost immediately, noticed a tiny bakery, with a display of the self-same rolls in the window. We were not deterred from eating a second one each as we strolled along the road. At one stage, we toiled up a very steep, hilly road where we saw a man savagely beating a heavily laden donkey which could not retain its foothold on the slippery cobbles. We all three berated the man who, naturally, had no English and simply regarded us in astonishment.

Eventually, we found our way into a small glass-blowing workshop, where I longed for a small bull we had watched a craftsman making. Fred blankly refused to buy it and, to this day, he cannot believe that he quibbled about so tiny an expenditure. Not long afterwards, he calmly bought a one litre bottle of a well-known gin for the equivalent of five shillings (25p). Neither of us had ever tasted gin and that bottle remained unopened for many a long year.

We found out during our walk that we could take a bus from Palma through the area where Georges Sand had lived with Chopin and then transfer to a little train to see the caves at Manacor, where our transport was replaced by a tiny boat. As we travelled on these minuscule vehicles, we were fascinated by the habit of the local people, who crossed themselves each time the transport set in motion. We were very impressed with the caves and, afterwards, the seaside isolation of Porto Cristo.

The attentiveness and hospitality of our hosts at the little pension enriched the swiftly passing days. We discovered that our rooms were tidied several times daily and that the wife produced generous packed lunches and very tasty dinners each evening, so that we were really given value for money. Their teenage son was an extremely affable and loquacious waiter, who loved to practise his English on us. He entertained us with the story of his English girl penfriend, who had sent him a photograph, as he had requested. His response was to write a passionate, Mediterranean style declaration of undying love, but her reply did not enchant him. She contributed a brief note, in which she portentously replied, "Last week my cat died". It was pretty obvious that, as a result, he believed that all English females must be very cold, since he added that he had no longer continued the correspondence.

Our happy stay had to end and we returned by the day ferry to Barcelona. We were greeted by our attentive protectors on the quayside and enjoyed an evening with them, as we took another lengthy stroll round the city, ending on a hill-top from which we could enjoy seeing all the lights. As we were saying "Good night", Juan tentatively asked us if we would be prepared to deliver a parcel from him to M. Vinas, back in Toulouse. We readily agreed, but were somewhat taken aback when, the following day, he accompanied us to our train and presented us with two beautifully wrapped, but huge, boxes, firmly tied with string. We pointed out that we would be questioned at the frontier about the contents of the packages and Juan calmly asserted that they contained two busts of Beethoven. The size and lightness of the packages aroused our suspicions and we fervently hoped that the contents would not turn out to be drugs. Once back at Puigcerda, we walked across the frontier and, as we had predicted, we were quickly pounced upon by two French customs officers who asked, in a sinister tone,

Qu'est-ce que c'est que ça? Hesitantly, Fred replied, *Deux bustes de Beethoven,* at which they were, for a moment or two, silent and uncomprehending, before one of them beamed with enlightenment *Ah, oui! Beethoven, le compositeur,* as he smartly chalked crosses on both boxes. Then his colleague majestically waved us through.

CHAPTER
SIXTEEN

Farewell France!

We were soon reunited with the Hillman to make our way back to Lardenne. Summer came quickly and tropically, so much so, that the flea population multiplied freely. I always returned from Auch having picked up a visitor or two on the train where, I suspect, they had been generously donated by none too clean peasant travellers. The creatures remained unnoticed until I got into bed each night after my journey. As I relaxed, I gradually became aware of their presence, running around my ankles and jumping on my back. By the time Fred had switched on the light and flung back the covers, they could be seen clearly on the bottom sheet, as our bed-linen was plain white. Fred became very adept at catching the pests and killing them between his two thumb-nails. We would often settle down to sleep when, once again I would have to create another disturbance, there being one or more little monsters plaguing me still.

As the term rolled by Fred became eager to acquire a teaching post back home. When he left for interviews in England, I had been foolish enough to tell the young Englishman who taught at the boys' school in Auch, about Fred's absence. He had repeatedly treated me to coffees in Auch and had come to Lardenne for a weekend sometime earlier. As I was on my own, Mme. Causse invited me to spend a day towards the weekend with her in her Toulouse flat and I gratefully accepted her offer. That evening, when I returned to our house, I found a note from the English lad, saying that he had come to keep me company, but had returned to Auch, having found the house unoccupied. I was angry as I digested the implications of his act and, the next time that I was in Auch and saw him, as usual, loitering at the school gates at leaving time, I made it quite clear that I never wished to see him again. On the day of Fred's return, I was at the railway station in very good time, anxious to know his news and to tell him all that had occurred during his absence. It was then that I discovered that the interview at Kingston had been unproductive and that Fred had accepted a post at Bordesley Green in Birmingham, with which information I was not particularly enchanted. At that stage, I could not envisage the happiness that we would eventually enjoy in that city. I, for my part, told Fred about my unfortunate experience with John, which caused him to be just as indignant as I had been.

With Fred's examinations safely out of the way, it was soon time to say our farewells to all the friends we had made in our schools and to pack the trunk and reinstall the sewing-machine in the car, having finally used it to make the only new garment I acquired in that sparse year — a black waffle cotton skirt. Fred, as usual, had worked out our return itinerary, passing through a series of exotic-sounding places, the first of which was Carcassonne. Having parked the car to allow us to view the city walls, I paid for the tickets and walked away, when I was called back by another Englishman, shouting *Ma-de-moiselle*! Billy! Billy", making me realise that I had forgotten to pick up the tickets. Our journey then took us to Nimes, with its spectacular amphitheatre and, then, to Avignon and its famous bridge: it was only then that I realised what risks they had taken when dancing on it. Onward, up the Rhone valley to Montelimar, where I was much aggrieved to find that the nougat was much too expensive for our meagre resources. In the torrid summer heat, I had the discomfort of an increasing gap in my floorboards, a source of great embarrassment as I stepped out of the car, displaying filthy feet and lower legs, only to be accosted by a very friendly Birmingham couple, delighted to know that we were now going to Birmingham in September and immediately insisting that we should visit them in Solihull, once we were installed. We did, in fact, take them up on their invitation and enjoyed their company. As we progressed through the Saar into Germany, where we had been invited to stay with Fred's friend Herve and his wife, Misette, we were astounded by the huge dungheaps adorning the fronts of many a farmhouse. Fred was sure that these dungheaps illustrated the wealth of the farmers. In spite of Herve's rather intimidating driving us at high speed through the Moselle valley and its hairpin bends, we enjoyed the lushness of the vine-terraced slopes, the like of which we had never before seen.

Parting from our friends, Herve and Misette, we set off towards Belgium, planning to spend the first night in Namur, where we found a small restaurant with rooms. It was still, at that time, a requirement to produce passports when registering in a hotel and the waiter/receptionist insisted that he inspect them, as he was making the entry. He laboriously copied the information that Fred was born in Ostrava with the name of Alfred Stiller and, despite Fred pointing out that Austin was his present name, he doggedly stuck to Stiller, while recording me as Mrs. Austin — we have always referred to it as our dirty night in Namur. The following morning, I was dismayed in this coalfield area by the ugliness of all the mines and steelworks, constantly seeking assurances from Fred that Birmingham was not going to be like this. As we travelled on through all these cobbled streets in the northern towns, very gradually, a spoke or two in our wheels began to show metal fatigue, but it was in Brussels that I was petrified when Fred discovered that he had no functioning brakes and we gently rolled into the back of a bus. As usual, my response was to panic, and this emotion increased as I saw a gendarme approaching us. I felt sure that we were due to spend a night in the cells, but his purpose was to direct us to a little garage where a repair could be effected. Flustered, Fred set off in the direction which the gendarme had indicated, only to find himself in a one-way street, with another gendarme gesticulating wildly. When Fred explained that he had no brakes, the policeman shrugged his shoulders, sighed and muttered *Ah! Ces Anglais!* and waved us on. He quickly located the garage, where they agreed to do the repair, pointing us to the adjacent Hotel du Nord, where we took our bags and settled in. The room offered a great deal more comfort than our last stop in Namur and we were astounded to discover an early television set on which we watched a Ray Milland film, after we had found something to eat in a neighbouring cafe.

By the next day, the car was repaired and we continued our journey via Ghent, where we could only afford bags of chips from the stall, which occupied a prominent position in the main square and then, on to Ostend. After the crossing, the drive up to Cleethorpes seemed endless and the spokes continued to rupture. We began to feel more relaxed as we drove into Lincolnshire, but then faced the setback of a puncture, which caused a further delay. Fred finally parked the car outside 70, Harrington Street, when he upset me considerably by snatching out his jacket from the back seat of the car, inadvertently tugging with it our main French extravagance, a bottle of Cointreau, which shattered on the pavement. My impossible family found this a highly entertaining event and my father said he had never before seen so many drunken dogs in Cleethorpes.

It was a delight to be back in our familiar surroundings, but I was surprised when I found it difficult to ask, when buying food for my mother, for pounds in weight rather than kilos. We slipped into well-practised routines. I found a job in an apron shop during the day and worked on various alterations to garments from the stock, which increased my earnings. I received a letter from a Black Country headmaster, who offered me an interview for a post in his school: I felt encouraged at the prospect and took a train to New Street in Birmingham and thence to Dudley Port on a small local train. I found my way to the Education Offices in St. James's Road and the Divisional Education Officer, Mr. Turley, drove me to Brierley Hill Grammar School, where I was duly interviewed and rejected for the post. Mr. Turley offered me a lift back into Dudley and he took me into his office, insisting on paying me my expenses at once. He then drove me to Castle Hill, where, he assured me, I would pick up a taxi easily which would take me to Dudley Port. No taxi appeared for what seemed an eternity, but, growing more and more convinced that I would miss my train, I was at long last driven to the station whence I travelled to New Street. Once there, I ran breathlessly to the platform for the Grimsby train and, as I reached it, it began very slowly to pull away. Luck was on my side: a man on the train saw my look of horror, opened the door and yelled, "Jump!" as I ran beside his carriage — and jump I did. The rescuer deftly caught me and I was soon safely installed on a seat. I had feared so much that I would have to face a night marooned in that unknown city, but all proved well thanks to that helpful gentleman and my own foolhardy nature. It was wonderful to find my ever-grinning Fred on Grimsby Town station, but, at that point, I gave way to tears —

partly of relief, but also of frustration, as the day had proved so fruitless career-wise. Later, my failure proved to be an advantage, because the school in question could only have been reached with considerable expense and consumption of time, since we were to be living in Selly Oak and had no idea where we would find a house that was within our means. I would have to settle on waiting until we were actually in Birmingham to find a post, by which time Fred would be installed and earning a salary. Little did I dream that such a large proportion of my later life would be spent in Dudley.

CHAPTER
SEVENTEEN

Life and Death in Birmingham

As my work at the apron shop drew to a close, another, slightly older, assistant asked me about our plans for accommodation in Birmingham. I explained our intention to buy a little house, upon which she, a council house tenant, demanded, "But have you got a deposit?" I enjoyed telling her that we had and, icily, she responded, "You are very lucky then." I did not explain about the meagre life we had led in order to accumulate something approaching £200, but, indignantly, replied that we were not lucky — just economical and determined to have a place of our own. Once we were both working in Birmingham, we were able to increase our savings for the various expenses we were likely to incur. I promptly reserved a New World gas range and was paying quarterly instalments so that it would be our property when we moved into our new house. We also budgeted for a small quantity of furniture and carpets, so that our environment would not be too spartan when that longed-for day dawned. In the meantime, we lived pleasantly enough in living room and bedroom rented from one of Fred's colleagues in Bordesley Green. By this time, I had obtained a post at City Road Secondary Modern school, where I adored my class of 11-year olds, found their querulous Birmingham accent very entertaining and enjoyed life very much more than I had at Elbow Lane in Leicester.

My Dad had died suddenly on the second day at work in a new job that he had taken on as a maintenance engineer on trawlers. He had, for years, flitted from post to post because of his chronic tendency to feel disgruntled at the workplace. Although his 60th birthday was only days away, he was still encountering no difficulty in gaining new employment almost as soon as he had quit the last. His mobility was a characteristic that my mother abhorred, fearing always she might have to revisit the insecurity of her early married life. Ironically, as he settled at the table for his evening meal after his first day at the new place of work, he reminded my mother of the impudence of his conduct at the interview with his new employer. He had brashly asked what was wrong with the firm and, in turn, he was asked why he had that impression. His response had been, "You can't be very supportive of your workforce, as you are constantly advertising for skilled men". Their sardonic response equalled his surliness, "Oh, we kill them off here." Dad's thought was that it would take them a long time to kill him off, as he considered he had not had such an easy job for years. The following morning he was working down below on a trawler when one of his workmates noticed that he looked ashen and asked my father if he was feeling ill. Dad admitted he had a bad chest pain and the other man suggested he went aloft to get some fresh air. The others helped him — perhaps too much — because they suggested, once on deck, that he should put on his heavy army greatcoat since it was a bitterly cold day. The struggle with the coat was too much for my Dad and he dropped dead on the deck. A postmortem later indicated that he had suffered a coronary thrombosis, which enabled us to understand why he had complained of chest pains for several months, though his GP had assured him, in spite of this, that there was nothing to worry about. Born too early, there was no way he would live to benefit from the immense progress in medicine that came later.

The memory of my being accosted by Fred as I stepped off a bus in Central Birmingham and my astonishment at unexpectedly seeing him there can still fill me with grief. Trying, as ever, to treat me with gentleness, he had attempted repeatedly to persuade me to go with him for a coffee. In astonishment, I reminded him that I was on my way to Sheldon to give a private lesson. He repeated his invitation, but his persuasiveness got him nowhere, so that, finally, he had to be brutal with me. "Pop has died", he announced. I was incredulous, distraught and totally uncontrolled as he ushered me onto a bus which would take us back to our digs in Selly Oak. As soon as he heard the news, our host, Don, displayed his warm, Brummie nature by producing a wad of notes and saying, "Borrow these and get the next train to Grimsby", which we did as soon as we had telephoned my Headmistress, Miss

221

Aston, to explain my enforced absence. The train journey is indelibly printed on my mind, as is our meeting with my brother Stan when we stepped off the train. Stan had been fulfilling his obligation to the Navy as a reserve in the RNR by attending a lengthy training. He had been flown by helicopter most of the way, but had finished his journey by train. He hailed a taxi and we were soon with my mother, whom we found to be overwhelmed with sorrow and shock.

Hastily, funeral arrangements were made and, after the ceremony, we promptly returned to Birmingham. The school holidays were just starting and we thanked Don for his timely loan, because my mother had decreed that we should wear black for the funeral: a coat for me and a black tie for Fred, together with a pair of black shoes. Before the funeral, Dad's body was brought to the house and placed in the front room. His was the only body I have ever had the courage to face and I have found the experience so awful that I have avoided further similar encounters. My father had lost his false teeth, apparently, as he fell and his mouth was agape, no one having had the presence of mind, in the panic, to close it before it was too late. At the hospital, they had stuffed it with cotton wool and a trickle of blood, probably a consequence of the post-mortem, had dried at the corner of his mouth.

It was an old-fashioned funeral, with masses of wreaths arriving at the house and, among them, was a huge anchor from his final work-place, which reflected their compassion and, probably, the employer's regret for his flippant remark at the interview. There was one ingredient of that sad day which set a new trend in our family. Dad was cremated because he had stressed his desire for this, for he believed that cemeteries swallowed up too much valuable land and also that cremation had to be more hygienic for the population in general.

Before we left, recognising that my mother would now have to survive on the meagre State Widow's Pension, as it then was, I told her that it was my intention to give her a regular £1 every week. Today, it sounds a paltry contribution, but £4 monthly was very acceptable in 1955. She demurred at first, but was finally persuaded and continued to accept it until she was incapacitated by a massive stroke in 1972. My elder sister then handed me a bankbook, which my mother had discreetly set up in my name, which demonstrated to me how sparsely she had used our contributions. Once she had bought her monthly supply of wool for her much-loved hobby — knitting — she had secretly banked the residue of the money we sent, to ensure that it did not fall into anybody else's hands if she were to die. After her death, I invested this unlooked for wealth in a ring with three lovely diamonds, as she would have encouraged me to do. She loved her children to have more luxury in their lives than she had ever known in her own.

When we returned, it was time to take over our new semi and it dawned on me that I had seen my dear little girls at City Road secondary modern for the last time, for I had been appointed to Aston Commercial School, selective, mixed and destined for pupils who had missed out on the 11+, but who had managed to succeed at the later 13+ exam, a tradition peculiar to the Birmingham education pattern. Fred and I worked hard on the house, which had been left in a very dirty state by the builders. We were able to make it habitable before it was necessary for both of us to start out in our new schools, Fred having also changed. We loved our work in the new establishments, formed good friendships with colleagues and, later, with pupils who, after leaving school, spontaneously called on us to inform us that they were accepted in a University or in firms where there was training in executive or administrative roles. Later, some brought newly acquired wives or husbands to receive our blessing. Many of my new friends had come to know Fred because of social occasions at school, just as I became acquainted with his Five Ways colleagues and pupils.

I was deliriously happy to use my English as a teaching subject at long last, to prepare my pupils for their "O" level English Language and Literature examinations. It soon became apparent to my Head, whose organisation in the school involved the segregation of the sexes in the classroom — "We are co-educational, but not co-instructional" — that I enjoyed the boys' classes and could control them with ease. Consequently, he asked me if I would take over more male classes. I readily agreed, on condition that I retained my own form of lovely girls. I still meet one of these from time to time and several of the boys have tracked me down and visited us.

After two years, I was encouraged to apply for a Head of English post in a Secondary Modern school and I was ready to move, as I had little respect for a new colleague who had been given the Head of English post at ACS. The new school was conveniently located close to our house, so I accepted the post, but found it difficult to quit the school which I had loved so much. My regrets soon multiplied as I became more familiar with the very unpleasant new Headmistress, who patently loathed me, a feeling which, I confess, I reciprocated. Fortunately, I was offered a similar post in a newly-opening, mixed school at the end of the school year. Bliss returned and I worked with delight and enthusiasm in my new environment for five rewarding years.

Very soon after moving into our Castle Bromwich home, we received a card with painful news: the death of our friend John Rutt, from a blow on the temple has already been referred to. When we had this piece of news, we both mourned John deeply and immediately jettisoned our plan not to try for a baby until we had spent one year earning extra money in Evening Institutes, so that our house would be fully furnished. We were now convinced that a baby was far more important to us then any number of sticks of furniture. However, that decision brought eight years of tears once a month, as I failed in my efforts to become pregnant. My family were notably fertile, so that my failures were all the more frustrating. I finally plucked up my courage to discuss this difficulty with my GP, who was considered to be an expert in dealing with problems of infertility: he recommended a consultant at the Women's Hospital. May Newman, parent of one of the Five Ways boys who, together with her husband had become firm friends of ours, and whom I called my Birmingham mother, always insisted on driving me to the Women's Hospital and remaining with me as long as I was needed there for tests and consultations. In the early 60's, such tests were far more rudimentary than they are today and, often, extremely painful. Having attended the full programme of visits, I was called into the office of the austere lady specialist, whose message was, "You are fine. Be a good girl, go home and have a baby." Totally disconcerted, I hastily returned to my GP, who displayed instant compassion, as he complained, "Yes, that consultant is very clever, but, in character, she very much resembles a sergeant major". He rallied me by promising a transfer to another gynaecologist of far gentler disposition, who worked in a small hospital, much nearer to my home. On my first visit to Marston Green, I was given a bundle of what I took to be hospital clothes and was asked to enter a cubicle and strip off and change into a hospital gown. I undressed and picked up what I took to be a string vest — funny? I tried to pull it over my head but could not locate a hole through which my head could emerge. I tried another struggle over my feet, with the same abortive result. Hearing a movement in the adjacent cubicle, I asked the occupant how one put on the string vest. I heard a ripple of laughter and my neighbour told me it was not a vest, but a bag designed to hold one's clothes. Red-faced, I eventually emerged from the cubicle, clad in the white gown, which I put on back to front in my confusion, and carrying my possessions in that mystifying bag. So, in the eighth year of fruitless hopes, I met this gentleman, who checked that Fred had been tested and was fine and then, in answer to my report about what had been the outcome of earlier investigations, his first recommendation was a D and C. The consequent minor operation led nowhere and, finally, my consultant suggested that, if I felt able to undertake a laperotomy, he would be able to investigate further. I told him that I was prepared to accept anything that he suggested and we agreed to go ahead. He allowed me to choose my date, so I selected the last week of term, when things were winding down for the Christmas holidays and, with my Headmaster's blessing, I went into Marston Green, bursting with hope and anticipation of progress at last. Unhappily, the findings were quite the reverse of my expectations. I was told that the left ovary was covered in small cysts, the Fallopian tubes were covered in adhesions — a consequence of my peritonitis operation — and the uterus was only the size of the average 11 year old's. Mr. Lester, my surgeon, gently told me that we should try to adopt, as it was most unlikely that I would ever conceive, with all the odds against me.

Fred had suggested many a time that we should apply for an adoption, but my only response had been, "But I want YOUR baby." My dear husband was not to be deterred, however, and wrote to Warwick Children's Department, after our applications to Hungary for an orphan and to the Methodist National Children's

Homes had both been rejected, the first responding with a straight request for money, but no offer and the latter stating that we were not religious enough. Our hopes increased when we received an invitation to attend for interview in Warwick. I was utterly terrified at the prospect of this for, by this time, I really believed that, at the age of 32, my fate was sealed and I would be for ever childless. In Warwick Council House, we met a gentle but positive lady, who asked us some very searching questions, all of which one or other of us managed to answer. Finally, she said to me, "Now, Mrs. Austin, for the most important question." Immediately, my hopes plummetted, as I wondered what was in store. However, she continued "Which would you like to adopt, a boy or a girl?" Relief swept through me, as I replied with no hesitation, "A boy, to start with." We had, for a long time determined that the first child should be a boy and had already chosen his name — David John: the first for my father, whose second name it was and the latter for the lovable boy who had died in Biarritz on that sad school trip. The Adoption Officer then explained to us that she would have to visit our house to see if it was suitable for a baby. Our delight was apparent at the amount of progress made that afternoon and I later very much enjoyed her visit to Castle Bromwich, when I showed her the bedroom destined for our future son. She seemed to be duly impressed and informed us that everything she had learned about us would have to be considered by her Committee and, in due course, we would receive a letter either of acceptance or rejection. That joyful news appropriately arrived on St. David's Day — a wonderful omen. The same lady paid another visit to our house to instruct us about the obligatory preparations we had to make so that a baby could be placed in our home at a moment's notice. I was instructed to resign from my full-time post as Head of English, so that I could spend all my time at home with the baby. I explained to her the rules of my contract which meant that the resignation date for that term had passed and that I would need to put in my resignation before the end of May for leaving after the Summer Term. I was also told that I would have to prove to her that we had installed all the necessary equipment for the baby, even to feeding bottles and Milton for sterilising them. What a pleasing demand — we would just love to acquire all that was necessary for him. Once we had fulfilled all these requirements, each waiting week seemed to be an eternity. I loved the school where I had taught for five wonderful years and where my pupils were a constant source of satisfaction — parting would be "such sweet sorrow" — but there are two of them that I still see quite frequently to this day and others have visited us from time to time. The 5th Form did me proud that final year, producing many good grades in English Language and Literature, as well as in French, which I had also taught them for the entire five years and, privately, I bewailed the fact that my 3rd Form of that year would not be mine for the two years that followed.

My departure on the last day of term was made memorable by all the good wishes that were expressed to me, accompanied by a great shower of gifts for the baby and for me. The 3rd formers bought a toy Panda, which proved to be David's most beloved toy until the day, many years later, when it finally disintegrated. During the following summer vacation, we took our final school party — consisting, this time, entirely of my pupils — to France and even mustered the courage to take them to Biarritz for a few days. Anxious to keep the costs as low as possible for the pupils' parents, Fred, who was now established as a Lecturer in Education at Leicester, had booked one of the Students' Union minibuses. It was a great blow when, at the eleventh hour, Fred was informed that the vehicle was no longer available, as it required a major repair. In despair, I mentioned this to my colleagues in the Staff Room and one of the ladies hesitantly told me that she knew someone in the Christadelphian Church she attended who might be able to assist. We contacted this gentleman, a garage proprietor, who told Fred that he had second-hand minibus that he would sell to us for £200 and that he would buy back for £50 less, if we returned it in the condition that we had received it in. Full of trepidation, we virtually emptied our savings account and accepted his offer. We warned the pupils that they would have to take great care of the vehicle, for any damage or vandalism would land us in Queer Street. How those concerned parents indoctrinated their children! One brother and sister assiduously cleaned the interior every single day and the entire group guarded our temporary property attentively. It was a really happy holiday — a fitting climax to my happy association with Hodge Hill.

Once back in Castle Bromwich, the excitement mounted as we waited for the arrival of the baby, for we had been told that we could hear from the Children's Department at any time after the middle of August. How I sewed and knitted as I dreamed of holding him in my arms. However, even the University vacation passed and Fred resumed his daily commuting to Leicester, leaving me to grow increasingly lonely and full of yearning when, daily, the postman brought me nothing. My ex-Headmaster telephoned me and asked if I would help him out on a supply basis and, with the acquiescence of the Adoption Society, I agreed. It fell to my lot to teach a most inappropriate timetable — Domestic Science stretched my capabilities, as did boys' PE, which, in my case, curiously resembled English in the classroom. The news of my return to education spread and I was subsequently invited to tackle some lecturing at the College of Advanced Technology in Gosta Green in Birmingham — a result of the garrulity of someone for whom I had worked in my Evening Institute days. There were other requests which I refused, in the hope that my destiny was about to change.

My mother recognised from my weekly letters that I was getting more and more depressed, so she diffidently asked me if her friend, after whom I had been named Margaret, a Spiritualist, could ask her medium about our baby. It was necessary to send something I was in the habit of wearing, so I sent a glove, which Auntie Maggie took along to a seance. We were both flabbergasted by the contents of my mother's subsequent letter. It first described the heart-rending distress of the medium when she spoke of Fred. She found the initials BA for him, which he later explained to me: apparently, at school, he had always been known as "Bunny" Austin, something he had never mentioned to me before. Of course, there was the other possible interpretation, his first degree providing the same initials. It appears that, after giving Maggie this information, the medium became distraught as she cried out "His poor mother! His poor mother! It is the most terrible thing I have ever seen." No one could have told this woman about the ghastly end to Fred's mother's life, because our only contact would have been through Auntie Maggie and she, like most of my mother's circle, had never been told, because of Mum's extreme discretion. When she was asked about the baby, the medium replied. "That baby is so near to her, he is almost in her arms." A few days later, the long-awaited letter arrived. I was, that evening, to meet Fred in Leicester, where his students and colleagues were throwing a party for him, since he was leaving to take up his first headship in the following January. Unable to reach him until the evening, I first telephoned my mother with the good news and then tapped on the lounge wall to alert my neighbour. Very promptly, she was on my front doorstep where, having taken one look at me, she squealed with joy, "You have heard about the baby, haven't you?" My mother was rushing round her friends in Cleethorpes, crying and laughing as she went to relate the glad tidings, while May, my neighbour, and I drank endless cups of coffee and May consumed all the mince pies that I had baked for our friends Millie and Ben, the parents of poor John, who were spending the following Sunday with us. Endlessly, we babbled about our forthcoming life and, repeatedly, May reproached me for leaving, first for Lincolnshire and then for Lancashire, thus depriving her and her husband of all contact with our baby.

Fred had been appointed to the headship of Nelson Grammar School just in time for him to resign from his lectureship in Leicester. The night after his successful interview was the only night in our entire marriage that I refused to share his bed: I spent that night on the settee downstairs. I was utterly desolate at that point, as the only qualification required by Warwick for adoption was the residential one. That night, I was terrified that we would not have the offer of a baby before we had to move to Lancashire: the result of his success in his career was likely to dash all my hopes. It was at this point that I had bemoaned my fate to my mother, which consequently led to the above comforting information from the medium, and which, I confess, I could not really believe. As I stepped off the train in Leicester, I saw, as ever, my husband's grin and poured out our news. What a deliriously happy evening that proved to be!

We decided to regale ourselves with an elegant lunch on our way to Warwick to see the baby for the first time but, as Fred says, I always have to have something to worry about: throughout the entire meal, I expressed my fear that the baby would have bright red hair, which I would have great difficulty in accepting. What a trivial woman I was! We arrived punctually at the foster-home, where we were received by the Adoption Officer, who conducted us into the living room, where we were greeted by the foster mother with the words, "So you have come to see this big baby". Apprehensively, I took the proferred child into my arms and recognised at once that I held the most beautiful little creature that had ever been born — he was neither red-headed nor big. Already nine weeks old, he smiled adorably and being minus a nappy, aimed a very good shower at the fireplace. We were asked if we would like to accept the child and, with enthusiasm, I asserted, "He is already our David." Arrangements were made for us to collect him on Friday, 13th December — only a few days away. We walked on air as we retraced our steps to the car. It was tough to leave him behind, moreover, to my horror, on the way home, I developed a streaming cold. Instead of returning straight to our house, we called at our GP's, who saw us at once. Full of panic, I explained that I feared that I would not be permitted to collect the baby if I had an obvious infection. Whatever Dr. Chitnis prescribed for me, I never knew, but, with the potency of a sledge-hammer, it had obliterated my symptoms by the following morning.

Once back home, we telephoned my Birmingham mother, the other May, who said at once, "He's not coming home in a b— Mini: I shall chauffeur you in our Wolseley." I carried the baby to May's car, but the Adoption Officer instructed me to place him in the carry-cot on the back seat. These were the days before seat-belts and child-seats. I so longed to hold him in my arms on the way home and, once we were well out of sight, May, sensing my desire and sympathising with it, brought the car to a halt and encouraged me to follow my instincts. That was the only time when, driven by May, it was a sedate, painstakingly careful journey.

Bottles were ready prepared in the fridge and the smart new bottle-warmer was plugged in to be used for this very contented child. He sucked with gusto and almost drained his Ostermilk. Now came the first nappy change. There were no specially designed changing-tables in 1963, the baby being dealt with on its mother's lap, the waiting nappy carefully folded into its kite shape. As soon as he was released from his wet nappy, he produced his fountain, this time all over our fireplace and I realised that I would have to adjust my long-established house-proud attitudes. Once comfortably dressed again, we placed David in the carry-cot on our settee and he settled into a blissful sleep. Soon, friends began to arrive, laden with gifts for our new arrival. The Welsh couple, neighbours three doors away, brought a christening mug and our dear friends, Andre and Gretl Drucker, entered, bearing a soft toy, a pale blue horse with a white mane, which we still have. Our neighbour Bob, May's husband, never a quiet man, burst in upon us and bellowed, "Where is that beautiful baby then?" in stentorian tones, at which David, nestling on Fred's shoulder, gushed out a projectile vomit. We were swiftly being inaugurated into the messiness of babies. Once Bob set eyes on him, he demanded, for the umpteenth time, that the child should be called Robert after him and, finally, we agreed to add it to David John, especially as his biological mother had named him Robert. That night, when it was time to give David his next feed, Fred brought him to me in bed, where I enjoyed watching him. However, when I raised him onto my shoulder to wind him, once again he displayed his expertise in projectile vomiting, which involved a complete change of all the bedding. It is a characteristic of David to guide us into sensible behaviour and that reaction taught us never to feed a baby in bed again. His first three displays — one on the fireplace, the second on Fred's shoulder and the third in our bed — were never to be repeated. He became a model baby, once he had made his point very clearly and we took note of his instructions.

The following day, frosty and bitterly cold, gave rise to a final piece of folly on my part. Longing to show off my prize, I wheeled his pram through the immediate neighbourhood and found his incessant crying unnerving. A friend, experienced as a father, approached and looked for a cause, immediately spotting that the poor little soul was cold. In my dreamy state, I had forgotten to dress him for the great outdoors. I hurried back to our warm house and, immediately, David was his normal, smiling self again.

As well as learning to cope with motherhood, I was having to pack our more treasured and fragile possessions for transportation to Foulridge, where we had found a newly-built house which suited our tastes

236

perfectly. Our difficulty was that the Castle Bromwich semi was still unsold so, of necessity, we had to arrange a bridging-loan to pay a deposit on the Foulridge four bedroomed house, the new debt being a source of concern to both of us. Fred and the friend who had pointed out that David was cold in his pram — John Garvey — each drove one of the Minis, laden with various valuables, to the house in Lancashire, where they left my car in the garage and, soon after their return, we said goodbye to our many Birmingham friends and to No. 20 and left to spend to spend Christmas with my mother, Clarice and family. What preparations had been made on our behalf! They had bought a second-hand cot for David and had arranged all the rooms for our welcome. My mother insisted that David's cot was to be located in her living room, because it had been thoroughly heated all day by her open fire, instead of installing him in the rather bleak bedroom, which had been allocated to him for the warmer weather later on.

The whole family was enchanted with the new arrival and my younger sister's husband, Steve, was especially enthusiastic, immediately christening David "Chickabiddy". It was a blissful holiday — one of the best we ever had. We particularly enjoyed watching the last feed of the day, when David, once fed, produced many a windy smile, which we thought hilarious. When he was winded and changed, he settled contentedly back in his cot and slept through until at least 8 o'clock the following morning. We congratulated ourselves on our parenting skills and were already enjoying the prospect of adopting three more babies, as we felt sure we were great experts, born to raise little angels. If only we had realised how much we still had to learn!

CHAPTER EIGHTEEN

A Lake Side View for Our Babies

We were soon back to a house of our own, this time much further north and, for a second time, discovered that the builders had left the place in a deplorable state. I quickly cleaned as much as I could around the furniture, which had been haphazardly dumped by the removal men, and then made sure that our little son had a pristine bedroom in which to start his Lancashire life. Next day, Fred left me amidst the chaos, so that he could familiarise himself with the new school. I swept and scrubbed and recalled my early days of occupation in the house in Castle Bromwich. There were mountains of cardboard boxes to unpack and, later, incinerated on the smallish patch of land behind the house, destined to be the garden. Its appearance that January defied the hopes I had nursed from the diagram supplied by the builder. Along with all the chores, I had my baby to care for, but he continued, fortunately, to be as good as gold. My only other contact with the human race was with the various workmen still doing jobs on the site, where I was the sole occupier. They were very supportive and one, a middle-aged plumber, took to calling a couple of times daily to see if all was well. One morning, as I bathed David, I noticed that one of his ears was full of blood. Immediately, I summoned my plumber friend, knowing he was experienced with children. He looked at the baby and suggested that David had scratched his ear with a sharp little finger-nail. He added however, that he would call a doctor, in case it was a sign of something more serious. Our phoneline had to go through a local operator, who frequently eavesdropped on our conversations. When a visit had been refused by the two doctors whom the plumber and I had found in the directory, the operator intervened in our conversation by stating, "if a baby is involved, I will put you through to Dr. Foggitt. He never refuses." She spoke to the doctor on my behalf and, in no time at all, the doctor arrived from nearby Colne and set about cleaning the blood from David's ear. Very quickly, he revealed the very scratch that the plumber had diagnosed and I was so relieved. I had already imagined that our baby would be removed from our care because it would be believed that I had neglected him. I really appreciated the compassion of the plumber, the doctor and the telephone operator. By the time that Fred rushed in from Nelson, everything was rosy again.

Gradually, the house became a home and we were able to afford some new furniture, having sold several items before we left Castle Bromwich. We bought new bedroom carpets which I fitted myself in order to save money, but I had skilled help for the open staircase and landing carpet. The lounge floor around the fireplace was carpeted and the dining area in our open-plan living room sported fitted rush matting, which proved to be not very serviceable.

During this period, I was nagged by a recurring thought that David's biological mother was, at any time, and without any warning, entitled to ask for the baby to be returned to her. I was haunted by this knowledge for several months, until we were called to visit a judge in Nelson, who would ask us many pertinent questions and, if he was satisfied that the baby had been rightly placed, he could sign adoption papers, thus making David our legal son. I knew I could not give him back so, without telling even Fred, I hoarded some money, determined to disappear to a hotel somewhere, to seek anonymous shelter if my fears ever proved correct. I suppose that, in my heart of hearts, I realised that my plan was both unrealistic and illegal, but the thought of losing that beautiful child was pure torture. Fortunately, we were regularly visited by a lovely lady, a member of another adoption society, and by Nurse Petersen, with both of whom we passed muster. The judge was satisfied about our worthiness, having received reports from both those ladies and from his own impressions. With a few encouraging comments, he cheerfully signed the papers and handed them to us. I can easily envisage the joy of couples carrying their first-born out of a maternity unit, but what we experienced when we left that house in Warwick and, later, the courtroom in Nelson, was certainly no less rewarding. It was not very long before

241

I was thinking of an application to the Manchester and District Adoption Society (to which our visiting lady belonged) for a second baby. As ever, Fred persuaded me to spend a few months enjoying the treasure that was now officially ours. We sent for his new birth certificates and settled down to a life of great contentment.

There were two important events during those first few months in Foulridge: one extremely sad, the other a great relief. My younger sister, Mavis, and I wrote weekly letters to each other and she mentioned, several times, to me that the infection we had seen in Steve at Christmas-time was still plaguing him. I visited a friend for lunch one February day, and remember commenting to her that I was concerned about my brother-in-law. That evening, after we had put David to bed and eaten our meal, we sat near the fire, Fred puffing away at a cigarette. He suddenly said quietly, "I had some bad news at school today". Immediately, I knew what he was going to tell me and interrupted with "Steve has lung cancer?" Astonished, he confirmed what I had said and I went on to explain that, during the morning, I had expressed my worries about Steve to Marge. I jumped up and snatched the cigarette from Fred and, stubbing it out, I added, "Don't let's smoke any more." He never did, having already thought along those lines himself, more aware of his responsibilities as a Headmaster and, even more, as a father. I made feeble efforts to follow his example, but failed dismally, partly because of my loneliness in the house, where I had my lovely baby but little adult company.

Eventually, I owned up to my failure and Fred never uttered a word of reproach. Steve's condition deteriorated rapidly and he died in hospital during the Easter holidays, whilst we were back in Cleethorpes. My brother, Mark, my brother-in-law, and Fred were wonderfully supportive to Mavis and Michael, her seven year-old son. The funeral took place before we had to return home, after which Fred and I discussed how we could assist my sister. We eventually offered to take responsibility for the purchase of Michael's clothes to assist her financially, for Steve, who had been a bricklayer by trade and only 36 when he died, had saved very little money. Our desire to help Mavis financially was made more of a realistic possibility when we heard from the estate agent in Birmingham who had arranged the sale of our Castle Bromwich house and enabled us, at last, to dispose of our bridging-loan. All went smoothly, the property was no longer ours and neither was the debt.

We felt that we had been singularly blessed compared with the difficulties which so many people had to face, so we decided not to have a holiday in 1964 but instead, to provide one for someone else, as a thanksgiving for receiving David and Fred's Headship. Having met the ex-husband of Fred's mother, Arthur Sommer, on our visit to Czechoslovakia during the summer of 1963, now with his third wife, we surrendered to his frequently expressed hints about coming to visit us. So, despite misgivings we had about him, we undertook to support them for a four-week visit to England. We knew that Fred's mother had divorced him after only one year of marriage and had grasped his habit of finding fairly wealthy women to marry. Having thrown caution to the winds — unusual for me — we met them at Manchester Piccadilly railway station, thus beginning several weeks of purgatory. He was intrusive, demanding and excessively greedy. His sweet-natured wife was just the opposite: she had owned the Bonny Baby garment factory until it was appropriated by the communists and was also a skilled seamstress who taught me a great many tricks of the trade. Between us, we made David a beautifully tailored blue overcoat. Childless herself, she immediately doted on our baby; her one failing, in our eyes, being that she was spoiling him. The weeks dragged, as Arthur's demands and complaints became more unbearable. It is true that he had suffered the evils of a concentration camp, but that experience had made him a very envious man: he resented even the simplest advantages we enjoyed, for example that the English could have their milk delivered daily to the house. They had brought with them some jewellery belonging to Elsie, though perhaps some pieces had been left by friends as they were being deported to camps. Elsie, a Christian, had not been persecuted and she guarded many such treasures for people who never returned. They showed us a large brooch, with several 2-carat diamonds in its elegant setting, cuff-links with diamonds set in jet and several other valuable pieces. They had hoped that we would buy them, as Arthur wished to invest the proceeds in a car that he could drive back to Czechoslovakia. That hope was forlorn for, after the expense of changing houses, the purchase of fresh furniture and providing for our son's needs, our savings had been reduced to little over £100. We suggested that we should accept a friend's offer of their house in Birmingham for a few days whilst they were away on holiday. Thus we were able to take our guests and their treasures to a manufacturing jeweller whom we knew in the Jewellery Quarter to see if he would be interested in buying the pieces. He was not interested, the diamonds being an unfashionable cut. He suggested the price they could expect if a retailer were persuaded to buy them, so we visited a well-established firm in Corporation Street, where the offer was £175 for the cuff-links and the brooch. They decided to sell, though we warned them that, even in those days, they could not buy a new car for that money. They then decided to go direct to London, where they hoped to buy several things that were unavailable in communist Brno where they lived. Their endless stream of demands continued until Arthur died in the early 70's. We have a beautiful decanter and matching liqueur glasses, which they brought as a present when they arrived, but they admitted that they were in their possession because the rightful owners were holocaust victims. On our visit to Czechoslovakia in the early 60's, we discovered that so-called friends of Fred's mother had been similarly entrusted, at the very least, with her and her daughters' jewellery. One of this family's relatives in England, whom they asked us to visit after our return, told us that she had given Ilse's ring to a grand-daughter — thus making our blood run cold, and we wondered if

245

those persecuted victims had been able to put their trust in anyone.

When we were finally freed from the tormenting presence of Arthur, we saw to it that we took a break to enjoy our life with David. He was standing up by this time and occasionally proved too ambitious, when he would fall headlong, often hurting himself quite badly. Whenever such accidents occurred, I was utterly terrified, as he would hold his breath for what seemed an eternity, turning first ashen and then blue. The only remedy I ever found to overcome this was to repeat his name gently and to stroke his head and face until, finally, he would gasp for air. These ordeals happened too frequently, but he could not understand the danger of his behaviour.

He was already making sounds that we knew to be his early efforts at speech. One of his first "words" was "De", his version of Panda — now established as his most precious possession. One evening, just before the News, Sooty was on television: David tried to grab the picture, screaming hysterically: "De! De!" I had to find the toy hurriedly to show him that the picture was not his beloved "De". On another occasion, whilst Fred and I were enjoying our evening meal, we heard David's wild screaming, once again, "De! De!". Racing to investigate, we found him shaking with fear and shuddering, because a black thread of wool, which had been part of Panda's nose, had become unravelled. We knew how the child found fringes on blankets, scarves and carpets to be horrific and this had given rise to his hysterical cries. While Fred calmed him down, I quickly stitched in the offending wool and peace reigned anew. Our nights were always undisturbed when David was a baby, but when he awoke in the morning, we could always hear him calling, "Big Ball". He loved his collection of balls and enjoyed sharing his cot with one all through the night. Equally, when in his pram or push-chair, he insisted on clutching a plastic skittle. We were queueing in the village shop one day when the Vicar strode in. I was filled with apprehension when he greeted David with, "Is life all beer and skittles with you, young man?" David had recently taken to uttering a sound that resembled an expletive — never learned from our lips — and I was afraid that it would be his response to the vicar. Fortunately, my fears were not fulfilled. On a later occasion, once again we were waiting our turn in the village shop, when David spotted a nun from the nearby convent. In a dreamy voice, he asked "What is it, Mummy?" and I told him, "That lady is a nun, darling." Ecstatically, he replied, "May I have one for Christmas?" A ripple of laughter went round the shop and the nun herself contributed to it.

Absorbed as I was in the upbringing of our first child, I began to yearn for another baby. At that stage, I was determined to raise a family of four boys. Of necessity, because of our change of address, we applied to the Manchester and District Child Adoption Society. In the meantime, David, now quite agile, loved to hurry from the bathroom after his morning dip, wrapped in his towel, which we both called his toga, would jump onto our bed and leap into space several times, as I sang, "Stand up! Stand up for Jesus!" Soon, he was able to join me in the hymn. I enjoyed the thought of having two angelic little boys providing me with such fun. Little did I know! I followed methods advocated by the District Nurse: I tried toilet training, to which David responded with no interest whatsoever. He also became quite an unwilling eater — probably a consequence of my anxiety if he did not eat well. I described my fears to our GP, who asked me if I had ever seen a puppy die of starvation. Green was David's favourite colour, so we took to offering David as many green foods as we could muster. These he enjoyed, as long as he was given his beloved "mammon" (salmon) or "mam" (ham). M was his favourite consonant and most of his nouns began with that sound. When we were clearing leaves in the front garden, he would look up at the large sycamore tree, shouting, "Mum on!", inviting further foliage to drop on the grass.

Soon, we were excited by the prospect of a forthcoming visit from my mother. We drove to Leeds to collect her from her through train and, when she stepped down from it, David, at 17 months, called out, "Nanny!" with obvious pleasure and recognition. My mother was impressed that he knew her, even though he had not seen her since the Christmas holiday and she expressed her usual opinion: "That child was three months old the day he was born." She always predicted his considerable intelligence. Almost coinciding with my mother's arrival, we received a letter from the adoption society which told us of the Committee's decision to offer us a baby boy. When I rang the

Secretary, Miss Hill, she told me that we could see the baby in the foster-home where he had been placed since birth. Swiftly, we made arrangements to visit and found the house, where the foster mother was caring for six babies, all sleeping peacefully when we arrived. We were shown our future son and felt he was just like a miniature Churchill, with his rounded, red face. He was only lacking a cigar in his mouth to complete the resemblance. The poor little mite was rosy-faced because of a heavy crop of pimples which, so we were assured, was merely a milk rash. We showed David this new little brother and asked him if he would like to take him home. There was an outburst of laughter when, with a great deal of assurance, David announced, "I would rather have the lady's cat!" Needless to say, his father and I did not concur.

CHAPTER
NINETEEN

Children Are Not All Alike

Arrangements were made for us to collect the baby in a few days. My mother shared our excitement at the prospect of yet another addition to the family and was delighted to be one of the party when we went to the Society's offices to collect him. When she held him, he produced a very lop-sided smile, which she found utterly enchanting. "God love him," she said. She was happy to cuddle him all the way home, whilst I hugged David so that he would not feel rejected.

The new baby slept happily on the journey home, so we were ready to congratulate him and ourselves. Back home, we found him very willing to consume his prepared feed, so we felt that all would be plain sailing as we tucked him into the small rocking crib. Having crept downstairs to attend to David's needs, we were very soon interrupted by loud yells from aloft. Thus began the period of interminable trials and errors. Peace would reign if we gave him a little boiled water, but not for many minutes. If we discovered a dirty nappy, we made him comfortable and hoped that the problem was solved but, once again, there was quiet for only 15 minutes. A bath was tried, but, again, success was very brief. By the time the three adults were more than ready for an early night, the screams had eventually subsided. Thinking back on David's arrival, we guiltily became aware that comparisons are odious, but we all hoped that Ian Christopher would be more like his brother once he had become accustomed to his new environment. We still had a lot to learn.

It was thus that our life changed and, for the next 19 or 20 months, we had a difficult time. Fred would wheel the baby round the village in the evenings and, even in the small hours of the morning, when we were on holiday in Bournemouth, because people in nearby bedrooms in the hotel were complaining to the management about his piercing screams. We were worried that we would be evicted from our accommodation if we took no action, after another young couple had met this fate when the chambermaid had reported their habit of leaving a bucket of dirty nappies in their bedroom. Disposables were not as common then as they became later: Fred preferred to take evasive action, so that he could protect the rest of our holiday. It was while this was happening that David rescued Fred from an almost grotesque error: as ever, David loved "green", continuing to call it "deen" and he called traffic lights by this name, whether they displayed green, red or amber. He was sitting beside his father — no seat-belts or child seats in those days — and suddenly cried out, "Deen, Daddy, deen!" on a busy Bournemouth road. Alerted from a reverie which, no doubt, stemmed from his broken night, Fred saw that he was about to cross on a red light, but was able to stop in time. He drove back to the hotel, where I had remained with Ian and proudly announced that David had probably saved both their lives.

As the months progressed, we eventually were able to enjoy another successful visit to the judge, who accepted our application for adoption and made us now the proud, legal parents of two little boys. Nurse Petersen, the health visitor, was still most assiduous in her home visits and noticed how fatigued I seemed to be. I explained the reason for my sleepless nights, whereupon Ian received his first official warning from this lady. Severely, she told him that he lived far too close to the lake across the road to be able to continue with his bad habit. Despite her threats, Ian continued with his usual conduct and my child policy remained unchanged. I recall the November morning in 1966 when, to my astonishment, I awoke in my own bed instead of on the lounge settee: was he mending his ways? It seemed as though I would no longer have to protect Fred's rest, to allow him to face his responsibilities in school on the following day. I remember the foster mother had told me, when we first saw Ian, that she always put a teaspoonful of brandy in the last feed that the babies had at night: very briefly, I tried this remedy. Though he drank his milk with gusto, he still behaved in the same way throughout the night. After two or three night feeds with the brandy added, I gave up that practice, because I was afraid that I would make him into an alcoholic and it did not seem to be working. Once or twice, I let him suck on an After-Eight mint, which he relished, but it brought no improvement in his sleeping. After a few months of being spoon-fed, he would frequently consume a tin of Heinz baby-food during the night, but even that treat did not solve my problem. Sometimes, I thought that he had gone to sleep in the travel-cot beside me and I would gratefully stretch out in a sleeping position on the settee, only to be greeted by the usual outburst as soon as I put my head on the cushion. After so long a period of sleep deprivation, I was rapidly becoming a zombie.

During the final period of torture, from mid-August to November, 1966, we were delighted to collect a beautiful baby girl, who demonstrated her sedate approach to life by behaving angelically both day and night. Helen was born in late July, on the birthday of the 5 year-old daughter of one of my nephews, the poor little girl having been killed by a car on Election Day the previous spring. When we received the letter about Helen, my mother produced one of her customary observations — "you have to lose one in order to gain one, so they say." We were so happy to have Helen, although we grieved with the rest of the family for the loss of poor Susan.

As soon as David had seen me give Ian a bottle-feed, he had rejected his own bed-time bottle, the only one remaining in his routine, and he adopted the same attitude to his night-time nappy once Helen was on the scene. He coped beautifully with both of those decisions. My two little lads adored their sister, who came to us when she was only three weeks old and was the smallest of our babies. If, in those early days, she uttered the tiniest whimper as she lay in her carry-cot, David would hurry over to her and say "It's alright, darling, I am here." It was my great pleasure to assemble my little group, with the baby lying inside the pram, Ian seated on the chair which attached to the foot of the pram and David clutching the handlebar beside me. I just loved being a mother. Each evening, after completing the day's ironing, I would set up my new Necchi sowing-machine and make a garment for one or other of them. I made my sons identical outfits, but I had to double or treble the number of trousers produced for Ian as, on average, the knees displayed huge holes within the first fortnight they were worn — a consequence of his lasting tendency to fall off his bike or simply tripping over when he was running. Fortunately, I had also become an expert on the local mill-shops, where I could buy inexpensive but good quality fabric, so that their clothing cost us very little. Helen, when she arrived, had been very lucky, in that everybody seemed anxious to buy her a pretty dress. Among my most satisfying products were the Chelsea Pensioner coats and hats for the boys — very elegant and not produced from mill-shop fabrics. For these, we had all travelled to Manchester to shop in Kendal's, the upmarket department store, where we bought lengths of fine quality, red, woollen material, together with black velvet for the trims and hats. I congratulated myself on another achievement, when I made a dainty little dress for Helen from a good quality, pretty piece of material which cost me exactly one shilling. My mother aided my efforts by knitting them countless sweaters, cardigans and even dressing-gowns, aided and abetted by my elder sister Clarice, who made the boys double-knit cardigans, with cowboys decorating the fronts. The sewing machine and knitting needles worked incessantly in those far off days.

We had a constant worry with David, which started not long after Ian's arrival on the scene, and continued until after he turned 3: I noticed that, when he was standing, he would frequently lose all awareness of his surroundings and the colour would drain from his face. When I mentioned this to our GP, he arranged a visit to a paediatrician, who thought that David might be epileptic and prescribed for "petit mal", explaining that the boy must be given this daily dose until he was three, when an expert on this condition would be able to do a brain scan. The examination produced the best imaginable result and the medical people decided that his problem was emotional, as a result of his no longer being the only child after Ian's arrival. It is still on my conscience that, on Ian's first birthday, while I was seated on the bed and changing Ian's nappy, David, who had repeatedly demonstrated that he was not totally enamoured of this little invader, rushed into the room, brandishing the baby hairbrush and smartly hit Ian across the face with it, whereupon I instinctively smacked David. This was the only occasion I can remember giving David a hard smack: he lost all his colour and held his breath. I carried him into the bathroom and sat by the handbasin, sprinkling water gently on his face and stroking his head, as I repeated his name over and over. Soon, I heard him gasp for breath and saw his colour return to normal, much to my relief, since I had been convinced that I had killed him.

In the midst of all this, that tiniest of our babies, Helen, continued to flourish. Her adoption was, in due course, approved by the same judge. I must explain why my origional intention to adopt four boys fell by the wayside: once Ian was firmly established in our family, it occurred to me that I had never asked Fred if he approved of my ambition. After a short, tactful hesitation, he admitted that he would quite like to adopt a little girl. I felt that my conduct had been unreasonable and I immediately told him that the choice would be his, on condition that there could be two little girls so that each could have a companion. Fred was delighted with this suggestion. After David's scan, our life seemed to be without anxieties, though there was the remaining problem of Ian, whenever we were out walking, going into hysterical panic whenever he spotted a dog and having to rush back to the house with one of us in order to calm him down. We never grasped why he was so nervous, but it was a passing phase. Some months after the trip to Manchester, David was offered a place in the local Nursery School. Fred would drop him there on the way to his own school and I would collect him at lunch-time. I was opposed to his spending a whole day away from home and, for the first few weeks he was very relieved to see me and return home. He had been very unwilling to stay when Fred delivered him and, weeping profusely, clung to his father. After a few episodes of this distress, Fred was very troubled, fearing the child was developing a school phobia and suggesting that we might have to remove him from the Nursery. However, he was persuaded by the staff to persevere a little longer and, one miraculous morning, David showed real pleasure at seeing his little friends, after which he never looked back in any of the schools he attended. When it was Ian's turn to go, he settled in immediately, only taking exception to the school lunch. I had refused to leave him for the afternoon session, really annoying the Headmistress in this, but she persuaded me to let him have a school meal. I arrived rather early one day and witnessed her pushing food that he did not want into his mouth and bullying him into swallowing it. As I watched Ian, who had started weeping because of her stupid treatment, I saw him suddenly vomit over the food which remained in his dish. This was too much for both of us and I refused to leave him beyond the end of the morning session after that. The Headmistress was furious with me and insisted that I was denying my son valuable experiences. One service for which I was very grateful to this domineering woman really impressed me. I had tried frequently to teach David, my left-handed son, how to use scissors, but had always failed: she knew how to deal with this problem because she was better informed about equipment for toddlers. She ordered scissors especially designed for left-handed children and was pleased to tell me of David's immediate success once he had a suitable tool.

While he was attending Nursery, he would repeat the tales that other children had told him. He wanted to know what one little boy meant when he announced that his grandfather had died: I explained in very simple terms what had occurred and, immediately, David asked what happened to the body after the spirit had gone to Jesus. I reminded him of the graves he had seen many times in Foulridge churchyard, where dead bodies had been buried. At once, he observed "I expect Kirks dig the holes," referring to the builders who were erecting new houses on what was rapidly becoming a small estate around us. Another little boy assured him that babies grew in Mummies' tummies. "I told him he was wrong," asserted David, "I know that you get babies from Manchester, because I have been there with my Mummy and Daddy to collect two." I pointed out that there was more than one method of acquiring a family and that his little friend had been telling the truth about his own family.

Time raced by and soon Helen was walking and talking, displaying these skills as precociously as Ian had done. They had now reached the stage of inventing imaginary roles. Often David, bearing a toy stethoscope, heard the other two demanding his attention because of their various ailments. In readiness, he had placed a large cardboard box at the bottom of our open-plan staircase and, after a cursory use of the stethoscope, he always prescribed a brief stay in the cardboard box, which the other two very much enjoyed for some weird reason. Another excitement resulted from attacks on the imaginary castle, where Princess Juliet, alias Helen,

258

resided with her baby — a favourite doll. She would emerge from their newly-constructed playroom and, plaintively, announce, "Those gangster boys are trying to kill my baby." She and the doll enjoyed the subsequent obligatory cuddle.

Ian had probably been the youngest to express himself in complete, clearly articulated sentences. He had long refused to call Fred "Daddy", giving him the name "Grandad", but, before that, his preference was for "Fred!" A very early sentence coming from his bedroom was, "Teddy's wet, Fred!" The next night, it was, "I've been sick, Fred!" On both occasions he was quite accurate with his facts. His vocabulary quickly expanded, sometimes inappropriately. I was washing the lunchtime dishes, when I heard David call from the cloakroom, "Mummy, will you wipe my bottom, please?" I dried my hands and hurried to satisfy my son's demands. Having washed my hands, I returned to my chore, whereupon the silvery tones of Helen proclaimed a similar need. I followed the same routine and, once again, had just resubmerged my hands in the sink, when the less dulcet tones of Ian voiced the instruction, "Mum, come and wipe my bottom." I decided that he would have to wait until I had finished the washing-up. Twice more he repeated his request and twice more I ignored him, when he yelled, "Will someone come and wipe my bloody bottom!" I ran to the little blackguard and performed my duty: when Fred returned home from school, I warned him that he would have to buy me a dishwasher. He was surprised at my urgent request and I explained the way in which

259

Ian's language was deteriorating and I needed to be jet-propelled in order to avoid a further growth in his use of expletives.

For the coming Christmas, we had large paper sacks prepared for Santa. The boys helped me to name theirs and, when it was Helen's turn, we could not use the name Helen under any circumstances, because Father Christmas knew that her name was really Juliet. This was during the period in her young life when her wish was my command. At about 16 months, she had a terrible attack of what the doctor told us was bronchitis. He prescribed an antibiotic and she made a gradual recovery but, on the first dreadful night of her infection, I had to hold her upright for hours while she gasped for breath. Our relief at her recovery was short-lived: two weeks later, another attack occurred, equally as appalling as the first, with the same medication repeated. So followed the same pattern through to the ensuing July. It was so predictable that I asked the doctor if we should go on holiday, as intended, when we were due to visit Margaret Garvie in Tooting, where she was Principal of the Furzedown Training College, and thence to Cromer. We don't think that Helen would have survived had he instructed us not to go: he gave me her normal medicine in powder form and told me to add water when required. After one peaceful night in Margaret's house, we took the children to Battersea Park, where Fred did some boating with the boys, while Helen and I admired the dinosaurs. We went on to Wimbledon, where we bought my mother's birthday present and into a department store for lunch. Suddenly, we heard that much-dreaded rasping from Helen and realised that we must return to our friend's house to deal with the antibiotic. Margaret was at home when we arrived and, having taken one look at our little girl, announced that she was not happy for Helen to be in her house without some medical supervision. To our delight, she asked permission to call in the College doctor, from whom we were ready to look for a second opinion. A towering, tweed-clad doctor, with a marked Scottish accent soon appeared and, having taken one look at Helen, snarled at me, "What the hell do you think you are doing, woman? That child requires oxygen urgently." Promptly, he telephoned St. George's Hospital in Tooting and, having booked an oxygen-tent for our daughter, instructed us to drive straight there. Leaving the boys with Margaret, we followed his directions and were soon in the ward where Helen was placed straight into the tent. It was wonderful to see some improvement in her condition, but the staff told us she would have to be admitted. They reassured me by telling me that I could stay with her all the time and offered me a small bedroom which could be mine for as long as Helen had to remain. We both felt that, perhaps, Helen would now receive more constructive attention, as we were weary of our GP's inevitable response whenever he was asked if more could be done for her: his one reply was, "Oh dear, I do hope that she will not be a chesty child!" Fred returned home to Margaret's to take over the boys and to collect a few necessities for Helen and me. Totally exhausted, I slept for a long time that first night and was horrified to learn, the following morning, that there had been a brief spell during the night when they feared that Helen would have to be resuscitated. I asked why they had not come for me, but they assured me that the emergency did not last very long.

I shall never forget the days that ensued. Helen was in a ward with a boy of 8 or 9, severely disabled by cerebral palsy, totally incapable of movement or speech. There was also a boy of 12/14 months, whose only difficulty, the nurses told me, was his habit of ruminating. Another little boy was suffering with a "flu-like" infection, but his mother was incapable of administering his medication correctly. He required four doses of an antibiotic during every 24 hours, but it had been discovered that the mother had been giving all four doses together, so the child had been admitted to rectify his treatment. It soon became obvious to me why the first boy ruminated: his parents came for no more than 20 minutes each evening and spent their time hugging and kissing each other, totally ignoring their beautiful little boy. After a few visits, the mother said that she had heard Helen talking to me and asked if I would take her child off her hands, because he would not talk for her: I had to control my indignation at her stupidity whilst I explained to her that Helen was approaching two, whereas her boy could not be expected to talk very much at his age. All that was really wrong with that child, I think, was that he received no attention from his parents. The incompetent mother of the other boy would arrive noisily, with a horde of children, all of whom were sucking on iced lollies. She

262

would then give a lolly to her sick little boy. She told me she only gave him tea in his bottle at home and added that he only ate sweets. Poor kids!

I rapidly noticed how busy the nurses were and happily took over the tending of the two little boys, as well as Helen. One day, I was asked to organise a walk-in cupboard where they had shelves full of donated children's clothing: dealing with such a mountain became an onerous chore. Fred and the boys came about lunchtime every day, as well as in the early evening. The nurses loved our family and were delighted to see our two healthy, intelligent boys. They always saved puddings for them at lunch and, one day, a nurse inattentively left a large bowl of stewed pears: before we noticed it, David had scoffed the entire contents of the bowl. He adored cooked pears and had made good use of the large serving spoon. As I walked along the corridor outside the ward, where most of my day was spent, I always looked at a poor little mite in an individual side-ward, who lay festooned with a multitude of tubes. A passing nurse stopped one day and explained that the baby's illness was terminal. I noticed that the child's name was pasted on one of the side windows and it was thus that I learned her name was Rebecca Peaceful. When Fred came that evening, I took him to see the lovely child, who always produced a brave little smile if her eye caught yours. It was really love at first sight for both of us and I said we should ask for another little girl as soon as Helen was cured and that she should be our Rebecca. Eventually, we were told that Helen had a collapsed lung and that, on our return to Lancashire, she must be placed in the care of a paediatrician. We succeeded in getting the same specialist in whose care David had been placed and he agreed to supervise Helen's treatment. He treated her with prophylactic antibiotics for three months, thus giving time for her lung to expand and for her health to be completely restored.

A letter was soon written to the Adoption Society upon our return to Lancashire, because already the gap between the third and fourth child had become twice as long as between the others, Helen's ill-health having caused the delay. In the nick of time, we were offered a beautiful little girl, who was already producing ravishing smiles at the age of three weeks, an accomplishment she has always kept. We eventually collected Becky the following June and I have always felt that she was the best birthday present I ever received. Like Helen, she was always a very contented baby and I valued my conversion to baby girls. Becky was one of very few babies now available through our Society and girls had always been more in demand than boys. When we learned how few babies were now being offered for adoption, we thanked our lucky stars. The change was the result of the introduction of legal abortion and my heart bleeds for childless couples who have been beset with failure because of the rarity of available babies. More than that, I am angry on behalf of those babies who have been denied life, rejected by their mothers-to-be and victims of the surgeon's knife. How many precious people have been lost to our world because of this — incipient artists, authors, scientists, teachers! When I think of the achievements of the four babies who were entrusted to us, my blood boils for those aborted embryos and for all those poor members of Fred's race who died in the Holocaust.

Helen and I had a new dimension to enjoy in our lives, but the boys started nagging for a dog. For some time, we turned a deaf ear. Unfortunately, Fred was accosted by the school Lab Assistant, who told him that her pedigree poodle had escaped while in season and had had an illicit encounter with a terrier. The consequence was a litter of unsaleable puppies: tentatively, she suggested that our children would enjoy owning one. As Fred passed this information to me, Ian, as ever, was eavesdropping and immediately broadcast the offer to the rest of the family. Inevitably, the following Saturday we all trooped to Nelson for a viewing. Only two of the litter remained — a tawny, shaggy mongrel, taller than his completely black brother. We could and should have predicted the outcome of this — David wanted the rough-haired puppy and Ian the roguish, black, curly-haired one. An argument ensued and, finally, we succumbed to Mrs. Riley's suggestion: we crazily took them both, adoption being our habit. Great discussions took place about names, David eventually deciding on Dylan and Ian on Dougal, demonstrating their allegiance to the Magic Roundabout. How our life was transformed — and not for the better — as we paid for our temporary brainstorm. Because there were two of them, we failed dismally with toilet training and it was not our good fortune to corroborate Mrs. Riley's claim that they were well on the way to being civilised. They displayed an infuriating capacity for destruction — I still begrudge the two beautiful baby dresses torn to shreds, a toilet-roll chewed, its residue widely littering the lounge carpet and furniture and Ian's prized new toy fire-engine, converted into an almost unrecognisable, mangled lump of metal (a birthday present received only about one hour and a half before). Weary of filth and devastation, we tried tying them up outside, but returned from our shopping to be greeted by irate neighbours, who remonstrated bitterly because the monsters had barked incessantly all the time we were absent. We were devastated to see the damage the dogs had wrought in our garden. Another setback occurred when Fred took them to school and found Dougal eating rat-poison, which had been placed there by the caretaker. The dog was rushed to a vet, who gave the offender an emetic. A few days later, that crazy creature slipped his collar and ran to investigate the foundations for a house, where he succeeded in impaling his throat on some reinforcing metal rods. Once again, we were faced with a vet's bill. At this point, that dog changed from sheer stupidity to malice, taking to growling and snapping. His final folly was once more to slip his collar and run into a passing car but, on this occasion, he was virtually unscathed. After all these setbacks, Dylan escaped our control on one occasion and was missing overnight and most of the following day. He came slinking into the house during the evening and cowered under the dining table, around which were seated some dinner guests. An abominable aroma filled the air and we noticed that he had been rolling in cow-dung. I tried to persuade him to emerge from his retreat, whereupon he was disgustingly sick. We were growing extremely disheartened and, almost immediately, on his late night walks with them, Fred, forlornly hoping that he would thus avoid the piles of faeces the following morning, began to experience what he diagnosed as breathlessness. At first, he was, as usual, dismissive, asserting that he probably had a chest infection or indigestion, but he reluctantly succumbed to my persuasion and our new GP, Dr. Alam, a very clever diagnostician, came to the house to see Fred. Having listened to the description of his symptoms, he examined Fred and then explained that it was not really up to him to reach such a conclusion, but he was confident that there was a heart problem and that Fred should see a consultant. We arranged an appointment promptly and were horrified to learn that Dr. Alam's diagnosis was accurate, as he appeared to be suffering from an angina of exertion. Just prior to this discovery, the longed for letter about a baby girl had arrived, inviting us to visit her in her foster home. Each of the children was permitted to hold her and arrangements for collecting her were going ahead when the shock about Fred's health came. Our first thought was to consult our GP, to find out whether we should continue to add to our family and I remember his words so clearly, "if you were pregnant with this baby yourself, Mrs. Austin, you could scarcely send it back. Mr. Austin, there are thousands of men leading normal lives and having no idea that they have serious health problems. You know now exactly what

267

your condition is and will adjust to it sensibly. Of course, you should take the child." It was with immense joy that we then took that familiar route to where our new treasure was handed over to us. We called her Rebecca Marie — Rebecca for the baby in St. George's Hospital and Marie for my mother, who asked us to change from Mary, her second name, to Marie, which she thought was prettier. How we gloated when all four were assembled in our own home! The only cloud to marr our contentment was Fred's newly-diagnosed heart condition.

In the meantime, a friend of ours, Ron, the husband of Marge and an ex-colleague of Fred's from Bordesley Green, living just a few miles away, was a very gifted craftsman and he offered to build a playroom on the back of the house, using Fred as his labourer. Progress was swift until Fred had to give up, having developed a tennis elbow. Always a joker, Ron found one of the children's toy tennis racquets and nailed it to the back wall of the house, which was now surrounded by the new structure. He did a wonderful job for us and the children were enchanted with their new domain and its bottom-warming floor, since it had under-floor heating built in. We laid a vinolay covering, ideal for their age-group: the design included road layouts, perfect for playing with Dinky and Matchbox cars and, elsewhere, there was Ludo and Snakes and Ladders on the vinolay. It was a great assistance on the countless very rainy days which had, hitherto, impeded their play and our lounge was no longer constantly littered during the day. Dr. David was no longer practising medicine, so the cardboard box sickroom no longer remained at the foot of the stairs. The large toy-box on wheels, which Fred had constructed a couple of years earlier, now resided in the playroom. The children also had an outside attraction, built by Fred on the lawn, known as his folly, but, in reality, a climbing-frame copied from Galt's catalogue. Helen was particularly fond of climbing to the top and, one day, she succeeded in escaping there without her nappy. For once, she was not the victim of her siblings, for she was able to cover Ian in an unexpected shower, as he loitered beneath her. This misdemeanour he found hard to forgive.

Before he was 5, David started at Park Infants in Colne. It was not too difficult to deliver him there, as we were still taking Ian to the Nursery. We were attracted to the Park School method of teaching reading, where they learned more symbols than in our normal alphabet, but the pupils succeeded in reading much more quickly with the ITA method, where each symbol had just one corresponding sound. David made very swift progress and was soon able to transfer to normal orthography. He was, however, easily discouraged by the number work, his teacher having told him that he lacked ability in that direction. Her approach marred his early number experience, but his true ability was quite apparent to his later teachers. One wintry afternoon, Helen and I arrived in Colne and, glancing at my watch, I realised that it was far too early to collect Ian, so we dawdled round Colne's tiny Indoor Market. Time seemed to be dragging until, suddenly, it dawned on me that my watch had stopped: I hurriedly drove to the Nursery, where I grabbed a bewildered Ian, the only child still in the school. We rushed to David's school and saw him all alone in the entrance. He hurled himself at me, pummelling me ferociously. When he could be persuaded to account for his anger, he explained that he had been bullied by a group of unpleasant classmates, who had snatched off his new anorak and stuffed it down the lavatory. It was drenched and the poor boy was shivering with cold. He did, however, subsequently, have the good fortune to strike up a friendship with a little boy called Peter, whose mother once invited David to their house for his tea. He was so thrilled and, after I collected him and was driving him home, he told me that, if I could only make apple pie like Peter's mother, he would always eat it. I asked him what was so different and his reply was, "The pastry was lovely: it was just like cardboard!" One day, when we picked him up at school, he was chanting, "Burnley, boom-boom-boom" repeatedly. When he tired of this, he asked, "Mummy, what is a Burnley, boom-boom-boom?" He had not, at that stage, been initiated in the world of football.

Eventually, Ian joined David at Park, where David had become devoted to Mr. Sunter, the Headmaster, and when we asked him the reason for this, he told us he really liked the trousers Mr. Sunter wore. As the latter sported really old-fashioned garments, we found David's fascination even more amusing. On the drive home, one afternoon, Helen, in her newly-acquired gruff voice, asked how many children Mr. Sunter had. I told her that he had only one boy, who was a pupil in her Daddy's school. In a tone of extreme disgust, she announced, "Well, he better "induct" another one, then." In those early days of his education, Ian raced ahead with ITA reading books, although he was later slowed down by decisions made on his behalf when we transferred to Dudley.

Although Fred had a secure job, his salary, like those of other Heads was none too generous and, with four children, we were beginning to feel the need to pinch and scrape. I continued to produce clothing for myself and the children, but decided to take up a firm's invitation to arrange party-plan evenings. I had the foresight to buy my selection of samples (non-returnable) in sizes and styles which I could use for our family, in due course. Though I hated the role of saleswoman, I was reasonably successful and managed to take over the responsibility for paying our rates bill. I had already withdrawn my teacher's superannuation in order to pay for the playroom, knowing that I could repay this in monthly instalments, once I was free to return to teaching.

Not far into the year 1970, David staggered into our bedroom a little earlier than usual and told us he was ill. We were horrified when he related how he had passed the night with repeated vomiting. I asked him why he had not come to wake me and his reply was, "You have to have your sleep, Mummy," which brought tears to our eyes. He told us his head really hurt and I found he was cold, his face ashen. We telephoned at once for our doctor and were delighted to see Dr. Alam at our door in no time at all. He examined David and

271

then asked to use our phone. We heard him request an ambulance and then he suggested we had clothing and other things that David would need in hospital ready for its arrival. I was permitted to accompany my little boy, whilst Fred delivered the other three to an ever-obliging friend, so that he could join David and me at Burnley General Hospital. We were reassured by the efficiency of the staff, but I was horrified to learn that David would have to have a lumbar puncture. I had read about this procedure in a novel and had learned that it was an excruciating experience. I was so worried for David, as he lay obediently in silence on the hospital bed! The process was almost complete when he quietly moaned, "Ohh". I was amazed at his cool response and courage.

We soon learned that David was suffering from meningitis and that news filled me with terror, as I feared possible brain damage, which might affect his undoubted ability. He, who had accepted this experience so patiently, proved a menace when it came to taking medicine orally, a phobia he had displayed many times when the GP prescribed medicine. In despair over his urgent need for treatment, his nurses felt obliged to give him injections, which he accepted in a totally relaxed way. Fortunately, this horrible condition was defeated with some alacrity. Whilst David was in the hospital, friends constantly appeared on our doorstep with gifts for him and, daily, I visited a small toy shop on his behalf. The day dawned when I asked him if there was anything that he particularly wanted me to bring on my second visit and his response was, "I would love a large piece of Edam cheese to eat without bread". I was filled with hope for his now certain recovery and, as the day of his discharge approached, we listened with relief to the information that the meningitis he had suffered was mumps-meningitis, a strain that caused no brain damage. To celebrate this news, I bought him a toy that he had long coveted — Matt Mason. Little could I know that, with that purchase, I engendered Ian's first act of rebellion and, for a few hours after David's return home, I became a very forlorn woman. On arrival, David was naturally anxious to display his newly-acquired trophies — gifts galore that had arrived in hospital. When, eventually, he brought out his Matt Mason, Ian, in a tone of utter disgust, proclaimed, "Now, that is the last straw! I am leaving." He raced upstairs, where we could hear him moving around at a great pace: he soon emerged, bearing a diminutive suitcase. "I am going to live with Auntie Joyce!" he announced and asked his father to drive him there. How I wanted to dissuade him from leaving: but he was adamant. Fred, quite unperturbed, took him to Joyce, who was just as matter-of-fact about it as Fred had been. When he returned, we tried to make that morning as routine as usual. As I served lunch, I longed to fetch Ian home, but his father insisted that I should not intervene. By mid-afternoon, I could no longer withstand the temptation to go, first, to the toy shop to buy another Matt Mason, and then to Joyce's house. I was ushered into the kitchen and when Joyce explained that her son, Simon, and Ian were in the lounge, she brought me up-to-date with

Ian's comments. His first question to her had been, "Where do you keep your car, Auntie Joyce?" and then, "Where is the playroom?" and, finally, "Where will you go on holiday this year?" To each enquiry, she responded in her lovely Lancashire accent that they had none of those luxuries in their lives. He had told her of his decision to change his name from Ian Christopher Austin to Christopher Bryan Green. That was just too much for me and I was about to rush into the lounge, when Ian walked into the kitchen. He was obviously surprised, as he said, "Hello, Mum, I mean Mrs. Austin." "How are you?" I asked him, thus opening the flood-gates and, as his tears subsided, he whimpered, "I think I'll come back home now. Simon Green won't let me play with any of his toys." Joyce later told me that he had asked if the Greens had a caravan and, when he learned that they also lacked that luxury, he said he intended to come to our house and help us load up when we were going away. Once in the car, I presented him with his new Matt Mason: the week was beginning to improve, with David's recovery and Ian's return, leaving only Helen with mumps and Becky with baby diarrhoea. The doctor had contemplated having Becky also admitted to hospital, but, fortunately, we were spared that.

Ian was the only one left attending school and another neighbour kindly collected him for me. There had been snow and severe frosts that week — a further trial — but, after school, Ian leaped out of the neighbour's car and rolled happily on our snowy front lawn. My neighbour was full of concern, but she calmed down when I said, "Leave him. He's the only healthy one I have and I want him to enjoy himself." The following Tuesday morning, Ian sported an obviously mumps-swollen face, which he bitterly resented. Fortunately, he, Helen and Becky, all made speedy recoveries and David's convalescence went well, too. David's departure from Burnley General ended for ever our visits there, though, some time before that, I had spent one night there for a minor operation and I had also made use of their Accident & Emergency Dept, when my doctors directed me there after I had been bitten, quite without malice, by one of our guinea-pigs: I think she mistook my finger for the carrot I was holding out for her.

We had been generously treated by the husband of our neighbour opposite, when he suggested that we borrow his caravan for a week or so, to encourage us to invest in something similar for our holidays. We took ourselves to Rhyl, where we decided that this type of break was ideal for a family like ours. Once we arrived, however, I was stricken with excruciating pain in my gums. Fred found a dentist quickly, as we were afraid that it was another dental abscess. We were told, however, that my upper gums had receded considerably, though the teeth were all quite healthy. As we were there so briefly, he recommended that I see a dentist once we returned to Lancashire. The choice of dentist proved to be a big mistake: he claimed it was essential that he extracted all of my upper set. He booked our doctor as anaesthetist when both were available to deal with my teeth. Sadly, it never occurred to either Fred or me that it might be wiser to seek a second opinion, but we were too concerned about my sudden and swift loss of weight and my lack of energy to delay the treatment, since the pain discouraged me from eating and drinking. Our priority had to be that I was well enough to look after the children. The deed was soon done and a denture inserted immediately into my mouth, a source of lasting disappointment, though the dentures later provided by Birmingham Dental Hospital are a jewel compared with that earlier encumbrance. My appetite was immediately restored; the moment we returned to the house, where my mother had stayed with our children, I astounded her as well as myself by consuming a great plateful of fish and chips, purchased on the way home and, that evening, I even managed a pork chop!

We followed up our neighbour's suggestion and bought a caravan — smaller than the one we had borrowed, but with an addition which was an important feature for me — an oven to add to the normal hob. Our first excursion fulfilled a dream I had long harboured: a return to those places I had so loved during the war in 1939-45. We first spent a couple of days in the garden belonging to my dear school friend, Avril, now married to George. Although I was well supplied with provisions, Avril refused to listen to my protestations and insisted we shared all the generous meals she produced for us and her own five children. She put on a display of real northern hospitality. She even insisted on mugs of hot cocoa and cake for Fred and me, before we joined our sleeping children in the caravan. Later, I proudly conducted the family around Axwell Park, still very beautiful, except for the emergence of rather ugly council houses which had been constructed behind the house that we had occupied. The people living there could no longer have the view of the small wood, where I spent so many happy hours in my girlhood. Only one thing blighted my day: David threw the most unexpected and raucous tantrum. Never before or since have we witnessed such a performance from him: we failed entirely to identify any cause for his outburst, so that we could only surmise that it was an aftermath of his dreadful illness earlier that year.

Out of the blue, our lives were about to change once more. Fred heard that his school was to lose its 6th Form and would be transformed into an 11-16 comprehensive school. He was quite unsettled by the news, but soon saw in his "bible", the Times Educational Supplement, an advertisement for the Headship of Dudley Grammar School, due to become a 6th Form College. After almost seven years' experience in a similar post, quite predictably, he was the fortunate candidate at the interview. Much as I loved the many friends we had made in Lancashire and the beauty of much of the countryside, I was delighted at the prospect of renewing my Midland contacts and to see Fred established in a school with such a superb history and a promising future. Furthermore, the new post would provide us with a Headmaster's house at a peppercorn rent.

Before we left the North, we were visited by my College friend Win, her husband and their brood. It

277

was shocking to see the deterioration in Tony's health and, every day, we tried to provide him with a restful period by taking the eight children on a variety of excursions. We were able to offer them the caravan on our drive as a bedroom but had a preference for putting Tony in the playroom where he would have a more peaceful night. Those brief reunion days passed swiftly and it did not occur to us, as we waved them goodbye, that we would never see Tony again since, by the following August, he had died of Hodgkin's disease.

CHAPTER
TWENTY

Caravan Adventure

The summer holidays in Lancashire, because of the Wakes weeks, always started in early July and, when the term ended, we set off for the north of France and Berck-Plage with the caravan and a large, borrowed tent in which Michael, Mavis's 13 year-old son — a late addition to the group — and Fred would sleep. From the word go, that trip was a disaster: Michael had borrowed an old-fashioned, padded sleeping-bag, on which he was horribly sick on the second night. Rain fell incessantly for a few days, so trying to clean and dry that cumbersome bedding proved to be a great trial. Seeing to the laundry became an insuperable problem. At long last, a new morning greeted us with watery sunshine: we wanted to profit from this unexpected relief and made our way to the nearby beach, to the delight of Michael and our three elder ones. I sat on the beach with Becky, who was still not walking and we played with the sand, letting it trickle through our fingers. Suddenly, my heart turned over as I noticed that my solitaire was no longer on my finger. Fred and I scrabbled in the sand in a forlorn effort to find my treasure, but this led to nothing. We reported the loss to the police, returned to the caravan, where I wept all the time, as I made lunch for Fred and the children. Once he had eaten, always Fred's priority, he decreed that we would leave that place of ill-luck and see if we could improve the situation by going to Holland, which could not be worse than Berck-Plage. As we drove along the north coast, I pondered on what the next mishap might be. Eventually, we found the resort recommended by the Caravan Club and were pleased to see that this was a much better organised site, enjoying a spell of fine weather to boot! Ian immediately reconnoitred the area on his bike — a prime necessity for him at all times — and, when he returned, he told us that he had found a playground with swings and other equipment on the fringes of the camp. We enjoyed a relaxed evening meal, despite the fact that I had singed the hair over my forehead and my eyebrows when I endeavoured to light the oven and had had to face a blow-back. The washing up completed and beds organised for the night, we accepted the children's demands and headed for the playground. It provided several ways for the children to enjoy themselves and we gave them the freedom to select whatever attraction appealed. Unfortunately, the 13 year-old Michael chose a spherical climbing apparatus and, within minutes, the inevitable happened. A rusty joint snapped and Michael, lying full-length on the ground, had the weight of the sphere on top of him. With great difficulty, we succeeded in freeing him, but our sighs of relief were premature, for he quickly assured us that he was unable to walk. It was, obviously, quite out of the question for Fred, handicapped by his heart condition, to carry Michael to the car so, that became my ordeal. I managed to install him in the car and then walked back to the caravan with my little crowd, while Fred drove our casualty to the nearby hospital, where he was examined carefully. We learned that he had suffered no serious injury and could return to us at once. In the meantime, when we reached the caravan, I clearly remember saying, "Come on, kids. They say that cleanliness is only next to godliness, so, I'll read you a bible story and you can go straight to bed, the great unwashed." I think my aches and pains, at that point, must have equalled Michael's. By the following morning, there was little evidence of his accident.

The next day, the children very much enjoyed playing on the beach which fringed a large lake, not far from where the caravans were parked. Becky, unable to walk, was jet-propelled in crawling, so that my day was spent in careering across sand and scrubby, coarse grass to intercept her before she plunged into the lake. She gave a good demonstration that she was to be a water-baby and, very soon afterwards, we discovered that she could swim before being able to walk. Helen and Ian, inevitably, were wet through in no time at all and proudly displayed their splendid achievement. A mishap was bound to follow: within two days they had both developed large patches of skin which were red and running with fluid. Once again, Fred went to find medical help for the two of them and learned that they both had impetigo — a result of their contact with what proved to be dirty lake water. As we had to ban them from all contact with the playground and the lake, we decided to take them into the nearby town. By this time, Ian had developed a further condition — botulitis — which transformed him into a puppy-like creature, unable to pass a tree or a street corner without the inevitable consequence. Neither he nor his sister relished the application of the prescribed ointment onto their impetigo so, as three out of the five had problems, we compromised and entered forbidden ground: a toyshop. The girls chose dolls' prams made of cane, the like of which we have never seen elsewhere: we hoped that Becky's would encourage her to walk. The boys chose yachts, despite the fact that the lake was out of bounds.

By this point, some of our food supplies were rapidly diminishing, so we shopped for fruit and vegetables in a market and, though we found bacon horribly expensive in a small grocer's, we discovered that it tasted as good as any we had ever had. As their activities in the camp had, of necessity, become more restricted, despite the fact that Ian had struck up a friendship with a little Dutch boy, who was equally fond of his bicycle, and both were talking freely to each other, one in English and the other in Dutch, and picking up the odd word from each other, we decided to move on. We now headed for Paris and, later, Daniel and Yolande's house in Vigneux-sur-Seine, an arrangement which resulted from their unexpected visit to Foulridge the previous summer. We were looking forward to seeing them again and, especially their little daughter Caroline, exactly the same age as our Helen, whose singing of *Sur le pont d'Avignon* had so enchanted Daniel and Yolande that they had determined to teach it to Caroline as soon as they returned home. As we arrived in Paris a day early, we spent one night on a caravan site in the Bois de Boulogne, where facilities were a great improvement on what we had so far encountered. The accommodation was even better once we reached Daniel's house, where the garage was large enough to house our caravan. Daniel's two elder daughters enjoyed bathing our children, who luxuriated in ample hot water, after their long deprivation. Michael's alarm was very obvious, for he feared that they were about to bath him, but he was relieved to find out that he was mistaken.

Our friends noticed that I had lost a great deal of weight since they were in Lancashire and they went out of their way to make life easier for me. Becky and their Nicolas were similar in age and their two older girls enjoyed having those two babies to look after. Fred and Michael were invited to sleep in the house, while the children and I stayed in the caravan in the garage. The holiday improved by leaps and bounds and we were able to take the three older children on little jaunts, while Becky stayed behind with Yolande and Nicolas. Soon, we were faced with the journey home and our next setback arose as we were leaving, when we discovered that the back door of our Hillman threatened to fall off and, therefore, had to remain locked. When we were half-way to the coast, we stopped at one of the "Aires" on the motorway to consume the picnic which Yolande had provided, but our evacuation was almost immediate, when swarms of wasps wanted to share our meal. We took to the road once more and I started, almost immediately, to be violently sick. For once in my lifetime, I hung out of the car window in order to protect the others from the mess. As if these adversities did not suffice, we were compelled to drive through a frightening thunderstorm and were relieved, finally, to reach a Boulogne camp site, conveniently located for the ferry the next morning. I was still incapacitated, so Fred persuaded me to stay in the car, while he made me a cup of tea and brought me two codeine tablets. As he passed these to me, he told me that he wanted to take me into Boulogne to buy the orange Le Creuset casserole I had admired as we passed through earlier. Plead as I did, I failed to dissuade him, so I drank my tea and, as I put the first tablet into my mouth, I thought how much better than usual it tasted. I swallowed what remained before examining the other pill, whereupon I realised that, mistakenly, he had given me Mogadon, a sleeping pill which I rarely used, but had been prescribed by the doctor for the occasional bout of insomnia. I had always limited myself to a half tablet, so that, when Fred returned, I handed him the second pill and pointed out the folly of attempting to take me into Boulogne: he remained adamant.

So, off we all went and made the purchase, returning to the caravan, where I began to mix instant potato, followed by custard for the dessert. I still recall sleepily stirring the latter, but nothing more. Apparently, sound asleep, I was undressed and put to bed by Fred and Michael. I did not stir until breakfast time the following morning, but managed not to delay our getting on the ferry. Later that day, we returned Michael to his mother in Gainsborough and complimented ourselves on our good luck, finding the car boot door still intact. Our serenity was somewhat shattered by an immediate outburst from Mavis, as soon as she set eyes on us: she had received a communication from the Dutch hospital where Fred had taken Michael and had immediately jumped to the conclusion that we had neglected him. Apart from Vigneux, it was certainly not the most successful holiday in our lives.

Our return to Lancashire, too, had its unpleasant side: almost as soon as we were back home, our friend, Margaret Thomas, died at the age of 41. As one of her executors, Fred was closely involved in sorting out her affairs, as well as winding up his work in the school, whereas I was kept busy, carefully packing what we regarded as our valuables, in readiness for their transportation to Dudley. Fred towed the caravan down to our new home, a useful way of delivering the china and glass. There ensued a period of hectic activity, overshadowed by Margaret's funeral and the farewells to our many friends. Joyce, whom Ian had attempted to appropriate as a new mother, dissolved into tears each time she saw us and I felt guilty at my failure to conceal my pleasure at the thought of returning to the Midlands. The prospect of living in that large house adjacent to the school, was very pleasant, its spaciousness being exactly what I had hoped for as the

285

family increased. It was impossible to envisage the uncomfortable conditions which the next four months would bring in School House. One of the problems we faced when finally loading our car, prior to departure, was producing accommodation for five guinea-pigs, David's budgerigar and two goldfish. All members of our little community were eventually housed in the vehicle and we set off, planning to stop on the outskirts of Blackburn, to partake in the only hot meal of the day in one of the very first Colonel Sanders Kentucky Fried Chicken outlets. We thought the pets had been left securely in the car, but we were greeted by chaos upon our return: David's male guinea-pig, ever assiduous in fulfilling his role as father of the clan, had escaped from his isolation and had had ample time to frolic with the females. Our fears that all four would now be pregnant proved accurate a few weeks later.

CHAPTER
TWENTY-ONE

The Children Grow and Flourish

Once we arrived in Dudley, we were warmly greeted by neighbours, who had a son in the school and had been forewarned of our arrival by the wife of the vicar, not long in Dudley herself, who had been a friend of mine in school in Cleethorpes. These new acquaintances ushered us into their house, where we were given refreshment, with the result that we entered No. 16 as twilight descended. The first setback of our new residence was immediately apparent: our predecessors had had the gas and electricity disconnected. We did our best to wash the children in cold water and then bedded them down on caravan mattresses. The next morning, I saw clean finger marks on the grimy tiles over the bath, the consequence of my putting my hand there the previous evening — how long since they had been cleaned, if ever they were? That morning, an electrician was called to reconnect the electricity and, once the removal-men had brought the gas-range into the kitchen, a gasman came to connect that, too. This was the stove's third home and it gave us stalwart service for another 16 years.

The Saturday and Sunday proved eventful, too: when we turned on the lights, as the evening progressed, alarming flashes and bangs in the fuse-box, located in the hall, resulted in the extinguishing of all our lights. The kind neighbour, who had offered us hospitality the previous night, came to our rescue and revealed skills which Fred neither possessed nor wished to. Our usual beds were now ready for occupation and we fell upon them in sheer exhaustion. Sunday morning brought its own tribulations: the heavy, solid oak door fell out of its frame into the dining room, landing, at an angle, on a packing-case, forming a tunnel where Becky was crawling, so that, by great good fortune, she emerged unscathed. David was not quite so fortunate, for the edge of the door struck his shoulder as it fell. When we took linen up to the airing cupboard, we found a huge nail supposedly holding the airing cupboard front, but several inches of which projected dangerously into the room at children's eye-level — that had to be dealt with immediately! The same day, we discovered the deplorable state of the house all over, so much so that I began to insist that we could not stay there with four young children. It did not take Fred long to contact the Director of Education, who, together with the then Chairman of Governors, came to inspect the scene and they were utterly appalled at what they found. They took immediate steps to call in the Local Authority Building Surveyors and, as a result, it was decided that the house needed rewiring, a new kitchen, which would combine the present breakfast room with the scullery, a relocated bathroom, the removal of the old Rayburn, to be replaced by a gas boiler, sufficient to allow the whole house to be centrally heated, and numerous additions and adaptations to make life there acceptable. All this was to be followed by complete redecoration throughout. A trial of my fortitude ensued, but, after three and a half very difficult months, we were finally clean, redecorated and the carpets we ourselves had bought were fitted in the nick of time for Christmas. We still had the worry of our unsold house in Lancashire, but I was beginning to enjoy No.16. The presence on some days of 14 workmen in the house had been an ordeal, but it had its lighter moments. I constantly heard the Black Country voice of the almost resident carpenter exploding with frustration, as he shouted, "Er's done it again!" He was alluding to Becky's habit of tipping up his container of nails and screws. She was still surprisingly mobile on all fours and fully enjoyed her illicit investigations, especially when paint brushes and cans of paint were left unguarded by the decorators. One day, she gave me a terrible fright when I found her, just in time to prevent her taking a nose-dive down the huge hole she had discovered in the dining room floor, where the workers had lifted up a trap-door. It was quite a drop down to the cellar below. In no uncertain terms, I told them that they must never leave trap-doors open, unless they closed the room door securely. The other children spent their week-days in more palatable conditions, the boys in a highly regarded Primary School and Helen, as a part-timer, in

289

a nearby Nursery School. Becky must have been the dirtiest child in Dudley when bathtime arrived, despite the frequent washes I gave her during the day. Now, the children each had a large, separate bedroom and, later, they were able to satisfy their desire for their favourite music in the privacy of their own domain.

The boys had been tested when admitted to St. Edmund's: David was well in advance of the standards in his age-group and was, therefore, placed in the group above, where he settled down immediately and flourished in his new environment. Ian, unfortunately, did not fare as well, at first, as he had the misfortune of not yet having transferred from the ITA reading scheme, being only five. His progress was on a par with David's at a similar age and he was able to read the ITA texts fluently; however, my request for him to make the normal conversion to standard orthography was immediately rejected, despite my offer to supply the last few ITA readers and Ian was compelled to start the Ladybird scheme from its very beginnings. His unhappiness persuaded me to spend the hour after we had eaten our evening meal training him to change to the school's normal scheme, though I did not inflict the early basic readers on him. He achieved a very high reading age very swiftly and an astonishingly advanced vocabulary. We could foresee a successful future for both boys and Helen, too, was revealing signs of significant ability. A further matter for celebration was that Becky had, finally, decided to get up and walk and her speech flowed freely. We put her delays in both respects down to life in that chaotic house, after the comfort of our home in Lancashire. She began to blossom and, very early, displayed a talent for drawing and other creative pursuits.

Because we were still paying the mortgage on our unsold property, I eventually began to feel the need to contribute to the family income once again. Fate proved generous, when Fred was approached by the Adviser for Remedial and Immigrant education, who had heard of my work with the latter group in Lancashire. He asked if I could work a couple of mornings and I did so gladly, but briefly. We had a very reliable cleaning lady, who agreed to look after Becky while I did my stint of teaching English as a Foreign Language, until, eventually, we had the good news that there was a buyer for the house in Foulridge, after our interminable wait of about 21 months. It was a paltry offer, but we accepted it to be rid of that anxiety.

When I was collecting Helen from the Nursery one day, I was approached by the Headmistress, who asked, "Have you heard your daughter scream?" "Indeed, I have," I replied, fully aware of the volume of noise this tiny girl could produce. She had reserved this potential for home use only until that day when the Headmistress spoke to me. For some time, it had been her habit to yell at the top of her voice out in the back garden and I had been told by the caretaker's wife that she and the school cleaners heard her regular outburst at 3.30 each afternoon. They knew by that signal that it was time to abandon their cups of tea and start on the cleaning.

The welcome we received from the school staff and neighbours was really heart-warming, so that we settled contentedly in our new environment. I was befriended by a lady, whose husband occupied a position in Dudley which brought them both into the public eye. Her friendship ultimately caused me considerable discomfort when she persuaded me to be the Treasurer of a charity of which she was the Chairman. My difficulties arose when she objected to my insistence on keeping detailed accounts. As a newcomer to Dudley, I found myself floundering in this situation until, as usual, Fred rescued me, offering his normal, level-headed advice. I was unable to attend the next committee meeting because of our attending the prize-giving in Nelson, so Fred's solution was that I should select a member of the committee whom, through my early contacts, I felt I could trust and ask him to read a letter, disclosing my difficulties and asking for a vote to see what course the majority of the committee would favour. Knowing when we would return to Dudley, my contact was good enough to telephone me to say that the vote had gone overwhelmingly in my favour. Another quandary solved by Fred!

As that first year progressed in Dudley, Fred developed an air of sadness and anxiety that was not a normal part of his nature. Eventually, I was able to learn that the cause was his own approaching of the age at which his father had died and, despite his habitual optimism, he was apprehensive about his own destiny. His heart problems were increasing and he found it difficult to walk uphill. As the months passed, however, he obviously had overcome these worries and the resulting confidence could have led to his downfall on one occasion. He had travelled to Manchester by train for an examiners' meeting and, having rushed back, he insisted on repeating the journey the following day. That evening, the Parents' Association had arranged a dance and Fred rejected my advice that he was too fatigued to attend. He brushed aside my worries and we went to the dance. Once there, he indulged in his accustomed style of vigorous dancing and I suddenly realised that he was in considerable pain. I asked him where his TNT tablets were and, with a hangdog expression, Fred admitted that they were on the dressing-table in our house. He was persuaded to sit down whilst I raced next door for the pills and found him ashen and weak when I returned. The pill under the tongue brought the usual relief and Fred succumbed to my urging to go home for a rest. I always, at this stage, avoided causing him any stress, if possible, but, the following day, I risked suggesting to him that he should seek further advice from a cardiologist. To my astonishment, he readily agreed and came back home with that doctor's warnings in the forefront of his mind. He was particularly delighted at the consultant's reaction to learning about the dietary restrictions which I had placed upon him. The specialist told him that I was as good as a doctor with my advice. That weekend of panic seemed to fade gradually, though I never lost those niggling fears through the years that followed.

Another worry haunted me. We heard that Philip Austin was somewhere in the Wolverhampton area. Though I was not eager to transmit my anxieties to David and Ian, as I wished them to enjoy the relative safety of the school grounds after school hours and during the school holidays, I was still vigilant and, without being explicit, asked our caretaker and groundsmen to keep a fatherly eye on them as they played. Helen was soon one of their companions and heaven help anyone who tried to intimidate either her or one of her brothers. One day, she was approached by a few of the Grammar School boys who asked, "Is Lumpy your Dad?" and she realised that they were being insensitive about the lump which Fred had developed on his forehead. Raising her clenched, but still tiny fists, she adopted an aggressive stance and threatened them with, "Don't you call my Daddy that!" Later, one of the boys concerned described her valour to me, as he had noticed that the offending blemish had been surgically removed. She very frequently displayed her quick thinking and courage: they had been indoctrinated never to accept sweets from strangers and, having completely absorbed this instruction, when a man invited them to take some sweets, Helen retaliated with her ear-piercing scream, inducing him to make a hasty exit. She came home at once to boast of her achievement.

Upon our arrival in Dudley, all four of them gradually became involved in the Sunday School at St. James's Church and, one by one, they joined the church choir. Whilst Ian was quite a newcomer to the choir, on New Year's Day, 1976, we heard of the death of Fred's Deputy, Wilf Clarke. That evening, whilst the boys were at choir practice, we were both still in a very tearful state, though I managed to conceal this when I heard them running along the side of the house towards the back door. I hurried to intercept them in the kitchen in order to explain that Daddy was very upset and was sitting very quietly in the lounge. Ian followed me and proferred a 10 pence piece to Fred, explaining that it was his choir pay, the first money he had ever earned in his life, and he wanted Fred to have it. Graciously, Fred accepted, as we both had faces dripping with tears. Not long afterwards, a neighbouring doctor, who had quite often stopped Ian on his way back from church to present him with one of his excess diaries or a coin or two, died equally unexpectedly. By this time, Ian was distraught and wailed "All our friends are dying." He was always the most sociable of our children and remains so to this day, though his siblings might dispute this claim.

Eventually, each one of them took up a musical instrument: Ian, with his tuba, proved the least enthusiastic or talented. Before his "O" levels, David had achieved Grade 5 on the piano; Helen was placed in the Dudley Festival with her violin and Becky's flute gave her a great deal of pleasure: in addition, both girls became quite skilful with the recorder. David had made great strides academically and succeeded in passing the entrance examination to King Edward's in Birmingham, where his ability continued to be apparent. The other three, in time, joined our school, though, by 1975, its

295

status had radically changed, as well as its pupil population. I now worked as a teacher in the newly-created Dudley School, into which the Girls' High School and two small Secondary Moderns had been absorbed.

I detested this transformation, which caused Fred a much increased workload, where he strove to produce a sound educational establishment, with greatly swollen numbers. My disapproval was far from groundless, as his health began to deteriorate rapidly; although they were quite apparent to me, few other people knew of the problems he was contending with. I also felt great concern for the children's well-being: we could live in our house for as long as Fred was in situ, but we accepted that, if he was forced to retire on health grounds, we would have to leave and, if he were to die, we could be homeless immediately. Meagre as our savings were, we decided to ask the Governors to sell us the property in which we were so happily settled, to give us a greater feeling of security. This request met with hard-hearted opposition, particularly from one businessman of sour and grudging disposition, who had considerable influence over his colleagues. Several meetings led to numerous rejections until, regretfully, we started house-hunting elsewhere. We soon found a property, not at all what we had come to require, but perhaps almost adequate. We put in an offer and Fred straightaway notified the Chairman of Governors of our plans. The latter revealed that he was flabbergasted by saying, "What do you expect us to do with that property?" referring to School House, and immediately altered his approach to the Governing Body. It did not take them long to reverse their earlier decisions and, soon, the District Valuer arrived at a price which we felt able to accept, having already received approval from a Building Society for a mortgage. I was encouraged to take out an endowment assurance policy to cover the mortgage because of our uncertainty concerning Fred's health. We paid interest only, allowing us to make regular savings over the coming years, in the expectation of paying off the mortgage completely when we came to sell the house. As we had the blessing of Fred's continuing survival, I then paid the insurance policy until its maturity, and it proved a very good investment, allowing me to pay off the mortgage and buy Fred a new car with the surplus.

Once the house was securely ours, my desires for further improvements were gradually met: in order to liberate the main lounge for the children whenever we were entertaining, we built an extension onto the dining area, to provide an additional lounge, above which we added a guest bedroom and a new bedroom for Becky. Her original room was then converted into a second bathroom, purely for the girls and the occasional guest.

We had already replaced our first caravan with a larger, more spacious model, offering a good-size oven and a refrigerator, a real boon. Our annual holiday in France had become a regular affair, although we sampled caravaning in the north of Spain, not far from Santander on one occasion. That visit provided the opportunity for all the family to see the cave paintings in the mountains, though the children were too young to retain the memory: we two, on the other hand, found the paintings most impressive. Some summers later, we bought an addition for the van — an awning — to enable us to take our dear friend, Auntie Millie, first to Brittany, where we collected Ian and Helen, who had been there on an exchange, and then to the Dordogne. Millie, despite her advancing years, thoroughly enjoyed her holiday and was first-rate at grabbing and hand-washing any smalls she found lying around and in entertaining the children with card games in the back of the car when we were travelling long distances. Fred had joined the Dudley Rotary Club in 1973, which led to a very pleasant expansion in our social life: so many of the friendships consequently formed have lasted well and later extended to further friendships in Brest, once that club — Cote des Legendes — was twinned with Dudley. We have many happy memories of the hospitality we received there and, on that occasion, Millie, too, was welcomed. We all enjoyed being on Daniel and Yolande's superb estate in the Dordogne, where they insisted, despite our protestations, that the caravan was superfluous to requirements and all of us, except the camping boys, were brought into the house. It was very pleasant to become acquainted with their rural way of life and we were introduced to many of the delicacies of the region whenever we went there. During one of our stays in later years, in addition to being plagued by his heart condition, Fred, having developed problems with his gall bladder, despite my insistence on his fat-free diet, was unable to restrain himself from eating the main dish, guinea-fowl, lavishly drenched in oil. Not long after we had retired, he was writhing in dreadful agony, a consequence of indulging in that rich and oily dish. As he was finding the pain unbearable, I sought out Daniel, still in the lounge and asked him to examine Fred, since I was afraid that the problem might extend to his heart. He quickly discovered that Fred was passing a gall-stone and, without further ado, drove to the chemist in Mussidan, persuaded the poor man out of his bed and acquired some pain-killing injections. The first of these was ineffectual, but a further effort proved successful and Fred was able to rest and, eventually, to sleep. That ordeal liberated me from the need to nag Fred about food, and once we were back in Dudley, we made an appointment with a kindly and skilful surgeon, who quickly arranged to operate on Fred.

During the years between 1972 and 1984, I was able to return to the classroom, at first the odd two or three mornings a week teaching my overseas boys English, but, in '73, I worked in a small primary school, having received an SOS from the Headmistress. Towards the end of that school year, I was appointed to an English post at the Girls' High School, where I settled with delight, enjoying the contact with superb colleagues and encouragingly motivated girls. I felt honoured to be working there and regularly assured Fred that I would go there willingly every day, even if there was no monthly cheque to reward me. Once more, my social horizons were enlarged and my educational frontiers reopened. Conscientious as I was in my work, I did, however, welcome the salary, which enabled me to meet the expenses of David's education for the next five years at King Edward's. He richly deserved the opportunities which that school afforded him, though, after five years of bus travel to and from Birmingham, he was suffering frequent bouts of crippling back pain. Naturally, we sought medical help, but the only result was a prescription for a support corset, which our son largely refused to wear. As he was approaching the "O" level examinations, his back troubles became more insistent and we suggested that he would perhaps feel better if he transferred into our 6th Form, a suggestion which he eventually accepted. We were all satisfied that he would not suffer academically by joining our 6th Form in Dudley.

Despite the success of our caravan holidays, previously described, 1978 was a disappointment because of the dominating bad weather, causing us to reach the decision that we would sell the caravan and use the proceeds to fund a holiday in the USA in the summer of 1979. The main purpose was to enable the children to meet Fred's relatives over there, to learn a little of American life and to visit areas on the Eastern seaboard. The American trip was a great success: the children received so much love from their newly-found relatives and responded with similar affection. Though all but one of the relatives has since died, the children's memories of life with them are still precious. Fred and I were blessed with an unlooked for freedom, for, whenever they asked if we could buy them jeans or some other item, we were always able to say, "Yes", since the rate of exchange gave us 2.25 dollars to the

£1, thus cutting down considerably on their long faces if we had to say, "No".

During the summer of 1980, the holiday began with a group visit to Clyro, each of the children being allowed to bring a companion: David invited Andrew from the school he was just leaving and Martin Yates, the son of a colleague in the Dudley School, who would be a contemporary of his in the 6th Form. Torsten, a German boy, whom we had accommodated for several months with no great enjoyment, was also in the group because his parents pleaded with us to hold on to him for two or three more weeks. We were housed in the Dudley School's Outdoor Pursuits Centre, a small converted primary school which the Governors had recently bought for that purpose and we planned to visit points of interest in the area. Our only problem was the German boy, who irritated every one of us and was tormented by all. Becky's little friend, Katie, an only child, had a few mild attacks of homesickness, aggravated by the visit of her over-anxious parents, who took her back home with them. To keep Helen company, we had also taken our lovely "Fifth child", Pamela, who was always capable of cheering everybody up. Our beloved mongrel, Tramp, was also there and thoroughly enjoyed all that was going on, as much as all the youngsters did. They appreciated our home cooking in the well-equipped kitchen which Fred and I had set up at the time of the remodelling of the building. Across the road from us, a potter of Yugoslav origin, a Mr. Dworsky, had his workshop and sales centre and I became both a customer and a great admirer of his work: three of his icons, a hand-moulded lady's head and a hand-painted box, done in the Swiss style, have all found their way into our possession.

A few days after our return, having made a prior arrangement with a gynaecologist, I was admitted to New Cross Hospital in Wolverhampton, ostensibly for a D&C, but, unexpectedly, to undergo a hysterectomy. Before the operation, I recognised one of our ex-pupils, who had created problems for many of her teachers, but with whom I had maintained a good relationship. The nurses found her difficult to contend with, but could not discharge her, since she was refusing to eat. To help them, I employed one of my devious tricks and pretended I was too shy to collect a meal from the trolley and eat alone: immediately, she sprang to my aid and offered to eat her meal beside me. As a consequence, she ate a substantial evening meal and a hearty breakfast, giving them the chance to be rid of her. A few days after my major operation, I was transferred to a different ward which was unbearably hot, being located above an overheated geriatric unit. I managed to escape this uncomfortable place on the 8th day by explaining to the consultant that my husband was coping at home with our four children, but insisted on visiting me twice daily despite the distance from our house to New Cross, his serious heart condition and his responsibilities in school. The ward sister was livid about the success of my ploy, but I could not be concerned about her, for I wanted to be at home to support the most important person in my life. Before I left, I was instructed to take three months off school to convalesce — some hope! The day after my release, the "A" level results came through and I insisted on being in the Visual Aids Room to give my students their grades. Waxen of face and halting in step, I was soon greeted by a lovely 6th former, the son of a friend who lived opposite to us: seeing how feeble I was, he offered me his arm and assisted me on my way in, where my anxious pupils waited. The success rate in English was superb that year. Together, we enjoyed the euphoria of the moment, until I was accosted by a colleague who told me forthrightly that I looked ghastly. "Hardly surprising," I replied, "as I had a hysterectomy just a week ago!" She remonstrated with me and pointed out that, after her similar operation, she did nothing foolhardy for the decreed three months, but I knew I would not do the same, because of the children and Fred's ill-health. 27 years later, I feel no remorse for my decision. I did receive a dressing-down from my GP, a very dear friend of ours, when he learned that I was back in school full-time at the beginning of the autumn term, but we reached a happy compromise when he agreed that I could teach all my 5th and 6th Form periods, if I rested for the remainder of each day. It took me a while to pluck up my courage to tell Eric (my GP) that, at the end of October, together with all the family, I was to go on the schools cruise as a working teacher. He teased me, saying that I was impossible, but continued to be my attentive and most affectionate doctor.

David had splendid "O" level results and, fortunately, was unperturbed by the prospect of changing to comprehensive school education after his five years in the refined atmosphere of King Edward's in Edgbaston, especially since his transfer released him from all his bus travel and enabled him to join all of us on the November cruise. It was normal practice to give the cruise groups all kinds of information about our forthcoming visits and to emphasise the type of records they were expected to keep. Although Becky was not yet in the school, she was allowed to attend these after-school classes: one such day, she rushed home and demanded to know how they were going to sail that enormous cruise-ship up the river to Clyro. We had to explain that this was nothing to do with the Centre at Clyro, it was Cairo that we were due to visit by coach, once we disembarked at Alexandria! Poor Becky came in for much teasing about that little confusion.

I had continued to fulfil many of my obligations in school and was becoming more and more weary, especially as I was stressed by having given up smoking before going into New Cross Hospital. I did not falter in my determination to give up cigarettes until, while waiting for our flight to Venice at Gatwick airport, together with family, colleagues and the other pupils, I thought I was hallucinating when I saw the figure of my elder sister in front of me: I burst into tears, fearing that I would be unable to cope with the duties in front of me. At that moment, my sister spoke to me in her usual harsh voice and scornful language and I realised she was no figment of my imagination. She told me that she and her husband were also waiting for a flight to some holiday destination and, as I was sitting there shakily, heavy smoker that she was until her death in 2002, she decided to stop my weeping by thrusting a cigarette into my mouth and lighting it. I explained that I had stopped smoking but, even as I said it, I was drawing deeply on the cigarette between my lips. She told me not to be so stupid (as she frequently did) and placed a packet of cigarettes in my handbag, thus ensuring my complete capitulation. I regretted my own weak will and her lack of sympathy, until February 20th, 1984, when my dear GP came to my rescue once again: with one single session of hypnotism, he cured me for ever of that abysmal addiction. I owe so much to that man and wish I had benefited much sooner from his skills, so that I would have spent fewer years subjecting Fred and the children to so much passive smoking. Fortunately, only one of them succumbed to the same bad habit: Ian then showed far greater willpower than mine by suddenly deciding to break off the addiction without any external help, despite the fact that he had smoked furtively and, later, overtly for a good many years. I admire his remarkable achievement.

Once on board the cruise-ship, my duties were taking their toll on me and the then Director of Education noticed that I was not at all well. I told him that I was still recovering from the operation: being a compassionate man, he at once insisted that my name be removed from the onerous patrolling rota each evening. Although I felt guilty, I was prepared, on this occasion, to take the easy way out. Our party of girls and boys were most amenable and the staff agreed that they were profiting from the experiences offered by the cruise.

The day we visited Crete, we watched a gardener ruthlessly pruning the bougainvilleas and my distress must have been obvious, as I displayed my regret for the fallen flowers. Noticing my reaction, the gardener cut a bunch for me, and presented it to me, together with a stolen kiss. Several pupils witnessed this little episode and rushed to Fred, believing that he should come and restrain the ardour of this encounter: needless to say, he was most amused by the incident. David had used the opportunity given him by the cruise to film, on cine camera, many aspects of life on board and ashore. This was preparation for his project for the "A" level in Communication Studies, in which he and Martin Yates were being used as guinea-pigs, and were being prepared by me and Martin's father. The English Adviser had wondered whether it might be a subject to encourage in future "A" level examinations and asked us to experiment with his idea. One of the options for the special project required by the examination could be a film and the associated story-board, which gave David an excellent opportunity to display his talent. We continued to cover the many other aspects of the syllabus which the Associated Examination Board prescribed, my colleague and I having to keep one step ahead of the boys, since this was a totally new course for both of us. Nevertheless, I insisted that, if the boys were to be involved in this programme, they would be entered for the examination at the end of that Lower 6th year, since their other "A" level subjects had, in the second year to be their priority. We managed to complete their preparation in

306

the reduced time and both boys succeeded in securing their "A" level, with David attaining a creditable "B" grade. He had learned a great deal from the experience of making the film and it sustained his interest in cinematographic work — though none of us realised how important that would be in his later life.

In the meantime, Ian was successful in his application for a Rotary scholarship, so that, at the end of August, 1981, he left for the USA, to spend the academic year in New Hampshire. He was accommodated there by several families in succession and achieved some pleasing results in the various tables in his school. Anticipating the hard winter which his hosts warned him about, he asked for some costly, but very special boots for the snow, for which we sent him the money: at the same time we had to send him the sad news of my mother's death, which distressed him greatly. At the end of the academic year, he also enjoyed an interesting month's tour which took him all over the United States. When the entire family congregated at Heathrow to welcome him home after his tour, he was disgruntled as he heard sniggers and comments from his siblings, who had immediately spotted the ear-ring he was wearing. One of the girls warned him that his father would make him remove the offending item as soon as he rejoined us after parking the car. Ian vowed to do no such thing, but I whispered to him that he should not disrupt the peace, just as Fred arrived. I was too late and Fred, having taken one look at his son declared, "You can take that thing out of your ear at once!" Fortunately, he did not argue. His newly acquired American accent sent his brother and sisters into paroxysms of laughter and Ian was beginning to seethe. On our journey back, we stopped at Woodstock for a break, by which time Ian had had enough of us and strode off down the High Street. Though he forfeited his drink, he thought better of risking losing his lift back to Dudley and rejoined us in the nick of time.

His American life had had a profound effect on him, which led to a few stormy weeks. Ian aspired to the lifestyle of his friends in America and, consequently, had asked Fred when he was going to buy a car for him. Fred's immediate response was, "Never!" After his year of singular benefits in the USA, we felt that he should be more than satisfied with the "welcome home" decorations that the girls had put up in the kitchen and the special cake emulating his favourite sweets — Polo mints — which I had baked and decorated. Nevertheless, Ian surprised us by having firmly decided that he would continue his studies in the 6th Form, meaning that now, after his year out, he and Helen would become contemporaries. There was the further coincidence that both of them chose to study English, French and General Studies, Ian's fourth subject being Geography, while Helen opted for Economics. In September, we were joined by Wallace, an American boy who was on a similar exchange to that which Ian had enjoyed. We decided on a different school for him in order to extend his contacts and to eliminate the risks we had run by allowing Torsten into our school, where he had been most indiscreet. Wallace

308

quickly became absorbed into the life of our family and we really enjoyed his being with us.

Early in August, David had received his "A" level results, about which we had been preoccupied for some time. It was the only year ever that I found myself too nervous to go over to school, until David had the results in his hand. As he had promised, he came back to the house, bearing the usual slip of paper. He came through the back door of the kitchen, where I sat quaking, and pulled a long face as he waved the paper at me. I took it with trepidation and failed to realise that I was, once again, having my leg pulled: he had been awarded "A" grades in all his subjects — a tremendous result in 1982 since the standards were, I am quite sure, so very much higher than they have come to be since. He had it in mind to qualify as an Anglo-French barrister, which required a degree in Law-with-French, a course provided by only a limited number of Universities. David had been successful in obtaining admission to Leicester, if his grades were good enough, as, of course, they were. He was admitted to the Faculty of Law and we were, naturally, delighted to have him following in our footsteps, remembering our own happy years there. Delivering him to College Hall for the beginning of his term was a memorable occasion for us and, looking back on my own Fresher days, I suggested to him that it would be a good place to find a wife which, in due course, he did.

CHAPTER
TWENTY-TWO

Affairs of Fred's Heart

Life was flowing smoothly along and Fred, as well as working hard at school, immersed himself in his duties as President of the Rotary Club. He had, in consequence, acquired even more responsibilities: one fateful night in November, it was demonstrated to his family and his colleagues at school, as well as in Rotary, how vulnerable and overstretched he was. Having attended a Primary School concert, designed to raise funds for Fred's chosen Rotary charity, an evening which had seemed to be quite relaxing, the tide turned early in the night when, heavy sleeper though I was under normal circumstances, I was disturbed by Fred's restlessness. When I asked him if he was unwell, I was met by his usual evasiveness. After observing him for getting on for half an hour, I realised that he was in serious pain and told him that I would call the doctor. Fred was adamant that I should do no such thing, being sure that he would soon be feeling better — a foolish claim, as the TNT tablets under his tongue had given him no relief. Two hours later, I ignored his protests, rang for the doctor, whose partner, Dr. Sant, came very promptly. He confirmed my worst fears and

I was astonished when he asked me to drive Fred to the nearest hospital, where they would be prepared for his arrival. As we were quietly preparing for our departure, the ever-considerate Wallace appeared on the landing, having sensed that there was an emergency. I explained what was happening and he burst into tears, for he felt sure that he would have to transfer to another family prematurely — my response, however, was that, of course, he would not have to leave, as he was, for the time being, a member of our family and would have to take the rough with the smooth. I added that I could not manage without him and I left him in charge whilst I went to the hospital with Fred. He was instructed to let the others sleep but, should they wake up, he was to tell them what had happened.

Having helped Fred down to the car and reaching the hospital in a trice, as I was supporting him through the door, I was accosted by the night sister in charge of the Intensive Care Unit. She quickly displayed her fury with me for letting Fred walk, but I had had no guidance from the doctor on this score. She seated Fred in a wheelchair and instructed me to take a seat in the waiting room, where I passed the worst night of my life, as I sat puffing away at one cigarette after another. Eventually, the sister returned, telling me that I could see my husband, as things were improving and, having guided me to his bedside, after a few minutes with him, she told me to go home. Fred told me later that this imperious woman was the mother of one of my 6th Form pupils. Mesmerised by the leaping lines on the machine beside his bed, I think I was even more terrified than I had been in the earlier hours of the incident but, at least, it was comforting to witness the calm with which Fred accepted his plight. As I climbed our own stairs, I discovered the restless Wallace, the only one stirring at this point. Attentively, he gave me one hot drink after another until it was time to wake the other three, as it was time for school. They were all distraught when I explained the situation to them, as was David when I telephoned him later. I also spoke to the Deputies at school to excuse myself from the morning timetable, which I felt unable to cope with after a sleepless night. Everyone rallied round and the support we both received was heart-warming. By the following Sunday morning, Fred had recovered sufficiently to be transferred from Intensive Care to a small ward. When I arrived there early that Sunday morning, the nurse, with a wry grin, informed me that Fred had helped her to hand round the early morning tea and, as soon as he set eyes on me, he was demanding a Sunday newspaper. By the end of that momentous day, he had written to book an Easter Caribbean cruise which he had just spotted in the Sunday paper and which he thought would be ideal for us and for Becky, since it brought us back to Florida. The three older children were each committed to activities connected with their French. The mere thought of a cruise filled me with consternation.

Fred had a treat that day, when the ever-thoughtful Wallace walked our lovely dog, Tramp, to the hospital and lifted her up to the window for Fred to see. After that afternoon's visiting, when I returned to the house, it seemed as though all hell was let loose: our cat, Melody, had brought in a dead rat. My mortal fear of rodents prevented me from tackling that emergency, but Wallace, a farm-boy from Vermont, reacted with enthusiasm, observing, "Oh, it's so cute! On our farm they're five times that size!" as he efficiently removed the offending creature. Meanwhile, Helen, hoping to please me, had baked a chocolate cake and attempted to make the chocolate cream that I always make: she must have made an error with the ingredients and had produced a runny, unusable mess which she poured into the dog's dish. Tramp tackled it with gusto but, shortly afterwards, wandered into our hall and vomited on the lovely oak parquet floor. I asked Helen to clean it up, as she was responsible both for that creation and her dog, but she totally rejected any idea of tackling the work herself. Approaches to Ian and Becky met with similar refusals but, once again, Wallace was ready to volunteer, earning my gratitude, since I knew that I would be sick myself if I attempted to clear it up. Soiled nappies had never been a problem for me, but sickness was always beyond my capabilities. What a kind lad our American proved to be, but I can still clearly visualise the precaution he took as he tackled the disgusting job: heaving uncontrollably, he pulled the neckband of his sweater over his mouth and nose, as he applied the dustpan to the foul pile, which he had already covered with a paper towel. Yes, Wallace was quite an asset in those overwrought days. He was such an acceptable guest that, when he asked if he could have a further period with us at the end of his stay in the Black

Country, we had no hesitation in acceding to his request.

As usual, once Fred was released from the hospital, he was itching to get back to his school duties and I did not succeed in deterring him after a few days of convalescence. Dr. Wilson, our GP, felt we were a completely outrageous couple of patients, but he was invariably kindly and unjudgemental towards us. Soon, Christmas was upon us. We celebrated Boxing Day, as had been our regular practice, together with a local vicar, his wife and their daughters and, included in his number, an American girl on the same exchange-scheme as Wallace. She was an embarrassing addition to all of us but, as all the other young people were impeccable in their behaviour, we managed to cope and, sometimes, overlook her inappropriate coarseness.

Wallace left us after Christmas for his host in Stourbridge, David left to resume his studies in Leicester and the rest of us returned to school. We confirmed the arrangements for the three that were spending the Easter vacation in France: David, being accommodated by a friend, was to spend time in a notaire's office, while Ian and Helen were destined for vacation courses in Nantes, not with any great jubilation once they knew that their little sister would be cruising in the Caribbean. Helen was reminded that she was invited to accompany Wallace to Vermont in the summer, whereas Ian was already booked to go as part of a Rotary team to clear a river-bed in Brittany. I hoped that the cruise that he had booked would further aid Fred in his recovery, but I had a few lonely days

314

whilst Fred rested, as he had developed bronchitis and Becky was out of action, suffering from a bout of tonsillitis. On one of those empty mornings, I entertained myself by consuming three breakfasts: the first was brought to our cabin by the steward and then I took the second, a buffet, served on deck; the third was devoured in the restaurant, sitting at our reserved table. Having selected baby lamb chops for the final excess, I was justly punished for my greed: I was trying to eat the value of the meals that we had all paid for, but, as might be expected, my reward was painful indigestion.

We managed to see all the ports of call, as my two invalids made fairly swift recoveries. We particularly enjoyed our hasty visit to Cozumel and were especially pleased to see the orderly cleanliness of Grand Cayman, having felt disgust when we saw the filth of Montego Bay, where we watched a grubby pig wallowing and snuffling in a dried-up river-bed, covered with a layer of filthy litter. However, in that very place we found the people lively and welcoming and took pleasure in buying the usual tourist souvenirs. All too soon, we were back in Tampa and collecting a hire car to drive across to the East coast of Florida to visit Fred's beloved cousins once again. Passing our first night on land after the cruise, we found a motel in Fort Myers, where, as we booked, the receptionist eyed Becky, clad in shorts and sporting a very short bob and then mortally offended our daughter by enquiring, "Is HE also staying?"

The next day, we drove further south to reach Alligator Highway, the prospect of which intrigued me because I had read that alligators could be seen and there was an Indian reservation close to the road. I was soon to discover the unutterable boredom of the landscape, with not an alligator or an Indian in sight, nor any sign of any other human presence. Later, that impression was dispelled: we were hoping that we were almost back to civilisation, when we had a puncture and, at the same time, down came the rain. As usual, I was very concerned about Fred's condition, but he was, typically, refusing to accept my help, even though, when he opened the boot, he was taken aback by the discovery of a minute spare wheel which looked nothing like the other four. As he stood there perplexed, a pick-up truck appeared, as if from nowhere, and young men, brandishing cans of beer and exhaling the stench of that beverage, yelled, "You gotta problem?", as they screeched to a halt. Full of trepidation, since I did not like the look of them at all, I admitted that we were in difficulties and they all piled out of the vehicle and filled my mind with imaginary fears of their evil intentions. Glancing at Becky and Fred, I was struck by their vulnerability. The new arrivals showed no interest in either of them and, instead, located the wheel needing to be changed and the tools to do the job. Their work was rapid: they were not intent on harming a hair of our heads, but wanted to make the car roadworthy once again. They worked quickly and efficiently and, soon, the driver was asking Fred if he knew how to deal with the car while running on its emergency wheel. Fred confessed that he had never seen a spare like it, so the young man warned him not to drive at more than 30mph and to call at the first "gas" station to have the puncture repaired and the original wheel replaced. The rest of this very affable group were climbing back into the truck, full of beer and good cheer, when, to my horror, Fred offered some dollar bills to the driver, saying, "Buy yourselves a drink." The response he received was, "Certainly not. Been a pleasure to help you folk. By the way, where you from?" When we told them, they said they thought so because we talked "kinda strange".

The rest of our journey to Boca Raton passed uneventfully and, when we reached Jack and Rose's house, we were, as always, warmly welcomed. They treated us with their usual generosity and we particularly remember a restaurant where they served delicious "hot cakes" to accompany their equally delicious fish. Jack very much enjoyed escorting us around the newly-constructed Town Centre, as similar Malls had not yet been built in this country. Jack had a boyish streak and was always full of mischief. In an elegant department store, he displayed this tendency by visiting each fragrance counter, flirting shamelessly with the young assistants and charming them into giving him a wide selection of free samples. He gave me a good share of his booty and, to this day, I have never had the heart to open a single one of them. He also demonstrated his enthusiasm for gadgetry by conducting us to his favourite shop, which specialised in his hobby. Typical Jack, he bought a heap of what appeared to us to be silly toys, but he was contented with his new treasures. All too soon, we had to say goodbye to the relatives and set off for home, to be reunited with the three older children. They were still quite envious of their little sister and had mixed feelings about their experiences in France. Helen and Ian had not specially enjoyed their holiday course in Nantes, while David had worked with the associate of a friend from Brest, who had enabled him to do some paid insurance work. Ian and Helen, in particular, had needed to improve their standard in French and this additional tuition seemed to have given them increased confidence. Their long faces when we arrived were not the consequence either of envy of Becky's good fortune, or of the experiences they had had in France, but purely due to the fact that the central heating boiler had broken down and they were shivering. Though this problem took a little while to sort out, all was soon put to rights and the last day of the holidays dawned.

Five of us were soon back in school and David returned to Leicester to complete his first year. The summer term was fairly fraught, as old animosities between the children reemerged, much to my dismay, since I was anxious to avoid any stress on Fred either at school or at home. On the whole, we succeeded in preserving the peace and soon Wallace returned, as supportive as ever. Helen was to be compensated for Becky's treat at Easter and Ian's year in the USA, for she was invited to return with Wallace to his family's farm in Vermont at the end of term. She was due to return after two weeks, to move on to an au pair arrangement in a French family, the father/grandfather being a retired naval officer: the intention was to further improve her French.

Expecting her return from Vermont to Heathrow, we arrived there in good time. The car was packed, ready for an immediate departure to Dover, where we were to take the cross-Channel ferry. In the car, we had Becky and Auntie Milly, who were to accompany us and explore the Loire Valley and its chateaux, after we had delivered Helen to a very choice apartment on the Boulevard Saint-Germain. We were relieved to see a swarm of passengers rushing along the concourse, but they thinned out and finally petered out completely, with Helen nowhere to be seen. Anxiously, we returned to the airline desk to investigate her absence. "How old is she?" demanded the surly stewardess. When she learned that Helen was approaching 17, the heartless woman displayed malice, as she observed, "Oh, she's probably gone off with a man somewhere. They do at that age." Bursting with fury, I defended my precious daughter, telling her that Helen was much too sensible and well brought up to behave in such an irresponsible manner. "Please find out if her name is on the passenger list," I begged. We were assured this was impossible, but insisted until we were certain that she had not joined that flight. Hurriedly, we telephoned Wallace's home, only to discover that Helen was still there with them, because she had failed to understand the dates on her ticket and thought her departure was not until the following day. Dispirited, we returned to Dudley for a night's sleep and food, to rise again the following morning for a repetition of our journey to Heathrow. This time, we spotted Helen, nonchalantly pushing her trolley laden with luggage. With relief, we carried on to our Channel crossing and reached the Paris apartment in good time, but a day late. We were hospitably received by her new employers, who regaled us all with light refreshments, leaving us with a good impression. Little did we realise what Helen would experience in the coming weeks. She wrote to us regularly from their holiday home, but did not betray the difficult aspects of her situation. She had always had a horror of spiders, but was immediately set to work in their summer home, where there was a massive accumulation of them. Not only was she made responsible for their grandchild, as arranged with Daniel, but was compelled to deal with all the table-laying and washing up for the large number of people in the house and she also had to bath a considerable number of other children there. Afforded very little free time, she dropped exhausted into her bed each night. As she toiled, we were busy enjoying a carefree holiday: the alarm-bells at Heathrow were a mere memory, but a second peal arose when Fred realised that he had left his heart medication in Dudley. We threw ourselves on the mercy of a kindly pharmacist, who sympathetically made up all of Fred's needs, enchanted, as usual, by Fred's excellent French.

Upon our return to Dudley, we were able to have longer telephone conversations with the two boys and Helen and were reassured that all were gainfully employed. It was only after we had met our relieved daughter in New Street station in Birmingham that we discovered the true horrors of her residence with that family. She reminded us of her ordeal with the spiders and enlarged upon her life of drudgery: she had worked very hard for a paltry sum of money and, furthermore, had been made to feel uncomfortable by the odd behaviour of the retired naval doctor. When the day arrived for her return to England, she was provided with a new anxiety when she learned that this man was to drive her and an old lady back to Paris. After the other passenger had been taken home, they were to go back to the Paris flat for one night. On the way to the flat, he indulged in inappropriate conversation, asking if she had a boyfriend and, not entirely accurately, she claimed she had. His next question floored her: had she had sex? In great astonishment, Helen replied "oui", before she had really been able to fathom out his meaning, having interpreted his question as: had she kissed him, the "him" being a figment of the imagination, anyway. She was filled with misgiving when she eventually realised what she had admitted to. At the apartment, she recalled that she would have to sleep on the sofa in the living room, a further source of anxiety. He furnished her with some sort of a meal and then observed that it was time to settle down for the night. She was determined not to undress until he stopped coming into the room, uttering feeble excuses. When it seemed safe to do so, she struggled to complete her undressing beneath the blankets. Once in night-garb, she feigned sleep and, at last, he must have realised that she had not shared his objectives. His crude behaviour — a grandfather, at least in his late fifties — shocked us. Our dear friends, Daniel and Yolande, who had made the arrangement for Helen, were horrified when they learned of this man's conduct and Daniel memorably proclaimed that he was "*un sale cochon!*" Having heard Helen's story, we decided that her au pair days were over. David, too, had had an unfortunate experience or two: as he waited outside a cafe for the bus which was going to take him to his "archaeological dig", he had to fend off the unwelcome approaches of an obviously homosexual man and, once arrived at the camp, was installed in a tent with a strange character who regularly brandished an ice-pick. Ian's spell in Brittany, where he was in a Rotary group clearing an overgrown river-bed, had passed far more pleasantly for him. David returned to Leicester and the rest of us were now back in the Dudley School, Helen and Ian pursuing their "A" level courses and Becky in the 4th year. We fervently hoped that they would work hard and enjoy the subjects they had selected. By this time, without any pressure from us, both Helen and Ian had decided that they would apply to University, Ian to study Politics and Helen English: both were ready to make their selection of colleges to put on the UCCA forms. Ian's favourites were Dundee or Essex and Helen favoured Leicester for English or Swansea for a combined course in English and American Studies. In both cases, it was their second choice which proved successful.

When Helen was due to go for interview in Swansea, with Becky and Auntie Milly in tow, we drove down

322

together. Two days before that, the 20th February, 1984, became a day to be remembered annually. I had repeatedly attempted to give up smoking and had failed dismally but, on that red-letter day, my attentive, kindly GP, Eric Wilson, hypnotised me in order to overcome my addiction and I have never touched a cigarette since. Whilst I was in the hypnotic state, I remember mentally criticising all the points he voiced to dissuade me from smoking, as I was utterly convinced that he would fail, just as I had done on many occasions. When he counted me back out of the hypnosis, I experienced a surge of jubilant freedom and the liberation I displayed as I walked home was witnessed by my dear friend Ruth Sweeney, who told me on the following day that she had never seen me walk past her house with such a jaunty air. I still feel a deep appreciation for Eric's success and I respect him for his dedication to his profession and his concern for his patients — a truly great man who broke an addiction in this intractable woman. Amazingly, neither of the girls had spotted that their mother was smoking no more, until Auntie Milly, on the journey down to Swansea, asked, "Has Mummy stopped smoking?" to which they replied, "No. Don't think so," at which point Fred and I smiled conspiratorially. At last, the "A" level exams arrived and the long wait for the results ensued. Helen and Ian both produced grades which satisfied their Universities and enabled them to follow in David's footsteps. Helen filled her mother's heart with pride when she achieved an "A" in English and both of them, though in no way distinguishing themselves, obtained satisfactory grades in French. All the excitement of preparing clothing, books and equipment for University followed and, when it was time for Helen to go to Swansea, I accompanied her to make possible the transportation of her mountain of luggage. Ian chose to travel alone to Colchester, despite my offer to accompany him.

By this time, I had come to accept the change in my life resulting from my retirement from school. My very good reason for wanting to free myself from school responsibilities was in order to reduce the pressure on Fred and his workload. It was very apparent to me that his condition was rapidly deteriorating, for all physical effort was becoming more onerous. He was still inclined to try and please me by taking on heavy tasks — for example digging in my allotment — despite my cries of horror each time that I discovered him indulging in such furtive activities. He became so ill that, having eaten a normal meal, he had difficulty in walking to our lounge to relax. His pallor increased daily and his skin was becoming loose and lifeless to the touch. He would never take even an hour off school and ploughed on relentlessly, fulfilling all his obligations, never once complaining about his disability.

The first Saturday morning after the end of that autumn term, we walked slowly into town and separated for Fred to go and pay for his papers at the newsagents, while I hurried to the Building Society to pay in the proceeds from the sale of the piano, which had been disposed of that morning. We arranged to meet in the Market Place after each of us had fulfilled our commissions. As I reached the Market, it began to rain and I spent an uncomfortable half-hour waiting for Fred to arrive. It soon dawned on me that he was not going to appear, so I returned to the newsagents to ask if he had been in to pay the bill. The two elderly sisters looked at me mournfully and admitted that they had not set eyes on him that morning. I told them I was very puzzled, as he had almost reached the shop when I had left him, whereupon I was horrified to hear one of the sisters announcing that she did not wish to alarm me, but a man had collapsed outside the nearby Saracen's Head public house and had been attended to by two ladies who were passing by. Apparently, one had given him the kiss of life, whilst the other telephoned for an ambulance, which had swiftly driven off with him. When that lady had said "collapsed" in her lugubrious tone, she had paused, convincing me that she was debating whether to add "and died". Overwhelmed by fear, I raced from the shop and hurried towards our house, in the hope that I could investigate further. I had walked about half-way home when I heard a boy say, "Hallo, Mrs. Austin." It was Robert, one of the caretaker's sons, a fifteen year old. I exclaimed, "Robert, I think something awful has happened to my husband," and went on to recount what I had heard at the shop. Very gently, he told me that it was Fred who had collapsed and, young as he was, he took my arm and walked me back to the house. As I dashed in, I found a distraught and bewildered Becky. Robert's mother then appeared on the scene

325

and told me that under no circumstances would she allow me to drive — she would take me. It was by this good-hearted family that Becky, alone in the house, had been told of the misfortune that Fred had suffered. In haste, I went to the reception in A&E and explained that I thought my husband had just been admitted. The receptionist insensitively failed to notice my distress and plied me with questions. His name — that was fair enough, but then she demanded our address and his date of birth, until I exploded with, "I want to know where he is and how he is." Eventually, she pointed to a little side ward and there I found him lying on a trolley: he was barely conscious, but, with relief, I knew that he was alive. He was promptly taken to the Cardiology ward and I was informed that he would be kept in overnight and possibly longer. Once I had seen him comfortable and returning to consciousness, I left, in order to let all the children know and to pack a bag of necessities for him, before returning after the children had had a meal. They all, naturally, wished to see him and accompanied me. He was recovering well, but it was decided that he should stay in hospital another day. We were all delighted to know that he would be back home with us in time for Christmas. Things would be normal, thank heavens.

A kindly Rotarian, Fred Jones, discovered that we had been intending, after the market, to buy a turkey for the Christmas meal and was about to acquire one from his butcher, but David had already determined to get up early and get one from Marks & Spencer's. He came home jubilantly bearing a beautiful bird and was never reproached for having spent a colossal sum on it. The Christmas atmosphere was returning for us all and we felt so blessed. With relief, we brought Fred back home and, as always, he started organising everyone and everything. Almost immediately after our return, I saw him walk outside, past the kitchen window and, suddenly, fall to the ground. Once again panic assailed me as I rushed towards him, thinking it was a recurrence of low blood pressure: I discovered, however, that he had slipped on ice as he was officiously, or he would say considerately, taking the rubbish to the bin. Admonitions rained down on him, as I escorted him to the lounge and told him to remain there if he hoped for a cup of lemon tea — his favourite — which he had been denied for days as a consequence of his fall in Dudley and his sojourn in hospital.

My early retirement in 1984 had been brought forward by my seeing the rapid deterioration in Fred's health and was also a direct consequence of my overhearing a very malicious exchange between two female members of staff, who were agreeing that a senior post, just advertised, had been tailor-made for me. This horrifying suggestion, that Fred would stoop to nepotism and that I would be a party to it, was the last straw as far as I was concerned. These factors, combined with the dispersal of the children to their Universities, led me into a rather severe depression in early 1985. Our future seemed bleak for, by this time, Fred had been seen by Dr. Clarke, his consultant, who had told him that nothing could be done for him because his left ventricle had been so damaged by his heart attack that the operation could only make things worse. Although he was entitled to six months' sick leave and then retire, he determinedly rejected this idea, which did not fit in with his philosophy. He was resolved to retire with good grace at the age of 57 and to leave his work for others to continue.

CHAPTER
TWENTY-THREE

Margaret Looks Back

After Fred's retirement at the end of the summer term, we decided, early in September, 1985, to visit Daniel and Yolande in Vigneux, as we both secretly feared that Fred had little time left and we wanted to spend a few days with our friends, possibly for the last time. At that point, I was addicted to plying Fred with cures which had been recommended to me by a variety of wiseacres. As a consequence, I had persuaded him to drink a cup of honey and cider vinegar with his breakfast. Daniel's younger son, Vincent, had overheard our mention of this and, one morning, when he was free from school, he asked if he could, with Fred's permission, watch him drink that witches' brew. Pottering around Yolande's kitchen, I heard Vincent exclaim in a tone of awe that Fred was sweating profusely and had lost all his colour. Recognising those familiar symptoms, I called for assistance. Yolande rushed into the kitchen and, seeing the situation, found a locum on the premises who, after one look at Fred, this doctor called an ambulance. I travelled with Fred to the Polyclinique, of which Daniel was a part-owner. When we arrived, a cardiologist greeted us in the entrance and instructed the porters to take Fred to a single ward. He then accompanied us and promptly examined Fred. He investigated Fred's medication, which horrified him, because the amount that Fred was taking — 17 pills daily — would only be prescribed by him for a man in his late seventies with one foot in the grave. In France, he explained, Fred would have had guidance concerning the spread of taking his pills, whereas Fred had taken them as an additional course at breakfast. He then advised us to see a friend of his, an echo-cardiologist who practised in Central Paris. Released from the clinique the following morning, Fred had agreed to the booking of an appointment for the next day, which was the day before we were due to leave. Daniel and Yolande insisted on accompanying us. The new consultant proved to be a Welshman who shared the disgust displayed by his colleague in the Polyclinique about the lack of thoroughness in Fred's Dudley treatment. John Evans, our new acquaintance, told us that the local man in Dudley had not tested Fred adequately and, therefore, was not in a position to arrive at his diagnosis about the left ventricle being so badly damaged. He offered to perform the tests he advocated, if we were able to remain in France but, otherwise, he recommended a cardiologist in Birmingham with whom he had been a student in Cardiff. As we had to return home to organise preparations for the departure of our own University students to Leicester, Colchester and Swansea, we elected to seek out Dr. Rob Watson, whom John Evans had recommended. Becky had accompanied us on the entire trip to France and David joined us at

Daniel's, having spent some time at the home of his French girl-friend, Valerie. This number was increased by the addition of the daughter of a Brest Rotarian, who asked to come and stay with us to improve her English. Imagining that she would be with us for a matter of weeks, we quite readily accepted her request, but lived to regret our decision when she told us that she hoped to spend at least two terms in our home. She offered help around the house to compensate for our hospitality but this was never in evidence once she had her feet under our table. Becky and she were quite incompatible and I often thought how much I would have preferred the return of Wallace.

Although we were to face further anxieties in the not too distant future, we all survived this difficult time and that courageous man of mine faced all his difficulties as coolly as ever. We lost no time in contacting Dr. Rob Watson, whom we saw within the week in his private rooms. Immediately, he arranged for Fred to be tested: first, by the nuclear examination of the heart muscle, which Fred was fascinated to follow on the screen, and then, at East Birmingham Hospital, in the first week of November, 1985, there followed the catheterisation, as a result of which Fred was hurriedly transferred to Walsgrave Hospital in Coventry to undergo a triple by-pass. That operation, which was performed on the following Thursday, was a considerably greater ordeal then compared with now, because the techniques were still in their infancy. Because of the seriousness of the operation, I was allocated a small room with a sofa bed, where Ian and I could rest. Eventually, a nurse from the

Intensive Care Unit came and invited me to see my husband, although he was still only semiconscious. His appearance was transformed by numerous tubes: his mouth was wedged open and, though he hardly looked like my Fred, he still sounded like him. The nurse told him that his wife was there and Fred emitted a very subdued, feeble, "Ho, ho!" Was he hallucinating, thinking himself to be Father Christmas? As ever, the "patient" patient made great strides after the operation, as his blood coursed around some complicated vessels on a structure alongside his bed. Filled with optimism, convinced that his future now looked more rosy, he was not yet able to see the huge relief in the family and, despite the discomfort which ensued, I never heard a single whimper or complaint from him. On the fifth day, he left Walsgrave, relying on his own legs and was reinstated at Dudley Road (now City) Hospital into the care of Rob Watson. Swiftly returning to normality, he took it upon himself to write a critical analysis of the condition and organisation of the large Nightingale Ward, designed to take 26 patients. Handing this masterpiece over to Dr. Watson, he delighted the latter, who saw it as an aid to increase his efforts for improvement. Whilst Fred objected to the ward radio being switched on at full volume at 6.30a.m. and voiced this opinion in the report, nevertheless he remembers with nostalgia when that very radio played Barbara Streisand singing *Moonlight*, encouraging his tendency to weep when he hears moving pieces of music. Whilst he was still in that ward, he was painstakingly instructed about foods he should avoid and was urged to undertake restrained exercise. Once home, he made a swift return to a healthy routine and, soon, that pale-faced man, who had frequently suffered intense chest pain, faded into our past. It became my turn to struggle to keep up with him, for he was usually several strides ahead of me. Anxieties allayed, the whole family felt greater confidence.

After a period of recuperation, two changes of house and the weddings of Helen and David, Fred, who had been working as a volunteer at Age Concern, took up a paid position there, which brought him additional satisfaction. Soon after his operation, Rob Watson had invited him to join in the formation of a new committee of the British Heart Foundation, which gave both of us the opportunity of putting something back into the NHS in our gratitude for Rob Watson's dedication. Ian's wedding to Cath followed in 1993 and Becky's to Nick in 1997: the wedding period was rounded off when Helen, having broken away from Andy, her American disaster, remarried, this time to another, but much more likeable, immigrant from France, Jerome.

After his five years at Age Concern, I had succeeded in persuading Fred that it was time to give up full-time work for the second time and to allow us to enjoy the freedom of retirement. In 1999, another setback had to be faced for, on the 30th December of that year, we were told that his PSA count indicated prostate cancer. Fortunately, Fred was in the hands of a very chirpy, but highly competent urologist who, while leaving the choice of treatment to us, suggested that the best would be to carry out a radical prostatectomy, the only

333

procedure which would be sure to bring about a complete cure. When we accepted his suggestion, he encouraged us to go ahead with the nine-week holiday that we had arranged and undertook to perform the operation as soon as we were back in Dudley. We would, by then, have had the opportunity of seeing something of New Zealand and Australia, following up with a three-week cruise which started in Hong Kong and ended in Vancouver, allowing us then to make a week's visit to Florida to see Rose. All through the six months which followed the diagnosis, leading up to the operation in June, 2000, Fred displayed the same positive attitude to his health prospects as he had at the time of his heart problems.

As I reach the final part of my account, this is probably the right time to write a brief testimonial to Fred, who has played such a vital role in my life. He is discreet, calm and considerate, as well as having a resourceful nature, qualities that his mother must have been fully aware of when she entrusted him into the care of fellow-passengers unknown to her, and then waved "good bye" to him on the platform in Prague. His innate sweetness he must have inherited from that courageous lady and, for 60 years or more, I have been a recipient of his kindness and love.

In addition to the blessing of Fred's part in my life, a further joyful quality has been added through the four babies that we were so honoured to be offered. As with all child/parent relationships, we have had our ups and downs, but, looking at them now as adults, it is a source of pride to see them all having developed into

334

wonderful people who are as conscientious as we could have hoped, both as parents and as professionals. The successes they have achieved are a constant pleasure to us both in our present lives. Their greatest gift to us has been those 10 superb grandchildren: I could never have dreamed of such an outcome when I failed for so long to become pregnant. The feeling of barrenness left me as soon as David arrived in 1963. Helen delighted us both when she invited us to be present at the birth of the twins. Though we were unable to witness the actual birth because of the rules surrounding a caesarian operation which was decreed by the medical staff, Jerome came out to join us immediately, to tell us very emotionally that there were two boys. He then ushered us into the room which had been prepared for Helen and the twins, just minutes after their birth, when Thomas was placed into Fred's arms and Sebastian into mine. We were similarly invited to be at Becky's house for the birth of Katie and, soon after that, for Molly. Equally, we hurried to the local maternity ward on May 4th, 1995, when Ian phoned tearfully to announce, "It's a boy!" and, on a later occasion, to take Jack, on May 6th, 1999, to see his mother, Cath, gazing adoringly at Megan, who had just been born. Our presence at Cousin Jack's funeral in Florida, which coincided with the birth of Grace in Hammersmith unfortunately prevented our being present there, but David promptly telephoned us at Rose's house to let us know of her arrival. Equally unfortunately, we were unable to be on the spot when Barnaby was born two years later. The last comer, Alfie, chose to be born in

335

the middle of the night but, having been installed in their house for all of the preceding week as chief cooks and bottle-washers, we were able to see this newly-born very rapidly, as we left to celebrate the New Year in Dudley, as planned, after I had the pleasure of holding this latest baby in my arms.

I could not have asked for more wonderful gifts, especially as we were allowed such close involvement in all of their arrivals. All the disappointments of my early days have thus been totally swept aside and I have often said to Fred that our efforts could not have produced such good-looking children. I was not destined to live with the sterility of a childless old age, something that I had long dreaded. One of my fridge magnets says it all — "If I had known how wonderful grandchildren are, I would have had them first". Nevertheless, the whole family would agree that my greatest gift was finding Fred: "Where did you find him?" my daughters have asked me more than once. They stare at me with incredulity when I respond with, "In a group of impudent youths in a queue at University." But the greatest, though unspoken, debt is to Fred's mother, who courageously sent him on that one-way journey, knowing that she would never see him again. She spared him so much, but he has repaid her sacrifice over and over again by serving his fellow-men, women and children: to me he is the embodiment of love.

Now that the year 2008 is drawing to a close, I have to look back on some painful occurrences which none of us can expect to avoid — the chief sorrow being caused by the death of our dear friend, Daniel. Such sorrow is, I am sure, the inevitable penalty for living so long. The compensation is that we continue to see our grandchildren, who will again be gathered for Fred's 80th birthday party where, once more, we shall have family love to cheer us on our way.

THE COLA

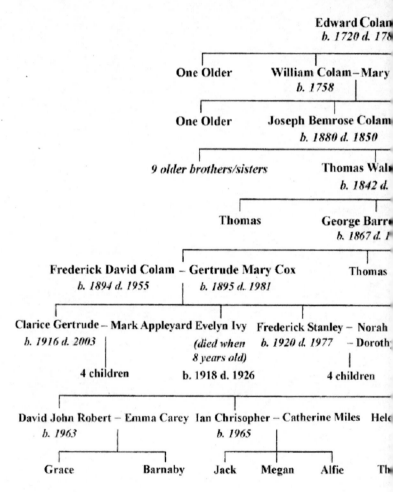

Edward Colam
b. 1720 d. 178

One Older   William Colam – Mary
b. 1758

One Older   Joseph Bemrose Colam
b. 1880 d. 1850

9 older brothers/sisters   Thomas Wal
b. 1842 d.

Thomas   George Barr
b. 1867 d. 1

Frederick David Colam – Gertrude Mary Cox   Thomas
b. 1894 d. 1955   b. 1895 d. 1981

Clarice Gertrude – Mark Appleyard   Evelyn Ivy   Frederick Stanley – Norah
b. 1916 d. 2003   (died when   b. 1920 d. 1977   – Doroth
   8 years old)

4 children   b. 1918 d. 1926   4 children

David John Robert – Emma Carey   Ian Chrisopher – Catherine Miles   Hele
b. 1963   b. 1965

Grace   Barnaby   Jack   Megan   Alfie   Th

AMILY TREE

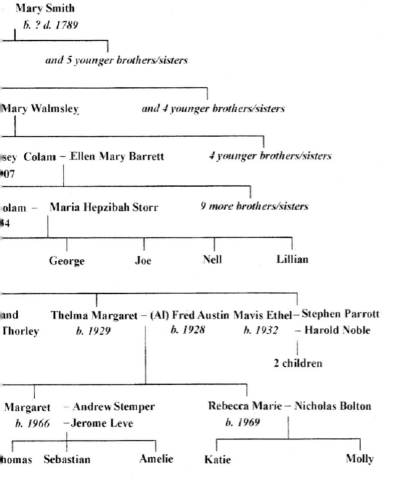

Mary Smith
b. ? d. 1789

and 5 younger brothers/sisters

Mary Walmsley   *and 4 younger brothers/sisters*

sey Colam – Ellen Mary Barrett   *4 younger brothers/sisters*
07

olam – Maria Hepzibah Storr   *9 more brothers/sisters*
4

George   Joe   Nell   Lillian

and   Thelma Margaret – (Al) Fred Austin Mavis Ethel – Stephen Parrott
Thorley   *b. 1929*   *b. 1928*   *b. 1932*   – Harold Noble

2 children

Margaret   – Andrew Stemper   Rebecca Marie – Nicholas Bolton
b. 1966   – Jerome Leve   *b. 1969*

homas Sebastian   Amelie   Katie   Molly

Also available in ISIS Large Print:

Bitter Fruit

Rod Broome

"The first twelve months of my career proved to be highly eventful. I was appointed to teach at a junior school . . . succumbed to a nasty dose of pneumonia caused — everyone said — by living in a cold, damp, rented flat; and on Christmas Eve I became engaged to Anita, the most wonderful girl in the world!"

In the final part of the "Broome" Trilogy, Rod Broome describes his early days in teaching; a head teacher who died in post, his first position as head teacher in a new open-plan primary school and how this caused staff to learn new methods of teaching. He recalls the day the school got its first computer, and the afternoon when the caretaker dressed up as a snowman!

ISBN 978-0-7531-9582-6 (hb)
ISBN 978-0-7531-9583-3 (pb)

Czech and Mate

Fred Austin

"I suppose that I had always (In my youthful experience!) been attracted by the smaller, darker-haired girls: they fitted better when you danced."

Fred saw Margaret for the first time in the queue for the Dean at the University College, Leicester. The year was 1947. He was making a fresh start and liked what he saw, noticing her little zipped dress.

His mother had sent him to England, at the age of ten, to escape the Nazis. Before 1939, Fred had lived happily with his mother and two sisters in Northern Moravia. Once in England, he soon adapted to a life, which was happy in school, but far from normal otherwise.

In meeting Margaret, Fred was, at last, encouraged to fulfil his potential and was able, in spite of setbacks to his health, to contribute to the life they made together.

ISBN 978-0-7531-9562-8 (hb)
ISBN 978-0-7531-9563-5 (pb)

A Birmingham Backstreet Boyhood

Graham V. Twist

"Mom bought me a second-hand pilot's leather helmet. It was miles too big for me, but I wore it day and night nevertheless. One day running up the street it fell over my eyes and I ran into the corner of a brick and concrete cover that they used to put over the cellar gratings."

Graham Twist's memoir is a fascinating, funny and poignant recollection of growing up in the slums of Nechells and Aston in 1940s Birmingham.

Despite hard living conditions and a distinct lack of money, a strong community spirit prevailed and families and neighbourhoods were close-knit. The womenfolk in particular took great pride in their homes, however humble. In those tough times you hoped nobody noticed you going to the "pop shop" to pawn precious valuables to get enough money to pay the rent or buy food for the family . . .

ISBN 978-0-7531-9580-2 (hb)
ISBN 978-0-7531-9581-9 (pb)

Poppies in the Corn

Fay Garrison

"My Father rented for us a rather run-down bungalow in the tiny Hamphire village of Redenham, a few miles from Andover. My mother, a city girl all her life, was horrified. Anything rural was anathema to her, from the dark country roads to the watchful cows in the fields."

When the Second World War broke out, Fay Garrison with her mother and sister moved from their native Birmingham. Her idyllic existence was then shattered by the news of her father's capture at Dunkirk.

Later in the war she returned to Birmingham, to a very different school system with new friends and teachers who shaped her future. A heroic aunt, captured by the Nazis who escaped to fight with the Resistance became a strong influence in her life. Eventually qualifying as a teacher she settled down in Solihull and married a journalist with whom she shared a love of music.

ISBN 978-0-7531-9576-5 (hb)
ISBN 978-0-7531-9577-2 (pb)